GAY FICTIONS
Wilde to Stonewall

Studies in a Male Homosexual Literary Tradition

Books by Claude J. Summers

Christopher Marlowe and the Politics of Power
Christopher Isherwood
E. M. Forster

Co-authored with Ted-Larry Pebworth

Ben Jonson

Co-edited with Ted-Larry Pebworth

The Poems of Owen Felltham
"Too Rich to Clothe the Sunne": Essays on George Herbert
Classic and Cavalier: Essays on Jonson and the Sons of Ben
The Eagle and the Dove: Reassessing John Donne
"Bright Shootes of Everlastingnesse": The Seventeenth-Century
Religious Lyric
"The Muses Common-Weale": Poetry and Politics in the
Seventeenth Century
Figures in a Renaissance Context (by C. A. Patrides)

GAY FICTIONS
Wilde to Stonewall

Studies in a Male Homosexual Literary Tradition

Claude J. Summers

A Frederick Ungar Book
CONTINUUM / NEW YORK

1990

The Continuum Publishing Company
370 Lexington Avenue
New York, NY 10017

Printed in the United States of America

Library of Congress Cataloging-in-Publication Data

Summers, Claude J.
　　Gay fictions : Wilde to Stonewall : studies in a male homosexual
literary tradition / Claude J. Summers.
　　　　p.　　cm.
　　"A Frederick Ungar book."
　　ISBN 0-8264-0466-9
　　1. Gay men in literature. 2. English fiction—20th century–
–History and criticism. 3. American fiction—20th century—History
and criticism. 4. Gays' writings, English—History and criticism.
5. Gays' writings, American—History and criticism. 6. Wilde,
Oscar, 1854–1900—Influence. I. Title.
　　PR888.G34S86 1990
　　823' .9109353' 086642—dc20　　　　　　　　　　　　90–1461
　　　　　　　　　　　　　　　　　　　　　　　　　　　　　　CIP

For
Terry Kihara and Michael Twomey
Jim Malek and Craig Pugh
Lynn Orr and Girard Miller—
and Ted again

love, having no geography, knows no boundaries

Contents

Acknowledgments

I am grateful to a number of friends and colleagues for commenting on portions of this book, including David Bergman, Joseph Cady, Chris Dahl, Neil Flax, Judith Herz, Dorothy Lee, Jay Parini, Sheryl Pearson, Melita Schaum, Michael Schoenfeldt, and Celestin Walby. Joseph Cady, James Malek, and Peter Thorslev made available to me unpublished papers. The editors of *Journal of Popular Literature* and *Modern Fiction Studies* granted permission to reprint revised versions of the chapters on Renault and Cather, which originally appeared as essays in their journals. Earlier versions of the chapters on Forster and Isherwood appeared in my books *E. M. Forster* and *Christopher Isherwood*, respectively, both of which were published by Frederick Ungar. My greatest debt is to my friend and frequent collaborater Ted-Larry Pebworth, whose interest, advice, and support sustained this project.

1

Introduction: From Wilde to Stonewall

This book is a study of *gay fictions*, by which is variously meant the fictional representation of male homosexuals by gay male and lesbian writers; the evolution of conceptions about homosexual identity; and the construction, perpetuation, revision, and deconstruction of fictions (including stereotypes and defamations) about homosexuality and homosexuals. The title, thus, refers both to specific works of literature that are designated gay fictions and to the changing ideas of what it means to be homosexual in particular places and times. As the subtitle intimates, there are many homosexual literary traditions and this book is offered as a contribution toward understanding but one of them: a particular tradition of fictional representations of gay males in twentieth-century Anglo-American literature.[1] My approach to defining this tradition is through the analysis of selected texts, chosen for their literary quality and representativeness.

Because all literary discourse is inherently (and sometimes triumphantly) rooted in political realities and social attitudes, and because all academic endeavors participate (either openly or silently) in the politics of social change, there ought to be no need to apologize for my hope that this book will contribute simultaneously both to an increase of knowledge and to a project of human liberation. But at the risk of courting the charges of special pleading and sentimentality that are so tiresomely and naively leveled against gay studies in general, let me confess at the outset that this book is not—to use a term favored by the now old New Criticism—"disinterested." While it is, I believe, free of propagandistic intent and unearned claims, it is at the same time unabashedly committed to the idea that the representation of gay men and lesbians in literature is a vitally important subject both for its own sake and for its consequences in the real world, where the aspirations of gay men and lesbians to full human rights is still disputed. As a contribution to literary history, the book scrupulously seeks to maintain historical and critical objectivity, yet it is constantly aware that history and criticism are never entirely objective or merely academic.

11

Even today gay studies in language and literature are delimited by what Louie Crew and Rictor Norton defined in 1974 as "the sociology of literature" when they noted that "homosexual literature is written, read, criticized, and taught within a generally hostile environment."[2] This environment of hostility toward gay literature and toward gay men and lesbians provides at once the subject and the context of this book. More specifically, this book is an exploration of selected texts that cumulatively constitute an important literary tradition focused on the homosexual's problematic relationship to society. Intended as a contribution toward the understanding of the gay male experience as represented in literature, it is neither a survey of gay literature nor even an account of gay fiction generally. It has no pretensions to comprehensiveness and it is circumscribed by historical and geographical parameters.

Focusing on Anglo-American fiction written in the advent and aftermath of the Wilde scandal of 1895 and in the period following World War II, but before New York's Stonewall riots of 1969—which ushered in the contemporary gay liberation movement—this book aims not to establish a canon of modern gay literature, but to explore strong representative texts that both reflect and reflect on the status of gay men in these earlier crucial decades. Although its interests are to some extent sociological and historical, the book's focus is preeminently critical. By means of practical criticism of important (and in most cases neglected and undervalued) texts, the book seeks both to illuminate significant works of literature and to help chart an evolving tradition of gay fiction in the twentieth century. Centered on the development of gay identity and on the relationship of the homosexual to (and within) the larger society, this tradition helps cast in relief both the history of gay people and the strategies of fictional discourse about homosexuality during this century.

Because discourse about homosexuality has until quite recently been fraught with all kinds of peril, and because homosexuality has itself been such a controversial subject, the texts discussed in this book are necessarily (though sometimes not obviously or deliberately) political. Although some of them are intent on reforming attitudes, while others espouse a more radical solution, they are all written in opposition to the prevailing prejudices of their times. Thus, this book is concerned with the interplay of artistic technique and social context. It views the particular novels and stories that it discusses as the joint products of individual visions and of concrete cultural and social tensions, and it attempts to place the fictions within their appropriate ideological contexts. But it takes care not to reduce them to the status merely of social documents or to emphasize their ideological positions at the expense of considerations of their craftsmanship and aesthetic achievements. Similarly, in cumulatively outlining a tradition of gay fiction, it makes comparisons and generalizations, but it also endeavors to respect the integrity of the individual texts as organic works of art.

Over the centuries, numerous theories have been offered as explanations of homosexual love and desire. Some of these theories—like Aristophanes' myth of the divided soul, or the psychoanalytic speculations of Freud, or psychobiology's postulation of an altruistic gene—are themselves dramatic enough to constitute gay fictions. But none is entirely persuasive and none currently enjoys universal acceptance. (Equally unclear, but less frequently the subject of speculation, is the origin of heterosexual desire.) This book does not endorse any of the pschoanalytical, congenital, or environmental explanations that are today most frequently espoused. While speculation about the origins of homosexuality is fascinating, and a frequent subject of discourse about homosexuality, such speculation is important to this book only insofar as it is featured in the particular texts under discussion. When it is so featured—and sometimes it is prominent by virtue of its absence— explanations of the etiology of homosexuality are usually significant primarily as embodiments of particular sexual ideologies that are themselves the products of the cultural tensions of the time.

Homosexuality itself is a fluid concept, encompassing more than a set of particular behaviors or emotions. Most people report (and probably all people experience) homoerotic feelings at various points in their lives. Many individuals repeatedly participate in a wide range of homoerotic behavior without defining themselves as homosexual, and some people define themselves as homosexual without ever participating in homoerotic activities. Although we typically think in terms of a dichotomy between homosexuality and heterosexuality, and between the homosexual and the heterosexual, with vague categories for bisexuality and bisexuals, the range of human sexual response and behavior is actually much less restricted than these artificial dichotomies suggest. Several students of sexuality have argued that the terms *homosexual* and *heterosexual* should more properly be used as adjectives rather than nouns, referring to acts and emotions but not to people. In such a view, there is no such thing as a homosexual (or, for that matter, a heterosexual). Yet the fact remains that sexuality is not completely plastic. For most people, sexual orientation is not merely a matter of choice or preference, but a classification that reflects an internal, as well as a social, reality.

Despite the arbitrariness and subjectivity of labels, and despite the dangers inherent in labeling and in accepting the labels of others, categorization as homosexual, bisexual, or heterosexual is not unimportant. It impacts both on sexual behavior and, even more decisively, on self-definitions. Since this book is less interested in any particular homoerotic behavior than in the developing concept of homosexual identity,[3] the phenomenon of accepting identification as a homosexual is a primary concern, whether or not there is in fact any such intrinsic or biological entity as a homosexual. The term as used in this book refers to those individuals who subjectively define themselves as homosexuals. These people differentiate themselves from others in society on the basis of erotic responses that the majority culture condemns and labels as deviant. Although rooted in erotic feelings, however, the consequences of identification as a homosexual reach far beyond the erotic, for sexuality is not a small, cordoned-off area of privacy. It affects all of life.

In the texts under scrutiny, homosexual identity defines not simply what one *does* but who one *is*. It is a process and product of self-discovery, and a validation of individual integrity and wholeness. It is a person's recognition of a primary sexual attraction toward members of his own sex and his acceptance of his capacity to love someone of his own sex. But it goes beyond recognition of sexual and emotional objects to reveal something important about the individual's very being and his relationship to a society that would penalize him for who he is. To arrive at a homosexual identity is to acknowledge a part of the personality that is repressed and denied only at heavy cost. In this sense, homosexuality is not a problem, but a solution to a problem.

Identification as a homosexual is frequently accompanied or preceded by feelings of guilt and shame and by a sense of (often quite justified) paranoia, for to be homosexual in most modern societies is to be set apart and stigmatized. But the isolation and alienation from the larger society that are typically concomitant with the attainment of homosexual identity often lead to a sense of solidarity with others of a similar nature. Hence, the achievement of a homosexual identity is intensely personal, yet inevitably social, for self-definition invariably impinges on one's interaction with others and on one's perspective toward the majority culture.

In the gay literature discussed herein, the acceptance of homosexual identity follows familiar patterns to the goal of self-recognition and acceptance. A gradual and frequently torturous process, self-definition as a homosexual is nearly always the culmination of intense introspection and evaluation. Homosexual identity is, thus, posited as a function of self-knowledge. But it is well to recall that homosexuality is not a single phenomenon, and that even those persons who identify themselves as homosexual are remarkably diverse. While the coming-out processes repeatedly portrayed in the gay fictions discussed in this book are variations on a basic pattern familiar to most contemporary homosexuals, they are by no means universal. These dramatizations are themselves implicated in the sexual ideologies that their authors affirm or challenge.

There has been much speculation about a peculiarly homosexual sensibility, but it is highly doubtful that such a quality actually exists. Homosexuals are far too diverse to share a single sensibility, and the manifestations of homosexuality are too various to permit sweeping generalizations. It is true that identifiable homosexual styles—such as, for example, camp—develop from time to time, but these styles are clearly the product of cultural and subcultural influences and they are never universally shared by all homosexuals. Even the stereotypical associations of homosexuality with effeminateness or, at certain periods, with hypermasculinity are time-bound, culturally reinforced social constructs. Insofar as there is a shared homosexual sensibility, it results not from any quality inherent in homosexuality itself but from the stigma attached to homosexuality. What modern homosexuals in the West share in common is the crucially important cultural experience of self-realization within a society that denies the legitimacy of their deepest instincts and most profound emotions. The basis for uniting and solidifying homosexuals into a distinct community is provided not by any particular sensibility or style, but by the feelings of alienation and oppression that stigma induces. This experience of "otherness" may foster certain recurrent motifs in gay literature, but gay literature is too broadly based and diverse to be summarized by any set of literary gestures.

Similarly, there is not much evidence to suggest that homosexuals are, as a group, any more intelligent, creative, or sensitive than heterosexuals. But certainly homosexuals are, at pivotal moments of their lives, more preoccupied with the implications of their sexuality than are their heterosexual counterparts, whose sexuality provokes less searching self-inquiry. The introspection that usually accompanies the coming-out experience fosters self-consciousness and self-knowledge and may thereby promote creativity. Moreover, as several of the included gay fictions imply, the homosexual's unusual relationship to society gives him or her a valuable perspective as social analyst and critic. Although homosexuals are usually able to pass as members of the dominant culture, they are, however, constantly aware that they stand apart from the culture and that they are likely subject to exclusion and punishment by it. This ambiguous relationship may encourage many homosexuals to question received ideas about the larger society and to develop insight into the arbitrariness and injustice of social forms and institutions generally. Hence, one of the important roles played by gay people in the texts considered herein, and in the real world as well, is that of social critic.

This book, which deals with literature written before the contemporary gay liberation movement, exists in a reciprocal relationship to that movement. On the one hand, the book explores the evolution of attitudes that culminated finally in a mass movement for reform. On the other hand, the book itself is made possible only by the climate of opinion that this movement created. That is to say, it is both a product of the intellectual and political ferment fostered by gay liberation and a contribution toward understanding, via gay fiction, the intellectual and emotional forces that ultimately coalesced into a liberation movement.

On the night of June 27–28, 1969, the police raid of a gay bar in New York City's Greenwich Village, the Stonewall Inn, ignited three days of rioting by gay men and lesbians and inspired the birth of gay liberation as an international mass movement. Modeled on the black civil rights struggle, the anti-war movement of the day, and the new wave of feminism, the newly militant gay movement challenged stereotypical ideas about homosexuality and boldly demanded social and political equality for lesbians and gay men. Its political agenda included the repeal of laws criminalizing homosexual activity, the modification of public policies that discriminate against lesbians and gay men, the guarantee of equal protection under the law, the combatting of harassment and defamation based on sexual orientation, the recognition of gay male and lesbian relationships, and the education of the public as to the meaning of the homosexual experience. More fundamentally, it demanded a change of consciousness, particularly in the consciousness of gay men and lesbians themselves, most of whom had understandably internalized the negative images of homosexuality and homosexuals with which they were constantly bombarded.

The gay liberation movement has, in the past twenty years, scored significant successes, ranging from the American Psychiatric Association's removal of homosexuality from its list of mental disorders; the repeal or judicial nullification of sodomy laws in many jurisdictions; and the adoption of numerous antidiscrimination statutes; to the acceptance of homosexuality as a normal variation in human sexuality by many mainstream churches; the election of openly gay and lesbian officials at all levels of government; and the mobilization against the AIDS epidemic. These successes have in turn inspired both conservative reaction and liberal consolidation. Gay men and lesbians in the United States and Great Britain continue to suffer legal and social oppression, and the struggle for gay rights has by no means reached a triumphant conclusion. Homophobia continues to infect British and American society, and both physical and verbal gay-bashings remain depressingly common, frequently inspired by religious fundamentalist propaganda. Besieged by the forces of the New Right, and necessarily distracted by the tragedy of the AIDS epidemic, which—at least in the West—has disproportionately affected the homosexual community, the gay political movement may even be described as currently embattled and defensive. Yet, given the status of gay people before Stonewall, its achievements are astounding and far-reaching.

In little more than twenty years homosexuals have significantly improved the quality of gay life. They have demystified homosexuality by making it visible in a wide variety of settings, and they have transformed an illicit and precarious sexual subculture into communities based less on sexual activity than on shared cultural experience. They have created an impressive array of community-based social and political organizations and institutions, and they have successfully altered the terms in which homosexuality is discussed and debated. By questioning the basis of gender roles and by reshaping private and public conceptions of homosexuality, they have contributed immensely to public discourse about sex roles and sexuality. They have sufficiently reduced academic prejudice against homosexuality to make possible a veritable explosion of studies of homosexuality and of gay men and lesbians and their roles in society. In so doing, the gay liberation movement has solidified what is surely its most important achievement: the recognition of homosexuals as a legitimate minority—with its own history and culture—among the sea of minorities that make up the social fabric of Western democracies.

In a very real sense, the overarching subject of this book is the change of consciousness that has made possible the creation of a homosexual minority: the change from conceiving homosexuality as a personal failing or social problem to a question of identity and the change from viewing sexual identity exclusively in individualistic terms to seeing it collectively. A mass movement based on erotic preferences presupposes the acknowledgment of sexuality as an indispensable element in the wholeness of personality and the acceptance of erotic interest as a distinguishing individual and social characteristic. These were the two necessary conditions for the evolution of gay liberation as a social and political movement. Thus, gay liberation transcends the narrowly political. Indeed, it is, foremost, a project of self-affirmation. But from the perspective of gay liberation, individual validations of the legitimacy of homosexual identity and experience are the *sine qua non* of social change. Self-acceptance fosters not only a sense of solidarity with others of a like nature but also an awareness of the anachronism of many social forms and prohibitions. Concerned as it is with sexuality as a function of self-knowledge, with the development of gay identity, and with the personal and social consequences of self-affirmation, this book, in effect, explores the necessary preconditions to gay liberation. Fittingly, it begins by examining a text in which the protagonist discovers his homosexual identity, only regretfully to reject this knowledge; and it concludes by analyzing a text that anticipates the gay liberation movement's insistence that homosexuals constitute an aggrieved minority.

The Stonewall Inn riots of 1969, which conveniently signify the "critical divide in the politics and consciousness of homosexuals and lesbians,"[4] mark the beginning of gay liberation as a mass movement. But Stonewall was itself the culmination of decades of activism, and the emergence of gay men and lesbians as a self-conscious minority has a much longer and more complicated history. Sexual activity between members of the same sex is undoubtedly coextensive with the history of the species; it has been documented in every civilized culture and in most primitive societies. In different times and places, homosexual activity and relationships have variously been celebrated or excoriated, institutionalized or marginalized. But, as Jeffrey Weeks and other recent historians of sexuality have argued, while homosexual behavior is universal, homosexual identity is culturally and historically specific.[5] The currently prevalent notion of the homosexual as a distinct category of person is—it is frequently argued—a modern Western social construct, datable to the nineteenth century and related to the rise of urbanization and industrial capitalism.

This social-constructivist argument is stated most forcefully in Michel Foucault's comment that

> The nineteenth-century homosexual became a personage, a past, a case history, and a childhood, in addition to being a type of life, a life form, and a morphology, with an indiscreet anatomy and possibly a mysterious physiology. Nothing that went into his total composition was unaffected by his sexuality. . . . It was consubstantial with him, less as a habitual sin than as a singular nature.[6]

Only in the late nineteenth century, according to this line of reasoning, did the homosexual become a class of person whose propensity for homosexual activity defined him or her. Whereas in the early modern periods of the West homosexual activity had been regarded as a sin and crime to which all individuals were potentially susceptible, in the nineteenth century homosexual desire became the salient characteristic of a particular type of individual, who in turn became the object of medical as well as theological and judicial intervention.

Foucault's powerful exposition of the sudden "invention" of the homosexual in the nineteenth century is an oversimplification of a more gradual and more complex historical development. The extreme social-constructivist position that sexuality is exclusively the product of broadly defined social forces has itself been attacked by essentialists, who hold that homosexual behavior manifests a biological or psychological essence within the individual.[7] They argue that, although sexual behavior may be socially organized and regulated in different ways at different times, sexual identity is a transhistorical essence or core of being, essentially similar from one period to another. Certainly, evidence exists that categorization of individuals on the basis of their sexual behavior predates the nineteenth century. Homosexual subcultures have been identified in medieval and Renaissance Europe; and, prior to the nineteenth century, at least some (and probably many) individuals developed what we would today define as a homosexual identity. Nevertheless, in late-nineteenth-century Europe an important change took place in the way in which people who engaged in homosexual activity were regarded and in the way in which they regarded themselves.

The late nineteenth century saw both a vastly increased visibility of gay subcultures throughout Europe and an increased hostility toward homosexuals, especially in England. With the adoption there of the 1885 Criminal Law Amendment Act (under which Oscar Wilde was convicted in 1895), all homosexual activity was criminalized.[8] This law had disastrous effects. Not only did it lead to the imprisonment of many individuals, but it exposed many more to disgrace and to blackmail. Significantly, however, it also had a positive effect. As Havelock Ellis remarked of the consequences of Wilde's prosecution, "The Oscar Wilde trial . . . with its wide publicity, and the fundamental nature of the questions it suggested, appears to have generally contributed to give definiteness and self-consciousness to the manifestations of homosexuality, and to have aroused inverts to take up a definite attitude."[9] Despite the perils of legal persecution and censorship, in the late nineteenth century homosexuality—previously a subject not to be mentioned among Christians, "the Love that dare not speak its name"— became the subject of ever-widening discourse and public scrutiny.

If the increased visibility of homosexuals prompted increased hostility and persecution, that hostility in turn sparked resistance. In the final decades of the century, there arose in England a loosely organized group of writers, artists, and philosophers dedicated to the goal of securing sympathetic recognition of the homosexual impulse in a repressive society. Calling themselves Uranians, these early gay activists attempted to explain homosexuality as a congenital condition related to gender confusion, and defined it as a transhistorical phenomenon that reached its apogee in classical Greece.[10] Appropriately, the term Uranian itself derives from Plato's *Symposium*, a text that will feature prominently in the gay fictions examined in this book. Given the overwhelming difficulties they faced in defending homosexuality in England's repressive climate, the Uranians deserve enormous credit for launching a homosexual emancipation movement. Although this movement had little success in its attempts to improve the legal status of homosexuals, it did contribute to the increased understanding of homosexuality and to the greater self-consciousness among homosexuals observable in the period. While it is difficult to speak of a homosexual emancipation movement in America at this time—possibly because there was then less of an organized hostility to homosexuality here than in England—the poetry of Walt Whitman both expressed and helped create an emerging homosexual consciousness. Indeed, it is scarcely possible to overestimate the importance of Whitman and his poetry in promoting homosexual self-consciousness in England as well as in America.[11]

The term *homosexual* was itself not coined until 1869, by a Hungarian legal reformer, Karoly Maria Benkert, and it did not become current until the 1890s. Not surprisingly, much of the discourse about homosexuality in late-nineteenth-century England (as in Europe) is medical and legal discourse, culminating in Havelock Ellis's collaboration with John Addington Symonds, *Sexual Inversion*. But homosexuality also became the subject of poetry and fiction and nonfiction apologias. Homoeroticism suffuses nineteenth-century British literature generally (including the work of poets as dissimilar as Byron and Tennyson), but in the waning years of Victoria's reign homosexuality is far more frequently and forthrightly expressed. Its expression varies from the pederastic poetry of the Uranian poets, who tirelessly evoke the precedent of classical Greece's golden age of intergenerational love, to the celebration of the Whitmanesque "manly love of comrades" by Edward Carpenter and others. It includes both the exuberant but sublimated sexuality of Gerard Manley Hopkins's "Epithalamion" and the wistful melancholy of A. E. Housman's *A Shropshire Lad*. It encompasses the biblically based homoeroticism of Sir Henry Hall Caine's *The Deemster* as well as the frankly decadent religiosity of John Francis Bloxam's "The Priest and the Acolyte." The homosexual discourse of the period includes both John Addington Symonds's earnest historical and critical studies and Walter Pater's fictional and nonfictional expositions of epicurean aestheticism, as well as a vast amount of pornography of varying explicitness.

If Carpenter and Symonds became the era's most persistent analysts of homosexual oppression and the leaders of England's inchoate homosexual emancipation movement (a movement never as strong in England as in Germany), Oscar Wilde both most fully exemplified a way of being homosexual at the end of the century and created the most enduring gay fictions of the day. The three gay fictions by Wilde explored in this book illustrate themes and attitudes that will reappear in various modifications throughout the twentieth century. The preoccupation with self-realization, the yearning for escape from moralistic prohibitions, the desire to recover an Arcadian past in which homosexuality is valued and respected, and the depiction of divided selves are characteristics of Wilde's gay fictions that are shared generally by those that follow.

Wilde's "The Portrait of Mr. W. H." (ca. 1890) is important not only for its claim to be among the earliest serious novelettes on a gay theme in English literature, but also for its originality as a foiled coming-out story. The protoganist discovers his homosexuality through the study of Shakespeare's *Sonnets* (establishing a connection between art and homosexual Eros that will also be repeated in other gay fictions), but finally rejects this self-realization for the safety of conformity even as he acknowledges the enormous loss involved in such self-denial. The ambivalence of "The Portrait of Mr. W. H." is equally obvious in the novel *The Picture of Dorian Gray* (1890, 1891), where self-realization is equated with dissipation and self-indulgence. Perhaps more responsible than any other single text in establishing the stereotypical link between art, decadence, and homosexuality, the work deserves credit as a pioneering depiction of a particular gay ambiance, yet it is divided against itself. But even as Wilde's novel enacts a moralistic fable, it also depicts homosexuality as a powerful attraction, guilt-inducing yet creative and potentially salvific. The homoerotic dream of a harmony between soul and body survives the moralistic conclusion to protest against an unsatisfactory reality and a tragic history of asceticism and medievalism.

Wilde's most important gay fiction is the poignant but exhilarating letter written in prison, *De Profundis* (1897), which translates the disaster of his disgrace into a ludic triumph. In his prison letter Wilde breaks free of the bourgeois mold that he had so often mocked yet to which he so tenaciously clung. Imprisoned and marginalized because of his homosexuality, he develops a new insight into the nature of the relationship between the individual and society, and he discovers in imagination (by which he means a critical alertness and attentiveness to received ideas and relationships, and a constant questioning of social codes and institutions) a way of liberating himself from the gay oppression that he experienced directly and that he came to symbolize for others. As a result of the social analysis and introspection occasioned by his pain and suffering, in *De Profundis* Wilde emerges as Saint Oscar, a kind of Harlequin Christ-figure who transforms his victimization into a martyrdom. In his martyrdom, he exemplifies the political realities of gay oppression and symbolizes both gay vulnerability and gay resistance. He revels defiantly in his exclusion from society and looks to nature for comfort and consolation. The rejection of society in *De Profundis* establishes radical separatism, either actual or metaphorical, as a potential response to homophobia and functions as a polar position in gay fiction's recurrent debate about the possibility of accommodation with a repressive society.

The other polar position is provided by Willa Cather in her remarkable story "Paul's Case" (1905), which is itself a direct response to the Wilde scandal. Her case study of an alienated youth almost mechanically moving to his suicide is enriched by an awareness of missed opportunities that might have rescued him. Her protagonist is not merely the homosexual victim hounded to his death by a persecuting society. The conformist and unimaginative American middle-class society that she depicts is culpable, but Paul himself also partakes of the lack of imagination that culminates in tragedy. The story in effect comments on Wilde's own fate as one that might have been prevented and as one for which he must share the blame. It

vividly depicts what at first glance may seem the inevitable fate of gay
people in an unsympathetic society, only to deconstruct this pessimistic assessment by subtly implying alternatives to alienation and suicide and envisioning possibilities of integrating homosexuals into the community, and
doing so without violating their individuality. Cather shares neither Wilde's
pessimism nor his blanket rejection of society. She implies that the solution
to the homosexual dilemma in an unaccepting society lies in assimilation
rather than separation. Her accommodationism places the burden of imaginative sympathy on society and the homosexual alike.

An overwhelming issue in gay fiction is the relationship of the individual
to society. The incompatibility between the needs of the homosexual and
the demands of a hostile and conformist society is the source of recurrent
conflicts. The polar solutions to this dilemma offered by Wilde and Cather
create a spectrum on which most of the subsequent gay fictions explored in
this book may be located. Those gay fictions optimistic about the possibility for reform in social attitudes toward homosexuality tend to embrace positions near Cather's humane accommodationism, while those pessimistic
about social reform adopt stances nearer to Wilde's justifiably bitter separatism. Since most gay people have had to practice various degrees of accommodationism—from the social invisibility of relationships to the
socially sanctioned hypocrisy of the closet—Cather's assimilationist position is likely to strike most readers as more realistic than Wilde's radical
separatism. But it should be pointed out that Cather's optimistic social
analysis is open to question and, based as it is on concepts as vague as
agape and *imagination*, her accommodationism is severely limited as a
practical response to homophobia. Reflecting the somewhat lesser degree of
hostility to homosexuality in America than in England in the first decade
of the new century, her social analysis may also be inapplicable in the face of
later organized campaigns of hatred and persecution.

E. M. Forster's gay fictions tend to be closer in spirit to Wilde than to
Cather. Although he embodies more fully than any other imaginative writer
of his generation a modern gay-liberation perspective, he became aware of
his own homosexuality in the climate of repression and self-consciousness
that prevailed in the aftermath of the Wilde scandal. Appropriately, *Maurice*, which may be described as the first gay-liberation masterpiece, is informed at every turn by *De Profundis*. Wilde's work is incorporated into
the very texture of Forster's novel, shaping the development of the hero and
leading to his embrace of the radical perspective on society conferred by
the outlaw status of the homosexual in 1913. Also deeply influenced by
Whitman and Carpenter, Forster's novel not only charts its protagonist's
achievement of a homosexual identity, but also traces his movement from a
platonized and sublimated homoeroticism to his salvation through a kind of
homosexuality that includes physical love and leads to a social analysis that
rejects class barriers and social conventions. Like Wilde, Forster has no

faith in reforming society; but, unlike Wilde's, Forster's pessimism is tempered by faith in personal relations. Hence, the escape into an Arcadian greenwood at the end of *Maurice* expresses Forster's radical critique of his society but also conveys his humanist faith in personal relationships.

In addition to *Maurice*, Forster's gay fictions include a number of excellent short narratives, such as "The Life to Come" (1922), "Arthur Snatchfold" (1928), and "The Other Boat" (1958), as well as some facetious tales. These stories, which might be described as priapic fictions, both celebrate and demystify sex. As a group, Forster's gay fictions illustrate his greatest gifts as a writer, and they are informed by the same concerns that animate all of his work: the quest for wholeness, the search for liberation, and the exploration of the inner life. Vital protests against gay oppression, the gay fictions embody a sophisticated social analysis, localized in Edwardian England, but remarkably contemporary. Because they were not published until after his death in 1970, Forster's gay fictions exerted no influence on subsequent ones (except possibly those of Christopher Isherwood, who read Forster's novel and stories in manuscript); nevertheless his work anticipates the second wave of gay fiction. In his choice of the *Bildungsroman*, or novel of education, as the mode in which to cast *Maurice*, Forster selected a genre particularly well suited to capture the complexities of the coming-out process. Not surprisingly, the *Bildungsroman* that culminates in the protagonist's acceptance of his homosexual identity is the most popular novelistic form of gay fiction.

While the first wave of serious gay fiction in English is the outgrowth of the early homosexual emancipation movement and the Wilde scandal, the second wave is part of the post–World War II literary boom, and it is predominantly American rather than British. The increasing urbanization of American life and the disruptions attendant upon the mobilization for the Second World War greatly facilitated the evolution of a visible gay subculture in the United States. As historian John D'Emilio observes, "The unusual conditions of a mobilized society allowed homosexual desire to be expressed more easily in action. For many gay Americans, World War II created something of a nationwide coming out experience."[12] Following the war, a number of reform organizations, such as the Mattachine Society, One, Inc., and the Daughters of Bilitis, formed to combat discrimination and to educate homosexuals and the public. Equally important, gay bars now appeared in almost every urban center, providing opportunities for socialization and for fostering a collective consciousness among homosexuals. Although the subculture centered around bars is often depicted very negatively in gay fiction, the institution of the gay bar contributed significantly to the developing sense of community among gay people in this period.

Two post–World War II publications were especially important in documenting the change that had occurred in gay life as the result of the war. In

1948, the Kinsey report on *Sexual Behavior in the Human Male* became a surprise best-seller. Its nonmoralistic, matter-of-fact discussion of sexual behavior permanently altered the terms in which sex could be discussed in America. Kinsey's discoveries, presented in dry, nonsensationalistic prose, were shocking because they indicated both a far greater variety of sexual behavior than expected and a far larger incidence of homosexual activity than previously acknowledged. He not only found that masturbation was a well-nigh-universal practice, but also that most males began regular sexual activity by the age of fifteen. His data on homosexuality was most startling of all. It indicated that 37 per cent of American males had had significant homosexual experience, that 12 per cent were predominantly homosexual for at least a three-year period in their lives, and that 4 per cent were exclusively homosexual as adults. He constructed a seven-point rating scale, ranging from exclusive heterosexuality at one end of the scale to exclusive homosexuality at the other, and demonstrated that human sexual response is fluid rather than fixed. Perhaps most important, Kinsey discovered that "[P]ersons with homosexual histories are to be found in every age group, in every social level, in every conceivable occupation, in cities and on farms, and in the most remote areas of the country."[13]

Kinsey's findings confirmed the emerging sense of gay men and lesbians in the late 1940s that they were not alone, that they in fact belonged to a group. This was also the burden of Donald Webster Cory's influential book, *The Homosexual in America*, which appeared in 1951. Cory argued more boldly than anyone previously for the rights of homosexuals as a group. He described the persecution and discrimination visited upon homosexuals, considered (though he did not dispute) the "sickness" theories of homosexuality, and indicated the diversity of homosexual lives. Most significantly, he conceived of homosexuals as a despised minority. "We are a minority," he declared,

> not only numerically, but also as a result of a caste-like status in society . . . our minority status is similar, in a variety of respects, to that of national, religious, and other ethnic groups; in the denial of civil liberties; in the legal, extra-legal and quasi-legal discrimination; in the assignment of an inferior social position; in the exclusion from the mainstreams of life and culture. . . . On the other hand, one great gap separates the homosexual minority from all others, and that is its lack of recognition, its lack of respectability in the eyes of the public, and even in the most advanced circles.[14]

Cory, thus, called for the change of consciousness and the collective response that would not materialize fully until Stonewall.

The greater visibility of the homosexual subculture following World War II made possible the emergence of a new openly gay popular literature.

While many of these works trivialized and sensationalized homosexuals and the gay subculture, Gore Vidal's *The City and the Pillar* (1948), one of the first explicitly gay fictions to reach a large audience, challenged the era's wide-spread contempt for gay people. Emphasizing the normality of homosexuals, it traces the coming-out process of a young man who is ordinary to the point of blandness. By providing an unsensationalized portrait of the gay subculture, it illustrates the vast range and diversity of homosexuals and the social dynamics, mores, and specialized language of a submerged society. While it concedes that the experience of being gay in an unaccepting society may foster neurosis, it also insists that this experience may lead to healthy introspection and valuable social criticism. Subverting important nationalistic and homoerotic myths, the novel exposes the false romanticism, particularly as expressed in the idealization of innocence, that was characteristic of American life at mid-century. Despite its melodramatic conclusion, *The City and the Pillar* is essentially optimistic, its accommodationist stance sustained by a belief in its own power to help reshape social attitudes.

While the intent of *The City and the Pillar* is to illustrate the basic normality of homosexuality, Truman Capote's *Other Voices, Other Rooms* (1948) and Tennessee Williams's *One Arm and Other Stories* (1948) and *Hard Candy and Other Stories* (1954) adopt a very different strategy. Rather than insisting on the ordinariness of gay people, the Southern writers revel in the extraordinariness of their exotic, frequently grotesque characters. Capote's novel is muddled and sensational, but Williams's gay fictions are altogether more affirmative. They are never designed merely to shock, even when they contain undeniably sensationalistic incidents. In stories like "One Arm," "Desire and the Black Masseur," and "The Night of the Iguana" from the first collection and "The Mysteries of the Joy Rio," "Hard Candy," and "Two on a Party" from the second, Williams focuses on individuals who have been bloodied by life, but who are still actively contending as they struggle against loneliness and isolation. Often heroic in their persistence and commitment, they arouse pathos and compassion. Too fully individualized to be merely stereotypical, Williams's characters are nevertheless too colorful and eccentric to exemplify the mundanity of homosexuality. While he is less interested in social context or explicitly political issues than in particular dilemmas, he nevertheless documents the cruelty and oppression suffered by gay people in mid-century America. Accepting the human in all its variety, and condemning only willful cruelty and mendacity, Williams wrote about homosexuality with a naturalness that was highly unusual in the 1940s and 1950s.

While Williams's gay fictions implicitly challenge the social stigma attached to homosexuality, Mary Renault's *The Charioteer* (1953) and James Baldwin's *Giovanni's Room* (1956) more explicitly confront this issue. Indeed, they may be (like Vidal's *The City and the Pillar*) defined as "homosexual problem novels" centered on the difficulties faced by the gay person in achieving dignity and self-respect in a nonaccepting society and within a sordid subculture. Written at the height of the 1950s backlash against homosexuality, the novels vividly document the increased homophobia of that era, when homosexuals were more aggressively and systematically attacked than at any previous time in modern Anglo-American history.[15] During this decade, gay people became the chief scapegoats of the Cold War, faced blatant employment discrimination, and suffered widespread harassment by local and national police organizations. In the United States and Great Britain throughout the 1950s, thousands of individuals were arrested and imprisoned for homosexual offenses. The popular consensus that homosexuals were immoral, emotionally unstable, and untrustworthy justified their punishment and stigmatization, and unavoidably engendered guilt and self-doubt in gay people themselves.

This guilt and self-doubt is apparent in *The Charioteer*, which mirrors the homophobia of its day even as it offers a portrait of homosexual love as potentially elevated and dignified and presents gay protagonists who are notably free of stereotypical affectations. The novel reflects the decade's received ideas about homosexuality in its adoption of a medical model to explain its characters' gayness, in its depiction of the gay subculture as pathological, and in its conception of homosexuality as a personal failing. At the same time that it absorbs the popular attitudes of its day, however, it also attempts to reform some of them, in the process reflecting the strategies of accommodation adopted by the small social and legal reform movements in England and America at that time. More successfully, Renault challenges the sexual ideology of the 1950s by sketching her characters as individuals responding to universal human dilemmas and by her insistence on the preeminent value of self-knowledge. Despite its apologetic tone, *The Charioteer* undermines its own calculatingly accommodationist approach to the "homosexual problem" and provides a happy ending for its lovers, who, against great odds, forge a relationship with potential for nobility and growth.

Baldwin's *Giovanni's Room* is also a coming-out narrative that both confirms and challenges stereotypical ideas about the gay experience, but in its confrontation with the homophobia of its day it is bolder and more sophisticated than Renault's novel. The ambivalences about homosexuality in *Giovanni's Room* not only vividly reflect the social reality of the day but also themselves constitute the core of the protagonist's inner conflict. A novel of the divided and deceitful self, *Giovanni's Room* is a searing account of the failure of integrity. But even as it exposes the moral cowardice of David, its indecisive protagonist, it places his betrayals within a larger context of a more generalized hostility to love. And even as it conveys the intense psychological suffering inflicted by homophobia, it also diagnoses the pressure for conformity as a fear of the terror within and exposes the American romanticization of innocence as a form of evasion. Most boldly of all, it illustrates the possibility of self-affirmation through confrontation with internal fears and it discovers in homosexuality a salvific quality, sketching the homosexual's potential role as a redemptive figure. Although it ends hopefully, its optimism is, finally, individual and personal rather than collective or social. In this respect, the vision of *Giovanni's Room* is nearer to that of Forster or Wilde than to Cather, Vidal, or Renault.

In the early 1960s, with the relaxation of censorship and the first stirrings of the (hetero)sexual revolution, homosexuality became even more visible. The virulent homophobia of the McCarthy years lessened somewhat and the election of a youthful president at the beginning of the decade signaled new hope for social-activist movements of all kinds, including the small homophile organizations. The medical consensus that homosexuals were sick, corrupt, and depraved was challenged as the study of homosexuality became the province of sociologists as well as psychiatrists. The homophile organizations were transformed from social and self-help groups to political action groups as the leaders who acquiesced in the notion of homosexuality as pathology were displaced by leaders who were more militant. These new activists rejected the sickness theories of homosexuality and insisted that gay people were a persecuted minority, deserving of equal treatment in a pluralistic society.[16] If in the early 1960s a huge majority of Americans and Britons (including a majority of gay people) still regarded homosexuality as pathological and homosexuals as unstable individuals afflicted with a personal problem, the seeds of the contemporary gay liberation movement were at least beginning to sprout.

Those seeds are obvious in Christopher Isherwood's *A Single Man,* which anticipates the gay liberation movement that would flower in the aftermath of Stonewall. In this novel, Isherwood humorously and movingly conveys the essence of homosexual resentment against a society that systematically denies the legitimacy of gay experience. He develops the context of gay oppression and places it within a still larger context of spiritual transcendence. But even as he articulates a transcendent vision in which a universal consciousness subsumes individuality, Isherwood also recognizes the need for gay solidarity. Unlike most of the gay novels explored in this book, *A Single Man* is not a *Bildungsroman* centered on the protagonist's acceptance of his homosexual identity. In Isherwood's novel, the protagonist's homosexuality is not the cause of agonizing self-examination, but a simple given, neither open to question nor a source of contention. Nevertheless, the hero is constantly and acutely aware of his minority status and he conceives of gay people as a legitimate minority with genuine grievances that need to be redressed. Isherwood's dual insistence on the common

humanity of gay people and on the need for a tribal identity among homosexuals are vital contributions to gay fiction. Especially distinguished for
its presentation of homosexuality as a human variation that should be accorded value and respect, and for its depiction of its alienated gay hero as
an Everyman figure with whom all readers can identify, *A Single Man*
is the masterpiece of the second wave of gay fiction in Anglo-American
literature.

The present book, then, traces a tradition of gay fiction that is roughly
analogous to the development of homosexual consciousness from Wilde to
Stonewall. Like gay life itself throughout this period, the gay fictions included are all circumscribed by homophobia; that is, they are all reactions
to the social and legal prohibitions against homosexuality, and, thus, they
are essentially defensive. Even when they most joyously and lyrically celebrate gay love, their celebrations are self-consciously defiant. But what is
most remarkable is the persistence and tenacity of the struggle for wholeness depicted in these fictions. Despite their acute awareness of the draconian legal sanctions and harsh social prohibitions directed against
homosexuality, these works nevertheless repeatedly affirm homosexual
identity. Collectively, the tradition of gay fiction traced through these representative texts defends homosexuality as an integral element in the fullness of personality, depicts gay people as complete human beings rather
than as case histories or curiosities, and illuminates the homosexual's relationship to the dominant culture.

Although the texts discussed in this book are products of particular and
immediate social contexts, they also transcend their historical moments and
continue to speak to the question of what it means to be homosexual: a
question that is important not only to gay people but to all who value justice and diversity. Cumulatively, these texts and this tradition constitute an
imaginative history of gay people and illustrate a variety of fictional strategies of representation of homosexuality in this century. The gay literary
tradition has been dis-esteemed, yet it is surprisingly rich. Despite the professional and personal hazards of writing honestly and sympathetically
about homosexuality in the years before Stonewall, the authors of the gay
fictions explored in this book created works that retain the ring of truth and
that continue to compel respect and admiration. These gay fictions deserve
recognition for their insight as well as for their courage, for their beauty as
well as for their compassion.

2

"In Such Surrender There May Be Gain": Oscar Wilde and the Beginnings of Gay Fiction

Modern gay fiction in English begins with Oscar Wilde. This is not only because "The Portrait of Mr. W. H." has claim to being the earliest serious short story on a gay subject in English literature or that *The Picture of Dorian Gray* is among the first novels in the language to feature (though blurred and inexactly) a homosexual subculture. Most profoundly, modern gay fiction may trace its beginnings to Wilde because of his role as a symbolic figure who exemplified a way of being a homosexual at a pivotal moment in the emergence of gay consciousness—the crucial final decades of the nineteenth century—and who ultimately functioned as Saint Oscar, the homosexual martyr. Although Wilde frequently (and sometimes self-servingly) asserted the impersonality of art, his own art is inseparably bound to his personality, or at least to the persona he so assiduously cultivated and promoted, and thus his works cannot be appreciated in isolation from his life. It is not merely that Wilde's work is, as Richard Le Gallienne remarked, "but the marginalia . . . of a striking fantastic personality"[1] or that Wilde, as he told André Gide, put his genius into his life and only his talent into his art.[2] What binds Wilde's life and art so inseparably is the fact that his greatest artistic creation is the complex and contradictory persona reflected equally in his work and in his life.

Certainly Wilde's life is as paradoxical as his works. Born to accomplished but eccentric parents in Ireland in 1854, he was educated at Trinity College, Dublin, and Magdalen College, Oxford, where he was almost equally influenced by the practically incompatible artistic doctrines of the moralistic John Ruskin and the epicurean Walter Pater. Leaving Oxford in 1878, he declared prophetically, "Somehow or other I'll be famous, and if not famous, I'll be notorious."[3] A master of drawing attention to himself, he quickly became known as the high priest of aestheticism, the intimate of artists, and the companion of actresses. A superb conversationalist and a

29

flamboyant dandy, he became a celebrity by virtue of his outrageousness as much as through his actual accomplishments.

Wilde married Constance Lloyd in 1884 and quickly produced two sons. Although he had flirted with homosexuality for many years and had aroused the suspicions and gossip of many (and later came to regard himself as having always been homosexual), he seems to have begun the sustained practice of homosexuality in 1886, when he met a young Canadian, Robert Ross, who was to be his lifelong and faithful friend and eventually his literary executor. In 1891, Wilde met Lord Alfred Douglas, the twenty-one-year-old son of the ninth Marquess of Queensberry, who was to hound Wilde to his spectacular fall. Douglas apparently introduced Wilde to the Victorian homosexual underground of male brothels and procurers and prostitutes who were to figure prominently in the sensational trials of 1895. Although Douglas appears to have been a thoroughly undisciplined young man, utterly unworthy of Wilde's devotion, the writer became so infatuated as to lose all sense of proportion and finally to embark on the course of action that was to culminate in his sentence to two years' penal servitude at hard labor. In hindsight, Wilde's association with Douglas seems a disaster. At the same time, however, the tumultuous affair may have inspired Wilde to some of his best work. Unquestionably, the discovery of his homosexuality liberated his art and marks a major breakthrough in his artistic maturity.

Wilde's brief period of serious achievement began in 1888 with the publication of *The Happy Prince*, a collection of fairy tales. Over the next six years he was to produce *The Picture of Dorian Gray, Intentions, Lord Arthur Savile's Crime and Other Stories*, and *House of Pomegranates*, as well as the five important plays: *Salomé, Lady Windermere's Fan, A Woman of No Importance, An Ideal Husband*, and *The Importance of Being Earnest*. This brief period of genuine accomplishment ended abruptly in 1895 when the Marquess of Queensberry left a card for Wilde at his club: "To Oscar Wilde, posing somdomite [*sic*]." Encouraged by Douglas, who loathed his father, Wilde stupidly sued Queensberry for libel: a suit that was won by the bitter and unstable Marquess and that was to culminate in Wilde's own prosecution for "gross indecency between males."

Wilde's penchant for self-advertisement and for audacious posing ought not to obscure the seriousness behind his apparent flippancy. The apostle of aestheticism and decadence, the dandy addicted to gold-tipped cigarettes and exquisite *objets d'arts*, the social butterfly who cultivated the lords and ladies of the aristocracy, and the witty epigrammatist who delighted in deflating Victorian pomposity while celebrating the trivial at the expense of the earnest was also a penetrating social critic who defended individuality and pluralism and attacked economic and social exploitation and injustice. In his remarkable pamphlet *The Soul of Man under Socialism* (1891), he enunciated a doctrine of libertarian socialism quite at variance with his mask of frivolity. For all its utopian idealism and arch wit, the pamphlet acutely dissects the harmful effects of private property on rich and poor alike. It is also filled with subtle insights into the nature of oppression, as when it redefines selfishness in terms of authoritarian morality: "Selfishness is not living as one wishes to live, it is asking others to live as one wishes to live. And unselfishness is letting other people's lives alone, not interfering with them."[4] Moreover, as editor of *The Woman's World* and in his plays, he consistently supported sexual equality and deplored the Victorian double standard. Wilde's anti-authoritarianism and his scorn for the philistinism of his late Victorian age are particularly important aspects of his persona and of his emergence as a symbolic figure, even as they are qualified by his almost equally strong need for social acceptance.

In the juxtaposition of his anti-authoritarianism and his self-promotion is found the ambivalence of his relationship to society: for all his gibes against the oppressive morality of his age, he had a deep-seated need for public approval. This need for social approval was, as he himself must have known, doomed to disappointment. For all his appearance as a respectable married man, and for all his success in attaining celebrity, by virtue of his Irishness and his homosexuality he could never be fully accepted into the upper-class society that he cultivated nor approved by the middle-class society he scorned. Perhaps, as James Joyce suggested, Wilde attempted to resolve this conundrum by deceiving "himself into believing that he was the bearer of the good news of neo-paganism to an enslaved people."[5] Mocking English hypocrisy and moralism, he made insincerity an artistic principle and lawlessness an ethical standard. Not surprisingly, the society whose values he so contemptuously dismissed eventually took its revenge, finally sacrificing him as a scapegoat for its sexual and moral insecurities.

Wilde is, it must be admitted, an unlikely martyr, and a deeply ambiguous one. His martyrdom, after all, resulted as much from his folly as from the viciousness of his persecutors, who were not eager to prosecute him or other homosexuals of high social standing or artistic prominence. Indeed, his trial and conviction for "gross indecency between males" and his subsequent severe sentence may fairly be blamed on his (and Alfred Douglas's) willed stupidity and penchant for self-dramatization, and perhaps as well on his unconscious need for exposure and punishment. The theme of martyrdom is a thread that runs through much of his work, early and late, and probably reflects the strong masochistic element in his personality, even as it also mirrors his sense of alienation. Moreover, his disastrous decision to prosecute the Marquess of Queensberry for alleging that he posed as a sodomite was itself reactionary rather than defiant in nature, reflecting both his ambivalence toward homosexuality and his desire to appear to conform to the Victorian standards that he so often ridiculed.

Even after the debacle of his libel suit against Queensberry, he could have escaped his own prosecution by fleeing to the Continent, a solution tacitly suggested by the magistrate who apparently delayed issuing the warrant for his arrest in order to permit him to go abroad. That he did not take this suggestion and go into exile, as so many prominent Victorian homosexuals had done when confronted with the prospect of scandal and prison, is a measure less of his rebelliousness than of his felt need to maintain his position in society. And even the eloquent defense in his second trial of "the Love that dare not speak its name"—"a great affection of an elder for a younger man as there was between David and Jonathan, such as Plato made the very basis of his philosophy, and such as you will find in the sonnets of Michael Angelo and Shakespeare. . . . that deep, spiritual affection which is as pure as it is perfect"[6]—is sharply undercut by the fact that the speech, largely untrue and certainly misleading, was designed to deny the physical expression of his homosexuality rather than to defend it. As George Woodcock has noted, "there is no cause to blame Wilde for denying the charges against him when he was faced with a thoroughly savage and immoral law, but the fact remains that he did not practise the defiance of a rebel, who would have admitted what was attributed to him, and defended himself by attacking the law."[7] Indeed, the only hero of the Wilde trials is the procurer, Alfred Taylor, who loyally refused to testify against Wilde and consequently shared his harsh punishment.

If Wilde is an unlikely and ambiguous martyr, nevertheless the severity of his punishment and the extremity of his suffering transformed him into a figure at once tragic and comic, Saint Oscar, both the symbol of gay oppression and of ludic triumph over adversity. Wilde's own folly and masochism may have brought him into the prisoner's dock at Old Bailey, but once there he was victimized by the bigotry and hypocrisy of a society that he had ridiculed and exposed and yet could never completely reject. This bigotry is palpable in the glee with which the philistines greeted his conviction and in the remarks of the presiding judge at his third trial. "It is the worst case I have ever tried," Mr. Justice Wills declared, adding almost superfluously: "I shall, under the circumstances, be expected to pass the severest sentence that the law allows. In my judgment it is totally inadequate for such a case as this."[8] Justice Wills's intemperate indignation here, his unctuous declaration that the acts of "gross indecency" with male prostitutes for which Wilde was convicted were in effect more heinous than murder or rape or assault or blackmail or theft or embezzlement or any number of other serious crimes, seems bizarre from our point of view today. But Justice Wills's attitude provides an accurate index of the intense hatred toward homosexuality that was felt by Victorian England and that continues to infect judicial decisions even today, as witnessed by recent opinions of the United States Supreme Court, such as the 1986 *Hardwick v. Bowers* case.

Hatred of homosexuality has a long and ignoble history in England. As late as 1861, sodomy, frequently described as the crime not mentionable among Christians, remained a capital offense, and executions for sodomy were actually carried out as late as 1835, long after nearly all of Europe had abolished capital punishment for the offense and after France had decriminalized consensual homosexual activity altogether. When the death penalty was abolished in England in 1861, the penalty for sodomy was reduced to penal servitude for life or for any term not less than ten years, while attempted sodomy was punishable by a maximum of ten years' imprisonment. The offense of which Wilde was convicted, an act of "gross indecency" not amounting to sodomy, became illegal in 1886, when the Criminal Law Amendment Act of 1885 took effect. The sponsor of this legislation, Henry Labouchere, publicly remarked when learning of Wilde's sentence that he regretted that the maximum penalty had not been made seven years instead of two.[9] Although the evidence indicated that Wilde was guilty of sodomy, he was probably charged with "gross indecency" rather than with the more serious charge because of the greater difficulty of proving the latter, which required evidence of penetration, and perhaps because of the reluctance of the prosecutors to subject the draconian British legal system to the glare of European publicity certain to be occasioned by the trial (and possible life sentence) of so prominent an author. This history of legal and social condemnation of male homosexuality helps explain the public outrage that greeted Wilde upon his conviction and the public humiliation that he suffered. As H. Montgomery Hyde reports, at the news of Wilde's conviction, some people literally danced with joy in the streets.[10]

This context of Victorian homophobia also helps explain the reticence and coyness of Wilde's depictions of homosexuality in texts such as "The Portrait of Mr. W. H." and *The Picture of Dorian Gray*. Wilde deserves enormous credit for bravery in even broaching gay themes at a time when it was dangerous to do so. Open, nonhomophobic discussion of homosexuality was, quite simply, impossible in the mainstream English press of his day. Even Havelock Ellis's pioneering and circumspect work, *Sexual Inversion*, was banned under the obscenity statutes in 1898. Nevertheless, Wilde's own (unsurprising) ambivalence—his internalization of homophobic attitudes—more fully explains why these texts are finally divided against themselves. Heir to a homosexual aesthetic tradition that stretches from Johann Joachim Winckelmann to Walter Pater and the center (in England) of *fin de siècle* dandyism and decadence, Wilde still remains curiously moralistic. In a play like *The Importance of Being Earnest*, he translates his ambivalence, epitomized by the very notion of Bunburying, into a complex parody of both himself and his society and thereby creates a masterpiece, perhaps the greatest comedy in the language. In the earlier works, however, the ambivalence fails to achieve resolution, and the result is a kind of imaginative paralysis: a rueful suspension between idealism and realism in "The Portrait of Mr. W. H." and a melodramatic moralism in *The Picture of Dorian Gray.* Only after his dizzying fall, in the painful but sly *De Profundis* (and as well in *The Ballad of Reading Gaol),* does Wilde achieve a vision at once unified and capacious enough to contain his contradictoriness, a vision at once tragic and ludic, deepened and purified by a felt understanding of the nature of suffering and its powers of redemption. In his imprisonment, Wilde is finally freed of the bourgeois attitudes that he had so frequently ridiculed yet nevertheless internalized. As a result of this painfully earned freedom, he finally is able to validate his sexuality and empower it both as a means to achieve wholeness of being and as a tool to explicate his problematic relationship to society.

"The Portrait of Mr. W. H." is a work on which Wilde expended great time and effort and it is one of the most revealing of his stories, although the revelations are characteristically shrouded. The original version was published as an article of twelve-thousand words in 1889, but Wilde became more and more obsessed with the subject and during the next four years he revised and augmented the story, in the process more than doubling its length. The manuscript of the expanded story, actually a novelette, was thought to have been lost in the chaos that accompanied the sale of Wilde's property after his arrest; many years later, it was discovered in the offices of Wilde's publisher, John Lane, and the revised version finally achieved print in 1921. Although the editor of Wilde's *Complete Shorter Fiction* prefers the shorter first version rather than the longer, revised story on the grounds that the additions "upset the balance of narrative framework,"[11] the latter is by far the more important work. By adding a long passage on neoplatonism and elaborating on the significance of friendship in the Renaissance, Wilde clarified the homosexual base of the story and made more meaningful the relationship between the narrative frame and the Shakespearean material.[12]

On one level, the story is merely a pleasant speculation on the identity of the young man of Shakespeare's *Sonnets.* Following suggestions by eighteenth-century Shakespeareans Edmund Malone and Thomas Tyrwhitt, and building largely on the basis of various puns in several of the sonnets, Wilde identifies Mr. W. H. as a boy actor named Willie Hughes and develops a detailed interpretation of the sequence and of the relationship of the *Sonnets* to the plays. Wilde may have originally intended the story as a satire on Shakespearean scholarship, particularly of the methods and conclusions of groups like the Baconians, who developed elaborate biographical theories on the basis of their analyses of word play. But as Wilde became more and more fascinated with the interpretation of the *Sonnets,* the satirical impulse receded. In its final version, the novelette is both an exercise in imaginative criticism and a defense of homosexuality. The "secret" to which Wilde referred in an 1889 letter to Robert Ross—"Now that

Willie Hughes has been revealed to the world, we must have another secret"[13]—is, in fact, the story's homosexual import, a meaning that is more clearly articulated as the result of the later additions.

Stripped of some of its fancifulness, Wilde's interpretation of Shakespeare's *Sonnets* could have been presented in the form of an essay, and indeed the story is sometimes included among Wilde's essays. But "The Portrait of Mr. W. H." is criticism made self-consciously fictional and dramatic. It is, as Lewis J. Poteet has noted, "an experiment in the mode of fiction as criticism."[14] The experiment confirms Wilde's famous definition of criticism as a form of autobiography, illustrating the point Wilde had made in "The Decay of Lying" that "the telling of beautiful untrue things, is the proper aim of Art,"[15] and embodies concretely his theory of the subjectivity of art. As Linda Dowling has demonstrated, the novelette both celebrates and subverts "the fin de siècle ideal of autonomous art."[16] But the elaborate fiction also works in a complex and tantalizing way to reveal the homosexual subtext. The narrative frame is itself both a distancing technique and a focusing mechanism. It places homosexuality in a distant past but also discloses a continuity of homosexual feeling that links the past to the present. "The Portrait of Mr. W. H." is at once a literary speculation, a meditation on idealized homosexuality, and a foiled coming-out story, Nabokovian in its complexity and irony.

"The Portrait of Mr. W. H." is divided into five sections, the middle three sections devoted almost entirely to analyses of Shakespeare's poems and his relationship with the young man of the *Sonnets*, the first and final sections devoted to the frame-story. The novelette pivots on the relationship between the Shakespearean material in the middle sections and the narrative frame established in the first section and resolved in the last. Significantly, both the middle and the framing sections are self-consciously homosexual in subject and tone. Whereas the Shakespearean material deals specifically with the attachment of Shakespeare and a young man, the framing sections are concerned with characters who are sketched in terms of an easily recognizable homosexual style—a style Wilde more than anyone else helped to establish. Leisured, aristocratic bachelors, Cyril Graham, Erskine, and the unnamed narrator are connoisseurs who interpret high culture to the middle classes. Although the homosexual relationships of Cyril and Erskine and of Shakespeare and the young man of the *Sonnets* are indicated implicitly rather than explicitly, the homosexuality that pervades both the critical sections and the frame-story is crucial to the work as a whole, and crucial in a way more important than simply a matter of ambiance or style.

"The Portrait of Mr. W. H." opens with a brief discussion of literary forgeries and Erskine's revelation that his beautiful and effeminate friend Cyril Graham, to whom he had been "absurdly devoted," had secretly

commissioned a forgery in order to convince Erskine that the only begetter
of the *Sonnets* was an Elizabethan actor. "I refused to be convinced till the
actual existence of Willie Hughes, a boy-actor of the Elizabethan stage, had
been placed beyond the reach of doubt or cavil," Erskine confesses. When
the forgery was discovered, Cyril committed suicide, offering his life "as a
sacrifice to the secret of the Sonnets." Although Erskine continues to doubt
the theory, the narrator is enraptured, pronouncing it "the only perfect key
to Shakespeare's Sonnets that has ever been made." Expressing admiration
for Cyril's faith and exclaiming, "I believe in Willie Hughes," he determines to vindicate the young martyr's place in literary history and pledges
to rescue Shakespeare himself "from the tedious memory of a commonplace intrigue." In sections two, three, and four, he investigates the texts
and contexts of Shakespeare's poems and confirms the truth of Cyril's theory. In the final section, he writes a long letter appealing to Erskine "to do
justice to the memory of Cyril Graham, and to give to the world his mar-
vellous interpretation of the Sonnets." The letter convinces Erskine, but the
narrator experiences a curious reaction: "It seemed to me that I had given
away my capacity for belief in the Willie Hughes theory of the Sonnets,
that something had gone out of me, as it were, and that I was perfectly
indifferent to the whole subject." He confesses his lack of belief to Erskine
and demands precisely the kind of proof that Erskine had earlier asked of
Cyril. Two years later, Erskine writes the narrator a letter saying that he
has failed to verify the theory and that, in consequence, he has determined
to commit suicide, "to give his own life also to the cause." The narrator
rushes to France to attempt to prevent his friend's suicide, but arrives to
discover that his friend is already dead, not of suicide but of consumption.

Central to the story is the notion that the *Sonnets* are "poems of serious
and tragic import, wrung out of the bitterness of Shakespeare's heart, and
made sweet by the honey of his lips." The theory assumes that the *Sonnets*
are addressed to an individual, to "a particular young man whose personality for some reason seems to have filled the soul of Shakespeare with
terrible joy and no less terrible despair." In defining his inquiry, Cyril proposes to answer the following questions:

> Who was that young man of Shakespeare's day who, without being of noble
> birth or even of noble nature, was addressed by him in terms of such passion-
> ate adoration that we can but wonder at the strange worship, and are almost
> afraid to turn the key that unlocks the mystery of the poet's heart? Who was
> he whose physical beauty was such that it became the very corner-stone of
> Shakespeare's art; the very source of Shakespeare's inspiration; the very incar-
> nation of Shakespeare's dreams?

Identifying Mr. W. H. as Willie Hughes, "some wonderful boy-actor of
great beauty" who portrayed Shakespeare's heroines, the theory is but-

tressed by an elaborate examination of the *Sonnets*. But Wilde's interest in "The Portrait of Mr. W. H." is less in the *Sonnets* than in the power of art and historical criticism to affect the lives of his lightly sketched characters, particularly the narrator. Thus, the point of the story is not the theory itself but the faith in the theory demonstrated by the three characters, one of whom commits first forgery and then suicide in order to indicate "how firm and flawless his faith in the whole thing was," and another of whom attempts to forge a suicide and thereby disguise his death as a sacrifice to the cause. Faith is the test by which the three characters in the novelette are judged, a test that the narrator—the character who is apparently the most truthful—finally fails.

A crucial context for both the *Sonnets* and the characters' responses to the theory is the homoeroticism and sexual ambiguity that were prevalent in the Renaissance, which—regarded nostalgically from the perspective of a tawdry present—is presented as a Hellenistic, Romantic age. The story's elaborate display of historical scholarship, tracing "the Romantic Movement of English Literature" back through the German *Aufklärung* and the Elizabethan and Italian Renaissances to the Hellenism of the ancient Greeks, illustrates the dictum enunciated in "The Rise of Historical Criticism" that speculation on the past "is part of that complex working towards freedom which may be described as the revolt against authority."[17] Associating Willie Hughes with Gaveston in Marlowe's *Edward II* and linking the love of the *Sonnets* with the neoplatonism of Ficino and Michelangelo and the Hellenism of Winckelmann, the theory constitutes a defense of homosexuality in terms very similar to the defense that Wilde would later offer for "the Love that dare not speak its name." For example, the narrator of "The Portrait of Mr. W. H." remarks: "I saw that the love that Shakespeare bore him was as the love of a musician for some delicate instrument on which he delights to play, as a sculptor's love for some rare and exquisite material that suggests a new form of plastic beauty, a new mode of plastic perfection." The love is one that transcends but does not deny the physical. "There was a kind of mystic transference of the expressions of the physical world to a sphere that was spiritual, that was removed from gross bodily appetite, and in which the soul was Lord," the narrator comments of friendship in the Renaissance. The *Sonnets* capture "the Soul, as well as the language, of neo-Platonism."

Neoplatonism is revealingly problematic for Wilde's story. In its dualism and its elevation of the soul at the expense of the body, neoplatonism is essentially antisexual. Yet it has in its idealization traditionally been used as a philosophical defense of (and euphemism for) homosexuality, and Wilde so uses it in "The Portrait of Mr. W. H." when he writes that

> In its subtle suggestions of sex in soul, in the curious analogies it draws between intellectual enthusiasm and the physical passion of love, in its dream of

the incarnation of the Idea as a beautiful and living form, and of a real spiritual conception with a travail and a bringing to birth, there was something that fascinated the poets and scholars of the sixteenth century.

But Wilde frankly acknowledges that the sixteenth-century philosophy that explains Shakespeare's passionate attachment to Willie Hughes would be denounced in the nineteenth century. In answer to contemporaneous critics, who see in the *Sonnets* "something dangerous, something unlawful even," the narrator defiantly asserts the superiority of the soul's affections to man-made law. And, in one of the most important passages in the novelette, the narrator recognizes both peril and potential in the kind of romantic affection Shakespeare felt for Willie Hughes or Ficino for Pico della Mirandola or Michelangelo for Tommaso Cavalieri or Winckelmann for the young Roman who initiated him into the secret of Greek art. "It is no doubt true that to be filled with an absorbing passion is to surrender the security of one's lower life," he writes, "and yet in such surrender there may be gain." This notion that there may be gain in embracing a higher truth than the security of everyday reality reverberates throughout the story, finally mocking the narrator himself when he rejects his own soul's truth. At the same time, however, the recognition of the perilous nature of self-discovery reveals as well Wilde's awareness of gay oppression, perhaps the single most crucial element in the formation of a modern gay consciousness.

But more important even than its idealization and cautious defense of homosexuality is the novelette's emphasis on the continuity of homosexual feeling from the past to the present. This continuity, rather than the identity of Mr. W. H., is the real secret of the *Sonnets* and the real connection between the frame-story and the critical sections. In "The Portrait of Mr. W. H.," to study the *Sonnets* is to recognize a personal affinity with the homoerotic passion of Shakespeare and Willie Hughes. As a result of his absorption with the text of Shakespeare's poems, Cyril, Erskine, and the narrator each finds reflected in the *Sonnets* an image of his own homosexuality. More accurately, they project onto their reading of Shakespeare's text their own homosexual sensibilities, discovering in the text the mirror of their own desire. The story in effect dramatizes the critic's power to reinvent and distort and rearrange a text, presenting art as essentially plastic, responsive to the changing needs of each viewer or reader. As Poteet comments, "The point of the allegation about Willie Hughes is not that it is true (it is in fact probably false, as the narrator learns) but that it is a piece of creative criticism that acts as a catalyst to insight."[18] Of greater relevance still, the criticism offered within the work is not merely subjective, but solipsistic, even autobiographical. Hence, it is not susceptible to independent verification, despite the demand first of Erskine and then the narrator for objective proof. The story confirms Wilde's assertion in "The

Critic as Artist" that the highest criticism is "the record of one's soul. . . . [Criticism] is the only civilized form of autobiography, as it deals not with the events, but with the thoughts of one's life; not with life's physical accidents of deed or circumstance, but with the spiritual moods and imaginative passions of the mind."[19] Thus, the search for the solution "to the greatest mystery of modern literature" finally reveals less about the *Sonnets* than about Cyril, Erskine, and especially the narrator.

The autobiographical basis of the Willie Hughes hypothesis is clearest in the case of Cyril, who bears a striking resemblance both to the portrait that he commissions and to the facts of Willie Hughes's life that he adduces. The painting is described by Erskine as

> a full length portrait of a young man in late sixteenth century costume, standing by a table with his right hand resting on an open book. He seemed about seventeen years of age, and was of quite extraordinary personal beauty, though evidently somewhat effeminate. Indeed had it not been for the dress and the closely cropped hair, one would have said that the face with its dreamy, wistful eyes and its delicate scarlet lips was the face of a girl.

Except for the period costume, this portrait of an androgynous young man might well be the portrait of Cyril himself, who shares with the hypothesized Mr. W. H. enormous personal charm and a histrionic gift for portraying Shakespeare's heroines, as well as capriciousness and sexual ambiguity. Moreover, just as Willie Hughes is supposed to have exerted such inordinate power over Shakespeare, so does Cyril affect others. As Erskine remarks, "I think he was the most splendid creature I ever saw, and nothing could exceed the grace of his movements, the charm of his manner. He fascinated everybody who was worth fascinating, and a great many people who were not."

Although less obvious than Cyril's creation of Willie Hughes in his own image, the narrator's discovery of his own soul's autobiography as the result of his criticism is nevertheless more central to the meaning of the novelette. The narrator's investigation of Cyril's theory, spurred by his fascination with the androgynous ideal represented by the portrait and deepened by his immersion in the *Sonnets*, serves to reveal his soul, both to himself and to us. As he remarks, "Consciousness . . . is quite inadequate to explain the contents of personality. It is Art, and Art only, that reveals us to ourselves." After he has refined Cyril's theory, he reflects: "it seemed to me that I was deciphering the story of a life that had once been mine, unrolling the record of a romance that, without my knowing it, had coloured the very texture of my nature, had dyed it with strange and subtle dyes. . . . I felt as if I had been initiated into the secret of that passionate friendship . . . of which the Sonnets in their noblest and purest signifi-

cance, may be held to be the perfect expression." In undertaking the cause
of Cyril Graham, the narrator discovers his own predilection for passionate
friendship, a predilection that (like sexual orientation itself) is less a matter
of conscious choice than a matter of being. He recognizes that

> The soul had a life of its own, and the brain its own sphere of action. There
> was something within us that knew nothing of sequence or extension, and yet,
> like the philosopher of the Ideal City, was the spectator of all time and of all
> existence. It had senses that quickened, passions that came to birth, spiritual
> ecstasies of contemplation, ardours of fiery-coloured love.

Notably, this passage, merging the life of the spirit and the senses, asserts
the superiority of the unconscious to the conscious. "The soul, the secret
soul, was the only reality," the narrator concludes at the moment of his
fullest understanding of the *Sonnets*.

But in "The Portrait of Mr. W. H." the soul's reality is realized only in art,
not in life. The novelette dramatizes the predicament that Matthew Arnold
speaks of in the poem "The Buried Life," the disjunction between the outer
and inner lives. If the historical study of Shakespeare's poems reveals (or
confirms) the narrator's homosexuality, the intrusion of the mundane
present imperils that reality and makes the soul timid. The implicit contrast
of the romantic Hellenism of the Renaissance and the philistinism of the
late nineteenth century measures the difficulty of homosexual love in the
real world of Wilde's own age, the danger implicit in that rare moment
when—as in Arnold's poem—"what we mean, we say, and what we
would, we know,"[20] and helps explain the narrator's inability to embrace
his homosexuality in his conscious life. His timidity contrasts with the romantic gestures of Cyril and Erskine, who in their different ways demonstrate their faith in an ideal rejected by their society. Like the poet Thomas
Chatterton, who is mentioned in the story's opening paragraph and whose
suicide Wilde regarded as a sacrifice to art,[21] Cyril dies for his faith and
Erskine contrives to make his death appear a sacrifice. But the narrator,
having found in the *Sonnets* "the whole story of my soul's romance," nevertheless rejects the theory, applying to it the very test of concrete evidence—
the mainstay of "the security of one's lower life"—that Erskine had earlier
demanded of Cyril with fatal results.

The narrator's repudiation of the Willie Hughes hypothesis is usually regarded as simply a Wildean narrative twist, illustrating the paradox "that
in convincing someone else of a belief you lose the belief yourself."[22] This
paradoxical explanation is offered as one of several possible reasons for the
failure of faith, but the narrator by no means endorses it as a definitive
explanation. Instead, he professes bewilderment. He cannot really explain

why he no longer believes in the theory, though he acknowledges that the result of his inability to believe is a feeling of loss. Nor does he understand why he can no longer respond to the *Sonnets* as he had before he wrote the letter to Erskine. "They gave me back nothing of the feeling I had brought to them; they revealed to me nothing of what I had found hidden in their lines," he confesses sadly. What has altered, of course, is not the text but the reader.

The best explanation of the narrator's repudiation is that it reflects an internal change within him. It is a reaction to the dangers of self-discovery. In exploring his soul through the experience of art, the narrator has become "aware that we have passions of which we have never dreamed, thoughts that make us afraid, pleasures whose secret has been denied to us, sorrows that have been hidden from our tears." Even in his disillusion, the narrator wonders whether his doubt is the result of his having "touched upon some secret that my soul desired to conceal," thus implying the impingement of the conscious upon the unconscious and implicating the higher life in the timidity of the lower. Significantly, in his initial despair at his inability to believe in the theory, he juxtaposes the conscious and unconscious worlds, saying to himself, "I have been dreaming, and all my life for these two months has been unreal." The narrator's repudiation of the theory he had so fully responded to is a choice of reason over romance, as well as a sublimation of his homosexual nature that reflects his (and Wilde's) apprehension of gay oppression. By demanding objective evidence for the theory, he allies himself with the philistines, forgetting both Erskine's reminder that the theory depended "not so much on demonstrable proof or formal evidence, but on a kind of spiritual and artistic sense" and Cyril's assertion of the insignificance of proof: "The only apostle who did not deserve proof was St. Thomas, and St. Thomas was the only apostle who got it." The narrator had put into his letter to Erskine "all his faith," and his curious reaction is one attendant upon a loss of faith.

In "The Portrait of Mr. W. H.," Willie Hughes is not merely the young man of the *Sonnets,* but the symbol of the Hellenic spirit—a symbol, that is, of idealized homosexuality. For Willie Hughes, Cyril and Erskine commit what the narrator describes as "the pathetic fallacy of martyrdom." He professes to regard their deaths as indicating a lack of faith, but this interpretation is more revealing of himself than of them. "Martyrdom was to me merely a tragic form of scepticism, an attempt to realise by fire what one had failed to do by faith," he declares. "Men die for what they want to be true, for what some terror in their hearts tells them is not true." Although the deaths of Cyril and Erskine remain ambiguous,[23] the deceit of the forgery and of the disguised suicide is not indicative of their failure of faith; but a reaction to the demand for physical evidence of desire, when desire by its very nature is nonmaterial, and a measure of the desperation

that they feel when faced with a philistine age. The narrator here projects
onto their romantic gestures a terror and a failure that are not theirs but his.

At the end of the novelette, the narrator, having inherited the portrait of
Mr. W. H., gazes at the forged artifact and muses, "I think there is really a
great deal to be said for the Willie Hughes theory of Shakespeare's Sonnets." For him, however, the theory remains an ideal impossible to realize
in the real world of consciousness, and his denial of this ideal signifies his
refusal to surrender the security of his lower life. Early in the story, the
narrator had insisted that "forgeries were merely the result of an artistic
desire for perfect representation . . . all Art being to a certain degree a
mode of acting, an attempt to realise one's own personality out of reach
of the trammelling accidents and limitations of real life." Now, however,
he rejects the revelations of art in favor of the "trammelling accidents" of
real life. His inability to sustain faith in the neoplatonic ideal indicts both
himself and his age. What is at stake is not merely the narrator's (or
Wilde's) belief in autonomous language or romantic criticism, but his capacity for translating vision into action, for achieving that rare wholeness of
being when—in Arnold's words—"what we mean, we say, and what we
would, we know." The difficulty may be implicit in neoplatonism itself,
which in dividing spirit from flesh and matter from essence sets up the
dualism that permits, even encourages, one not to act honestly on one's
feelings. In a sense more ironic than he could have imagined, Erskine was
correct when he told the narrator early in the story, "For heaven's sake,
my dear boy, don't take up the subject of Willie Hughes. You will break
your heart over it."

In "The Portrait of Mr. W. H.," Wilde enacts a parable about the difficulty of maintaining homosexual idealism in the late nineteenth century,
illustrating how the age was—in Cyril's words—"afraid to turn the key
that unlocked the mystery of the poet's heart." Implicated in forgery and
fraud, this idealism, this gay fiction, nevertheless represents a higher truth
than the security of the lower life of consciousness and reality, a truth that
demands not proof but faith. Although it is a projection of his own truest
being, this idealism is rejected by the narrator. His need for proof of the
theory is a failure of faith in the ideal that Mr. W. H. represents. The narrator's renunciation of the Willie Hughes theory is at once a sublimation of
his own deepest nature and a decision to live in the mundane reality of a
philistine world. "The Portrait of Mr. W. H." both defends homosexuality
and regretfully—perhaps prophetically—rejects it.

A similar ambivalence informs *The Picture of Dorian Gray*, Wilde's flawed
yet haunting and puzzling experiment in the gothic novel, the first version
of which was published in *Lippincott's Monthly Magazine* in July 1890. The
revised, expanded version was published as a book in June 1891. Since
Wilde probably revised both *The Picture of Dorian Gray* and "The Portrait

of Mr. W. H." during the same period, it is not surprising that the two works share a number of similarities, including their homosexual ambiance and tone.[24] More specifically, both the novel and the novelette pivot on portraits of androgynous young men, who are extraordinarily beautiful and adored by somewhat older men. Both stories allude to famous homosexual artists and lovers in history and they both assume a significant connection between homosexual Eros and art. In addition, both works reveal Wilde's characteristic concern for issues of self-realization. In a real sense, however, the ambivalence of *The Picture of Dorian Gray* is far deeper than that of "The Portrait of Mr. W. H." Whereas the novelette depicts regretfully the failure to attempt a potentially liberating self-realization, the longer work risks satirizing the very notion of self-realization by (perhaps unintentionally) equating it with mere dissipation and self-indulgence. Most crucially, however, the novel's fascination ultimately resides in a disturbing discrepancy between its obvious moral and its contradictory tone. This discrepancy is the result not merely of narrative confusion and imperfectly mastered generic conventions, but also of the author's own divided vision.

When the story was first published in *Lippincott's Magazine,* it was roundly denounced as immoral. That these attacks were largely in response to the homosexual ambiance of the story is apparent from the description of Dorian as "Ganymede-like" in the dismissive *Punch* review; from Samuel Henry Jeyes's protest in the *St. James's Gazette* that the story "constantly hints, not obscurely, at disgusting sins and abominable crimes"; and from the remark in the unsigned notice in the *Scots Observer* that Wilde wrote "for none but outlawed noblemen and perverted telegraph boys," a clear reference to the Cleveland Street scandal of 1889–90, in which post office messenger boys and aristocrats were exposed as participants in a prostitution ring.[25] Significantly, even homosexual apologist John Addington Symonds found the story "unwholesome in tone," regretting in a letter to Horatio Brown "the unhealthy, scented, mystic, congested touch which a man of [Wilde's] sort has on moral problems."[26] Wilde responded to such charges not only by asserting the morality of the work, but by so revising the novel for book publication that the homosexuality of Basil Hallward is somewhat less obvious and the intended moral of the tale somewhat more so. He also, apparently in an attempt to undercut the moralistic assumptions of the reviewers, appended a "Preface," consisting of amoral aphorisms asserting the independence of art from questions of morality. Clearly, Wilde's responses to the charges of immorality were contradictory, reflecting in effect the incompatible impulses of the novel itself, which mocks conventional morality while enacting a moralistic fable.

The moralism of the novel is apparent from its plot structure, which emphasizes the fall and punishment of a narcissistic young man who makes a Faustian bargain to preserve his youthful beauty. Adored by the artist Basil Hallward, the innocent Dorian Gray is seduced by the cynical Lord Henry

Wotton into a life of selfish hedonism, justified by the Pateresque notion that "Nothing can cure the soul but the senses, just as nothing can cure the senses but the soul."[27] Influenced by Lord Henry's worship of youth, Dorian looks at the wonderful portrait of himself painted by Basil and mourns for his natural susceptibility to age and decay, declaring that he would give his soul if only the picture would grow old in his stead. To his surprise, he soon discovers that this wish has been granted. The marvelous portrait registers the effects of a life that is increasingly dedicated to betrayal, dissoluteness, and the exploitation of others. Responsible for the suicide of a young actress who loved him and for numerous other scandals and, finally, for the murder of Basil, he maintains his youthful appearance while the portrait grows increasingly ugly, the visible manifestation of his inward depravity. Finally, in an attempt to destroy his conscience altogether, he stabs the portrait, only to kill himself. At this point the mysterious process is reversed. The picture returns to its original appearance and the body of the dead Dorian Gray is discovered, "withered, wrinkled, and loathsome of visage."

But neither this plot outline nor Wilde's own explanation of the story's moral in terms of excess can account for the tale's true interest. Wilde summarized the moral as follows:

[A]ll excess, as well as all renunciation, brings its own punishment. The painter, Basil Hallward, worshipping physical beauty far too much, as most painters do, dies by the hand of one in whose soul he has created a monstrous and absurd vanity. Dorian Gray, having led a life of mere sensation and pleasure, tries to kill conscience, and at that moment kills himself. Lord Henry Wotton seeks to be merely the spectator of life. He finds that those who reject the battle are more deeply wounded than those who take part in it.[28]

What this explanation neglects is the tension in the text created by the discrepancy between an imposed moral and a contradictory tone. Because the good characters in the novel are weak and passive while the corrupt ones are glamorous and strong, and because the ambiguous narrator frequently "seems to be seduced by the views of his own wicked characters,"[29] the novel remains enigmatic despite the rigorously moral plot structure. Notwithstanding the retributive ending of the book, the Faustian dream of an escape from human limitations and moral strictures ultimately triumphs over the condemnation of excess and thereby subverts the apparent moralism. It is not irrelevant that in the popular imagination the name Dorian Gray conjures not an image of evil but of preternaturally extended youth and beauty bought at the trivial price of a disfigured portrait. Surely, one reason the sometimes awkwardly written novel continues to fascinate is that the Faustian dream is rendered more appealingly than the superimposed lesson of the dangers of narcissism.

Homosexuality is an important aspect of *The Picture of Dorian Gray,* and the novel deserves credit as a pioneering depiction of homosexual relationships in serious English fiction. The depiction of homosexuality in the book is undoubtedly—though perhaps unconsciously—shaped by Wilde's personal ambivalences toward his own sexuality, which found expression both in idealized love affairs and in liaisons with prostitutes. But it is important to stress that the novel's primary interest is literary rather than biographical, and that, especially in the final version, Wilde hints at homosexuality rather than expresses it directly. And it is necessary to insist that the work's homosexual subtext is far more complex and subtle than has frequently been acknowledged, complicated by the extreme difficulty of writing sympathetically about a taboo, though titillating, subject for a popular audience as well as by an unclear authorial vision. Homosexual readers would certainly have responded to the book's undercurrent of gay feeling, and may have found the very name "Dorian" suggestive of Greek homosexuality, since it was Dorian tribesmen who allegedly introduced homosexuality into Greece as part of their military regimen; but Jeffrey Meyers's homophobic view of the novel as being "really about the jealousy and pain, the fear and guilt of being a homosexual" is simply wrong, a distortion based on egregious misinterpretations and on the *a priori* assumption that homosexuality is the root of all evil.[30] Wilde purposely leaves the exact nature of the sins of Dorian Gray mysterious and vague, suggested but not defined. Characteristically playing hide-and-seek with his readers, he alternately exposes and conceals the homosexual dimension of the novel. In response to the attacks on the book, he remarked, with some justice if not complete candor, that "Each man sees his own sin in Dorian Gray."[31] But whatever they may include, the dissipations of Dorian Gray are by no means exclusively or even primarily homosexual. Those that are specifically cited, in fact, are explicitly heterosexual. The evil in *The Picture of Dorian Gray* may encompass homosexual (as well as heterosexual) excesses, but it should by no means be identified with homosexuality per se.

Wilde's attitude toward homosexuality in the novel may best be seen in his portrayal of Basil Hallward. Hallward is the character most clearly delineated as homosexual, and it is significant that he is presented as the most morally sensitive character as well. So passive as to function largely as a choral figure, he nevertheless speaks as the voice of moderation. His love for Dorian seems altogether noble, especially in contrast to the blandishments of Lord Henry, his rival for the young man's affection. In the triangle formed by the competition of the two older men for the attention of the beautiful boy, Basil represents an idealized, platonized homosexuality, linked to a long tradition of art and philosophy. Indeed, he has been affected by Dorian in much the same way that the homosexual artists and thinkers celebrated in "The Portrait of Mr. W. H." have been affected by

their lovers. Dominated by the beauty of the young man, Basil sees in
Dorian "an entirely new mode of style." Actually, he is in love with him
less as an individual than as the embodiment of a Hellenic ideal, the "harmony of soul and body." Tellingly, however, the idealized homosexual love
that Basil feels for Dorian—"such love as Michael Angelo had known, and
Montaigne, and Winckelmann, and Shakespeare"—is regarded by the artist
as a shameful secret, a love that dare not speak its name.

The implied link between homosexual Eros and creativity is clear in
Dorian's effect on Basil's art. Dorian's beauty and the ideal that he represents cause Basil to see the world afresh and inspire him to his greatest
work as an artist. For this, Basil is profoundly grateful to Dorian, but at the
same time he expresses ambivalence, for he sees his homosexually inspired
art—indeed, his homosexuality itself—as both a gift and a curse. Declaring that "It is better not to be different from one's fellows," Basil early in
the novel comments on the fatal aspect of the mark of difference. "Your
rank and wealth, Harry; my brains, such as they are—my art, whatever it
may be worth; Dorian Gray's good looks—we shall all suffer for what the
gods have given us, suffer terribly," he remarks prophetically. Basil's ambivalence is apparent at the very beginning of his relationship with Dorian.
When he first feels irresistibly attracted to the young man, whom he sees
across the room at Lady Brandon's party, he literally attempts to escape.
And however much he comes to appreciate the new vitality his love for
Dorian gives to his art, he desperately fears exposure. His reluctance to
exhibit the picture of Dorian, because "I have put too much of myself into
it," indicates both his self-doubt and his fear of the world's contempt
should it guess his secret.

Basil's ambivalence is evident in his guilty characterization of his love
for Dorian as idolatry. "You became to me the visible incarnation of that
unseen ideal whose memory haunts us artists like an exquisite dream," he
explains to Dorian, confessing that "I worshipped you. I grew jealous of
every one to whom you spoke. I wanted to have you all to myself. I was
only happy when I was with you." This revelation is made after Basil's
infatuation with Dorian has faded somewhat and he has overcome his inhi-
bition against exhibiting the portrait; yet it is still permeated with guilt.
Even the idealized homosexuality that Basil represents inspires shame and
fear, and is condemned in theological terms as idolatry.

Tellingly, the confession of Basil's secret inspires only condescending
pity in Dorian, for there "seemed to him to be something tragic in a friendship so coloured by romance." At the same time, the narcissistic youth
characteristically wonders whether he might himself ever be so dominated
by another. "Was that one of the things that life had in store?" he muses,
as though Basil's love for him were simply another sensation to be tasted
on his quest for experience. Later, however, he will wonder whether "Some

love might come across his life, and purify him, and shield him from those sins that seemed to be already stirring in spirit and in flesh—those curious unpictured sins whose very mystery lent them their subtlety and their charm.''

But Basil and Sibyl Vane, the young actress who commits suicide when Dorian rejects her, are the only characters in the novel capable of love for another, and the depth of their devotion serves to underline the shallowness of Dorian's addiction to pleasure and Lord Henry's devotion to emotional voyeurism. Interestingly, although the connection of each to Dorian involves art, both Sibyl and Basil value love before art. Early in the book, when Dorian laments the fact that the picture will mock him by remaining young as he grows old, Basil offers to destroy the painting. He is dissuaded from ripping up the canvas only by Dorian's revealing plea, ''I am in love with it. . . . It is part of myself.'' Later, after the fiasco at the play when Sibyl performs poorly precisely because she has discovered the reality of love, Dorian complains bitterly but Basil remarks, ''Love is more wonderful than Art.'' Basil's devotion to love is, in fact, the quality that ultimately redeems him.

Wilde conceives of Basil's homosexual love for Dorian as something positive but dangerous, an emotion that inspires guilt and fear: measures, respectively, of the internal and external condemnations brought to bear against homosexuality. Perhaps more pertinently, Basil's love is clearly, if imprecisely, implicated in the strange events that culminate in Dorian's loss of a moral sense and in his murder of the artist. When Basil confronts Dorian about the widespread tales of his corruption, pleading with him to deny the rumors, Dorian responds by offering to show him the picture, ''the diary of my life from day to day,'' for ''You are the one man in the world who is entitled to know everything about me. You have had more to do with my life than you think.'' Dorian unveils the portrait, and Basil shrinks in horror from the hideous face on the canvas, while Dorian observes the scene calmly, like an amused spectator, with merely a flicker of triumph in his eyes. The younger man blames his predicament on the artist, who taught him to be vain of his good looks. Although protesting that ''There was nothing evil, nothing shameful'' in his love, Basil nevertheless accepts responsibility. ''I worshipped you too much. I am punished for it,'' he tells Dorian, adding: ''You worshipped yourself too much.'' As he implores Dorian to pray for forgiveness, he is stabbed to death, Dorian receiving from the ugly portrait—his own debased conscience—a directive to murder.

The idealized homosexual love of Basil for Dorian, then, is presented ambiguously. On the one hand, it is repeatedly described as noble and its power is confirmed by the transformation of Basil's art that it effects. On the other hand, it is the source of guilt and fear, and the very art that it inspires is ominous, for that art culminates in the sinister portrait itself. By presenting the naive Dorian with a surprising image of himself (i.e., the artist's own image of him), by awakening him to his beauty and thereby encouraging his vanity, Basil may be said to initiate the entire tragedy. The diabolism of the painting may be dismissed as a gothic plot device, but Wilde's serious purpose in implicating Basil in the corruption of Dorian Gray is to underline the major theme of the work, the wickedness of using others. This theme is most clear in Dorian's heartless exploitation of others, and in the amused, detached voyeurism of Henry, but it is involved as well in Basil's reduction of Dorian to "simply a motive in art" found "in the curves of certain lines, in the loveliness and subtleties of certain colours." Although Basil is by no means the villain of the piece, he too partakes of the objectification of others that the novel most vehemently condemns. Yet his fault is not that of loving Dorian, for as Dorian himself recognizes, Basil's love might have saved him from his ugly fate. Rather, his fault is that of not loving him openly and disinterestedly, of appropriating his image as art.[32] Basil's aestheticization of Dorian is analogous to Dorian's aestheticization of Sibyl Vane.

If Basil is to blame for objectifying Dorian, so too is Lord Henry Wotton. Whereas Basil reveals to Dorian a new image of himself, so Henry more deliberately attempts to shape Dorian and to experience through him sensations and emotions that he is too fearful and too detached from life to experience firsthand. Although Basil and Henry are at first glance extremely dissimilar—the one earnest and idealistic, the other cynical and disillusioned—the rivals share an artistic impulse. They both want to transform and re-present reality, a desire that may be a psychological compensation for their essential passivity. Basil's artistry finds expression in painting, Henry's in the exercise of influence. Tellingly, Henry's homoerotic attraction to Dorian is whetted voyeuristically by Basil's worship of the young man, and Henry is thereby roused from his characteristic languor to a desire to influence—that is, to shape—Dorian, a process that is itself a sublimated expression of homosexuality.

The rivalry of Henry and Basil centers in fact on the question of who will exert a shaping influence on the naive youth. Soon after meeting him, Henry determines to adopt Dorian as his protégé. "Talking to him," the aristocrat reflects, "was like playing upon an exquisite violin. He answered to every touch and thrill of the bow." This suggestive passage reveals the interconnection of art and sex, dominance and submission in Henry's response to Dorian, whom he regards as "a marvelous type" who "could be made a Titan or a toy." The worldly cynic undertakes as his goal the "making" of Dorian much as a poet or a sculptor might shape a work of art. "There was something terribly enthralling in the exercise of influence," he muses:

> To project one's soul into some gracious form, and let it tarry there for a moment; to hear one's own intellectual views echoed back to one with all the added music of passion and youth; to convey one's temperament into another as though it were a subtle fluid or a strange perfume: there was a real joy in that—perhaps the most satisfying joy left to us in an age so limited and vulgar as our own, an age grossly carnal in its pleasures, and grossly common in its aims.

Significantly, he later thinks of Dorian as "his own creation." The deliberate callousness of Henry's decision to influence Dorian is cast in relief by his early statement that "All influence is immoral" because it inhibits self-development, the perfect realization of one's nature. Henry's agenda is to substitute for Dorian's unformed nature his own, which he is too timid to explore directly.

Interestingly, Henry's artistic aim in shaping Dorian is to create a harmony of matter and spirit, a synergistic balance of body and soul akin to Basil's Hellenic ideal. In a pivotal passage that profoundly affects the naive Dorian, Henry announces a credo that is strikingly congruent with Basil's idealistic vision, however divergent their ideas and means may appear. "I believe that if one man were to live out his life fully and completely, were to give form to every feeling, expression to every thought, reality to every dream," Henry asserts, "I believe that the world would gain such a fresh insight of joy that we would forget all the maladies of mediaevalism, and return to the Hellenic ideal." As Henry explains his "new Hedonism," a philosophy based clearly if tendentiously on Pater's (in)famous conclusion to *The Renaissance*,[33] he tells Dorian that "The moment I met you I saw that you were quite unconscious of what you really are, of what you really might be."

Just as Basil's portrait offers Dorian a revelation of his own beauty as filtered through the artist's transforming vision, so Henry's belief in the mysterious interanimation of body and soul reveals to the youth a hitherto unsuspected potential. Dorian, in fact, murmurs his fatal prayer for unchanging beauty while Henry's suggestive words ring in his ear and Basil's instructive painting shines in his eyes. And just as Basil is fearful of the secret love for Dorian embedded in the portrait, so is Henry fearful of his own doctrine of self-realization. "People are afraid of themselves, nowadays," he remarks, and the comment is more applicable to himself than to anyone else.

Henry displaces Basil in the competition for Dorian's attention, yet his triumph is more illusory than real. Although the younger man accedes to Henry's statement that "All through your life you will tell me everything you do," in fact he tells Henry very little. "If I ever did a crime, I would come and confess it to you," Dorian tells him, but Henry naively believes his protégé incapable of crime. "People like you—the wilful sunbeams of life—don't commit crimes," he remarks. Blithely unaware of the extent of

Dorian's depravity, he persists in believing that he represents to the youth all the sins that Dorian lacks the courage to commit, when precisely the opposite is true. Even when the younger man hints that he may have murdered Basil, the elder dismisses the suggestion: "It is not in you, Dorian, to commit a crime." And, unaware of the horror of his friend's existence, Henry admires Dorian's "exquisite life," telling him near the end of the book that "You have drunk deeply of everything. You have crushed the grapes against your palate. Nothing has been hidden from you. And it has all been to you no more than the sound of music. It has not marred you." The sentiments expressed here are, of course, mocked in the novel's final scene, just as during his life Dorian's unblemished appearance is mocked by the ugly visage of the portrait.

The central irony of *The Picture of Dorian Gray* is that the Hellenic ideal of "the harmony of soul and body" pursued by Basil and Henry alike, and localized in their separate visions of Dorian, is not realized largely because they project onto the young man their own unbalanced and fragmentary images. None of the three principal characters is complete or harmonious; hence, they appear mere caricatures. Each is fragmented, unable to achieve that wholeness of being implicit in Arnold's desire for a transcendent moment when "what we mean, we say, and what we would, we know." Basil says what he means in the homoerotic portrait he paints, but he is unable to act on what he knows. Similarly, Henry lives vicariously through Dorian, precisely because he too dares not act on what he feels. And in the corrupt and materialistic world of late-nineteenth-century London, Dorian's project of self-realization amounts simply to a self-indulgence that mocks both Basil's idealism and Henry's tendentious (mis)interpretation of Pateresque epicureanism. Rather than harmonizing, in the course of the novel Dorian's soul and body become increasingly disconnected and finally separated entirely, as symbolized in the increasing disjunction between the unaging beauty of Dorian's body and the hideous representation of his soul (i.e., the picture). This irony suggests that the Faustian theme is by no means confined to the gothic diabolism of Dorian's supernatural bargain for a youthful appearance. By assuming godlike powers of creation, Henry and Basil also partake in the Faustian desire to escape human limitations. Consequently, they too are implicated in the tragedy. In their unbalanced pursuit of the Hellenic "harmony of soul and body," they contribute to the disharmonious dualism represented by Dorian's external beauty and his internal ugliness.

The poignant tone of the novel derives from its conclusion that the romantic quest for wholeness and balance cannot be achieved either through the representation of an artistic ideal or through the vicarious realization of the new Hedonism. These defeats, rather than the gothic plot centered around the preternatural portrait, are at the heart of the book's haunting irresolution and the discrepancy between its tone and moral. Dorian's Faustian bargain can be dismissed as mere gothicism, and the novel's moralistic plot and retributive ending can be classified as melodrama. But the yearning for a new moral order, an escape from the "maladies of mediaevalism," and a return to the Hellenic ideal persist even after the contrived, conventionally moral conclusion. Dorian's recognition that mankind's distrust of the senses has led to a profound loss may be qualified by his own subsequent history of reckless abandon, but it nevertheless resonates with meaning:

> As he looked back upon man moving through History, he was haunted by a feeling of loss. So much had been surrendered! and to such little purpose! There had been mad wilful rejections, monstrous forms of self-torture and self-denial, whose origin was fear, and whose result was a degradation infinitely more terrible than that fancied degradation from which, in their ignorance, they had sought to escape, Nature, in her wonderful irony, driving out the anchorite to feed with the wild animals of the desert and giving to the hermit the beasts of the field as his companions.

In *The Picture of Dorian Gray*, homosexuality is a powerful and fatal attraction, guilt-inducing and dangerous, yet enormously creative and potentially salvific. The worship of Basil and the voyeurism of Henry are finally condemned for their objectification of Dorian and for their Faustian aspirations. Nevertheless, the romantic dream of an idealized harmony of soul and body—a dream that in the novel is clearly homoerotic in inspiration—survives the moralistic conclusion to protest against an unsatisfactory reality and a tragic history, linked to asceticism and medievalism. In this sense, the novel is a gay fiction, however ambivalent its depiction of homosexuality. The *Picture of Dorian Gray* is a text divided against itself, but its creative tensions yield both a poignant sense of loss that the world cannot be re-created and made whole and an implied vision of an imagined world at ease with homosexuality, a world in which sensual enjoyment has been made an element of "a new spirituality, of which a fine instinct for beauty was to be the dominant characteristic." Perhaps more responsible than any other single English work in forging the stereotypical link between art, decadence, and homosexuality, the novel—for all its moralistic posturing—mourns the loss of a golden age and art's inability to re-create that homoerotic harmony of flesh and spirit of which Hellenism is the nostalgically evoked *locus amoenus*.

Wilde's most important—and least ambivalent—gay fiction is the remarkable letter written in prison, *De Profundis*, a work that creatively transmutes the disaster of his prosecution and imprisonment into a ludic

triumph. Written over a period of three months early in 1897, after he had
been imprisoned for some eighteen months, and addressed to Lord Alfred
Douglas, *De Profundis* is far more than merely the recriminatory attack of a
disenchanted lover or a self-serving, self-pitying tract. Although it is in the
form of a letter and has obvious generic relationships with autobiography
and confessional as well as epistolary literature, as so often in Wilde's
work generic distinctions are deliberately blurred and not altogether helpful. The epistolary form of *De Profundis* was dictated by the fact that
prison regulations permitted Wilde to write only letters. This work, undoubtedly among the longest letters ever written, was self-consciously designed as a vindication and reflects the author's unwillingness to "sit in the
grotesque pillory" to which he had been assigned by public opinion.[34] It
might best be described as Wilde's attempt to create and present a complex
and contradictory but nevertheless authentic self (however artificially constructed), a self to displace or qualify the masks he had himself created
earlier and the ugly images attributed to him in the popular press. Certainly, it is not merely a personal letter, for Wilde clearly intended its eventual publication and took elaborate measures to assure its preservation. The
address to Douglas provides a focus for an imaginative dramatization (and
reconstruction) of Wilde's personal experience. Thus, *De Profundis* may
be regarded as either a work of fiction in the service of autobiography, or
vice versa.

The book has often been denigrated as "insincere," and many of its details have been challenged. Even the famous account of Wilde's humiliation
on the platform at Clapham Junction railroad station, where he was allegedly jeered and spit upon by an angry crowd, may be fictional (although
recent biographers accept it as true). But the charges of inaccuracy are
more than a little beside the point, since *De Profundis*—an artistic construct written under horribly difficult conditions—should be judged not on
the basis of factual accuracy but on the success of its creation of a symbolic
character, the martyred artist. The importance of Wilde's prison letter for
gay literature (and gay liberation) is that in it Wilde finally breaks out of
the bourgeois mold he had so frequently attacked yet to which he so tenaciously clung. As a result of his imprisonment, he discovers a new freedom
and emerges as Saint Oscar, the victim of gay oppression who finally triumphs over a philistine society.

The title *De Profundis* was given to the letter by Robert Ross, apparently
at the suggestion of the British publisher and writer E. V. Lucas.[35] The
title, which echoes Psalm 130, is a good one, for it captures the complex
tone of the work, a combination of prophetic utterance forged in the crucible of suffering and self-consciously daring wit that approaches campy self-
mockery. But the title Wilde himself suggested for the letter, *Epistola: in
Carcere et Vinculis*, is equally telling, for it calls specific attention to the

conditions under which the letter was written. Not only does Wilde continually refer to the painful realities of his imprisonment, but the authentic self that emerges in the work is, at least in part, a product of those realities. As Regenia Gagnier has demonstrated by placing Wilde's letter in the contexts of prison literature and of the specific conditions of his imprisonment, particularly his solitary cellular confinement, "The self in his letter is a self constructed in a particular imaginative act of resistance against insanity and against the material matrix of prison space and time, that is, confined, segmented space and timelessness."[36] Several problematic aspects of the work, including the tactic of alternating passages of romance and realism, the obsession with precise chronology and the meticulous rehearsal of minute details, are explained by the conditions under which Wilde wrote *De Profundis*, which is both a protest against prison regimentation and an exercise in the saving grace of imagination.

Imagination is, indeed, the key faculty in the authentic self that Wilde creates in this work. In the first half of the letter, he sketches a bitter portrait of Douglas, linking him with satanic hatred and Judaslike betrayal, while in the second half he associates himself with Christlike attributes, re-creating himself in the image of a romantic Christ-figure martyred by a philistine society and a satanic lover.[37] He is both a victim of a fateful classical tragedy and a participant in the Christian comedy. But in both sections, imagination is the quality most prized. All of the charges against Douglas are finally subsumed in the accusation that he lacked imagination. "Don't you understand now," Wilde writes, "that your lack of imagination was the one really fatal defect of your character?" He repeats like a mantra the motto "The supreme vice is shallowness. Whatever is realised is right." Douglas is condemned because he lacks the capacity either to realize himself or to imagine the sufferings of others. In theological terms, he lacks *agape;* he has no desire to help bear the burdens of others, including the pain of Wilde, who is in prison as a result of their friendship. Wilde tells him that "by your actions and by your silence, by what you have done and by what you have left undone, you have made every day of my long imprisonment still more difficult for me to live through. . . . The sorrow you should have shared you have doubled, the pain you should have sought to lighten you have quickened to anguish." Wilde admits that Douglas has not intended such results: "It was simply that 'one really fatal defect of your character, your entire lack of imagination.' " Significantly, Douglas is presented not as an outsider or rebel against an unjust society; rather, in his lack of imagination he is explicitly associated with society—which, Wilde asserts, "also has the supreme vice of shallowness."

Wilde means by the terms *shallowness* and *imagination* not merely judgments on the contents of Douglas's character but on his way of being; that is, his lack of self-realization. These are preexistentialist terms for the faculty of the individual's attentiveness to received ideas and relationships. As Joseph Cady has written, "For Wilde 'shallowness' is ultimately a deadness of soul, a petrification of the spirit . . . it is an appalling lack of alertness to our own experience, to the meaning and consequences of our actions, to the fact that we inevitably live . . . in relationship, and to the corrupting power that social institutions can have over us."[38] Shallowness is a function of philistinism (itself an Arnoldian conception) and the result of not saying what one feels and not acting on what one knows. Imagination is the opposite of shallowness. It indicates a liveliness of the spirit, an awareness of the meaning of experience, a critical alertness to the nature of one's relationships both to others and to society and social institutions, and a constant questioning of established social codes. In this sense, *De Profundis* is an important document in preexistentialist thought, for it enacts Wilde's developing awareness, as the result of his pain and humiliation, into the nature of the relationship between the individual and society, and it marks a significant enlargement of his characteristic concern with self-realization. These are subjects in which Wilde had always been interested, but in *De Profundis* he reaches a profound insight into the function of the imagination (as defined above) as a necessary component in the process of self-realization. Imagination is now conceived as a means of liberating himself from his problematic relationship to society, an insight that is a direct result of the gay oppression that he experienced directly and came to symbolize for others.

In contrast to the shallowness of Douglas, Wilde conjures Christ as a romantic artist, who is characterized by "an intense and flame-like imagination," as in fact someone very much like himself. Christ possessed, Wilde writes, "that imaginative sympathy which in the sphere of Art is the sole secret of creation." Christ is presented not as a supernatural being but as a fascinating artist whose power of imagination "makes him the palpitating centre of romance." The embodiment of *agape*, Christ understands the sufferings of others. He is aware, on the one hand, that since there is "no difference at all between the lives of others and one's own life," man thus has "an extended, a Titan personality" in which each individual mirrors the history of the world. At the same time, however, Christ is portrayed as a Blakean proponent of radical individualism: "he had no patience with the dull lifeless mechanical systems that treat people as if they were things, and so treat everybody alike: as if anybody, or anything for that matter, was like aught else in the world. For him there were no laws: there were exceptions merely." Rather than consisting of moralistic prohibitions, Christ's "morality is all sympathy."

The most daring aspect of *De Profundis* is Wilde's simultaneous depictions of Christ in his image and himself in Christ's image. Not only has he been betrayed and humiliated as Christ was—like Christ, he is betrayed by a false friend's kiss, and he accuses Douglas and his father of throwing "dice for my soul"—but he also depicts himself as suffering for the sins of others, namely Douglas and his family.[39] The portrait of Christ as the romantic artist martyred by a philistine society functions for Wilde not merely as self-aggrandizement but also as a means of attacking the religious base of philistine morality and as an element in the artificial—and essentially comic—construction of his authentic self. He co-opts the very personification of Christianity itself and reconstructs Christ as an all-embracing spirit of the imagination, the supreme individualist, who is indifferent to the petty "sins" that so agitate conventional moralists. He recruits Christ as his ally in an assault on his persecutors—those moralists who thirsted for his blood. He evokes Mary Magdalene and the prostitute who anointed Christ's feet with spices and quotes his injunction, "Let him of you who has never sinned be the first to throw the stone at her." He casts the faithful Robert Ross as John the Beloved Disciple and stresses again and again that Christ's morality is not that of laws or prohibitions. "All that Christ says to us by way of a little warning is that *every* moment should be beautiful, that the soul should *always* be ready for the coming of the Bridegroom, *always* waiting for the voice of the Lover," Wilde writes, pointedly (and wittily) employing the Christian language of mystical desire even as he demystifies Christ. Indeed, Wilde slyly inverts the orthodox version of Christ's attitude toward sin, writing that "through some divine instinct in him, [he] seems to have always loved the sinner as being the nearest possible approach to the perfection of man. His primary desire was not to reform people. . . . To turn an interesting thief into a tedious honest man was not his aim. . . he regarded sin and suffering as being in themselves beautiful, holy things, and modes of perfection."

Significantly, just as he links a shallow, uncritical Douglas to a corrupt society, so Wilde depicts Christ as an imaginative social critic, alert to the injustices of society and waging a war against social tyranny. Christ's (and Wilde's) antagonists are the philistines, who never question the dehumanizing and limiting social codes that they enforce, codes that have created a thoroughly inhumane prison system, incarcerated Wilde for his homosexuality, and robbed him of his children. Philistinism is the epitome of shallowness, for it is "that side of a man's nature that is not illumined by the imagination"; and its "heroic figure" is Queensberry, memorably sketched as unimaginative and degenerate in his "stableman's gait and dress, the bowed legs, the twitching hands, the hanging lower lip, the bestial and half-witted grin." Christ, Wilde alleges, "exposed with utter and relentless scorn" the "cold philanthropies, the ostentatious public charities, the tedious formalisms so dear to the middle-class mind." Making him sound very much like himself, Wilde asserts that Christ's chief war was against the philistines and "their heavy inaccessibility to ideas, their dull respect-

ability, their tedious orthodoxy, their worship of vulgar success, their entire
preoccupation with the gross materialistic side of life, and their ridiculous
estimate of themselves and their importance." He adds: "That is the war
every child of light has to wage."

The term "child of light" is a playful inversion of the biblical concept
(cf. Luke 16:8, John 12:36, Eph. 5:8, and I Thess. 5:5) and it is undoubtedly meant to suggest Uranian as well. In *De Profundis* Wilde defends his
homosexuality, or Uranianism, obliquely but strongly, and the letter deserves a prominent place in the literature of homosexual apologias. Skeptical of the medical model of homosexuality emerging in the late nineteenth
century, Wilde refers dismissively to Cesare Lomboroso, an Italian crimi-
nologist who believed homosexuality was a congenital dysfunction, to be
treated in insane asylums rather than prison; and Wilde's depiction of
Queensbury as degenerate may itself be intended as an ironic reversal of the
medical view of homosexuality as a symptom of degeneracy.[40] Although
open to a theoretical connection between homosexuality and artistic creativity, as implied by homosexual apologists like Symonds and Carpenter and
endorsed in *The Picture of Dorian Gray* and more openly argued by other
Uranians of the era, Wilde observes laconically that "the pathological phenomenon in question is also found amongst those who have not genius."
Rather than belaboring the causes of homosexuality, he is defiant of those
who would condemn him, expressing a fierce awareness of the reality of
gay oppression. He resolutely denounces the "wrong and unjust laws" of
the "wrong and unjust system" that convicted him, and he concludes:
"The one disgraceful, unpardonable, and to all time contemptible action of
my life was my allowing myself to be forced into appealing to Society for
help and protection. . . ." This new awareness of his problematic relationship to a society whose code he violated yet naively looked to for protection is an important measure of his growth in imagination as a result of his
experience.

In terms of Wilde's frank acceptance of his homosexuality as an integral
part of his personality, perhaps the most significant passage in *De Profundis*
is his response to a friend who protested that he did not believe a single
word of the charges against him. "I burst into tears at what he said,"
Wilde writes,

> and told him that while there was much amongst [Queensberry's] definite
> charges that was quite untrue and transferred to me by revolting malice, still
> that my life had been full of perverse pleasures and strange passions, and that
> unless he accepted that as a fact about me and realised it to the full, I could
> not possibly be friends with him any more, or ever be in his company. It was
> a terrible shock to him, but we are friends, and I have not got his friendship
> on false pretences.

In his suffering, Wilde has realized that however painful the truth might be, "To be forced to tell lies is much worse." In this acceptance of himself, he makes his homosexuality an irreducible part of his authentic self. His frank admission that his homosexuality is "a fact about me" translates his sexual identity into an element in the new self-knowledge he has gained in the crucible of suffering and one that he will not willingly deny or surrender. It is true that Wilde here and elsewhere in *De Profundis* tends to obfuscate the role of sexual desire in forming homosexual identity by making his "perverse pleasures and strange passions" seem simply part of a Pateresque quest for experience, but this mild evasion is undoubtedly a concession to the predominantly heterosexual audience he conceived for the letter.

Wilde confutes the popular image of himself as a monster who exploited a young and innocent aristocrat and replaces it with an image very different. He denies that he corrupted Douglas, telling him that "of all the people who have ever crossed my life you were the one, and the only one, I was unable in any way to influence in any direction"; and he ridicules the version of history that makes Queensberry "the hero of a Sunday-school tract," Douglas "the infant Samuel," and he himself ranked somewhere "between Gilles de Retz and the Marquis de Sade." He casts the selfish and shallow Douglas—who, so far from being an innocent, knew not too little but too much about life—as the villain of the affair, motivated by hatred of his father. Wilde regrets much, including his allowing his "unintellectual friendship" with Douglas to dominate his life entirely and to lure him "into the imperfect world of coarse uncompleted passions, of appetite without distinction, desire without limit," yet he does not recant his sexuality and he finds some solace in the fact that, for all their affair's debilitating effects, Douglas did love him, at least insofar as the young man was capable of loving anyone.

Wilde admits to having indulged in sexual excess, but with little or no remorse. "Tired of being on the heights I deliberately went to the depths in the search for new sensations," he writes. "What the paradox was to me in the sphere of thought, perversity became to me in the sphere of passion. Desire, at the end, was a malady, or a madness, or both. I grew careless of the lives of others." The point of this admission is made clear by his earlier statement that "Sins of the flesh are nothing. They are maladies for physicians to cure, if they should be cured. Sins of the soul alone are shameful." Thus, Wilde can sound boastful as he describes the pleasures of "feasting with panthers," but sincerely ashamed of misusing others. He refuses to promise any moral reformation, for "Reformations in Morals are as meaningless and vulgar as Reformations in Theology." And even as he acknowledges the dull repetitiveness of unrestrained indulgence, he refuses to express repentance. "I don't regret for a single moment having lived for pleasure. I did it to the full, as one should do everything that one does to

the full. There was no pleasure I did not experience. I threw the pearl of
my soul into a cup of wine. I went down the primrose path to the sound of
flutes. I lived on honeycomb,'' he boasts. But he adds: "to have continued
the same life would have been wrong because it would have been limiting.
I had to pass on. The other half of the garden had its secrets for me also.''
Those secrets in the other half of the garden include the self-knowledge he
gains as a result of his season of sorrow.

Perhaps the most moving aspect of *De Profundis* is Wilde's graphic account
of the mental and physical pain he has undergone in prison. Deserted by
Douglas, humiliated by a vengeful public, branded and cast out from society, he describes his life as a veritable "Symphony of Sorrow." But the
supreme theme of the work is the meaningfulness of suffering. Through his
disgrace and imprisonment, Wilde discovers a new humility that gives his
experience meaning, that leads him to "a fresh mode of self-realisation"
and enables him finally to triumph over a world of philistines. Although he
has not yet completely achieved that desired humility, he hopes to reach the
point where he can view his imprisonment as one of the positive turning
points of his life, a *felix culpa* that leads to a *vita nuova*. He would like to
be able "to absorb into my nature all that has been done to me, to make it
part of me, to accept it without complaint, fear, or reluctance." Thus, he
embraces sorrow and its lessons of humility, for behind sorrow there is always a soul. In a crucial passage at the heart of the letter's lesson of the
redemptive power of his painful experience, Wilde declares that suffering
"is really a revelation. One discerns things that one never discerned before.
One approaches the whole of history from a different standpoint." Through
suffering, he hopes to achieve that great goal of romantic art, "the unity of
a thing with itself: the outward rendered expressive of the inward: the soul
made incarnate: the body instinct with spirit." In other words, through his
oppression, he expects to complete his authentic self and to possess his own
soul before he dies. He concludes that "to have become a *deeper* man is the
privilege of those who have suffered."

It is the deeper man, the Wilde whose eyes have opened to an imaginative apprehension of the loveliness and sorrow of the world and to a critical
analysis of society, who triumphs in *De Profundis*. His persecution has en-
abled him to see the world differently, to realize the injustices of his society
and the meaningfulness of suffering, and thus he can accept himself and his
plight without bitterness. Wilde's triumph here is a ludic triumph, a willed
conversion of a grim disaster into a comic victory. In *De Profundis* he
emerges as a kind of Harlequin Christ-figure, a martyred clown who enjoys
the last laugh.[41] If he complains that "the dreadful thing about modernity
was that it put Tragedy into the raiment of Comedy," and that his own
tragedy has been a grotesque comedy, he is nevertheless able to create a

persona—indeed, an authentic self—who combines the imagination of Christ and the grotesquerie of a tearful clown. "We are the zanies of sorrow. We are clowns whose hearts are broken," he says as he recounts the painful mockery he allegedly experienced on the railroad platform at Clapham Junction. "For half an hour I stood there in the grey November rain surrounded by a jeering mob," he writes. "For a year after that was done to me I wept every day at the same hour and for the same space of time." But the measure of his triumph is that "now I am really beginning to feel more regret for the people who laughed than for myself." As the result of his having come to understand the philistine lack of imagination, he can exercise his own imagination to translate his martyrdom into a triumph analogous to the Christian comedy implicit in Good Friday and the Resurrection.

For all its bitter recriminations and painful accounts of suffering, *De Profundis* is finally comedic (or at least tragi-comic), as George Bernard Shaw recognized when he wrote that "It is really an extraordinary book, quite exhilarating and amusing as to Wilde himself, and quite disgraceful and shameful to his stupid tormentors."[42] The comedy of the painful letter is implicit in the success of Wilde's imaginative triumph and in his resistance to despair. His strategic, parodic subversion of conventional Christian morality by re-creating Christ in his own image, the defiance of his defense of his homosexuality, the profit he makes of his intense suffering, his sly wit and even his histrionic self-dramatizations and obvious insincerities and exaggerations: these all contribute to the comic mode of the work. In this mode, Wilde records the triumph of an indomitable spirit and creates a new self, a martyred artist who is at once a tragic figure and a grotesque clown.

The new self that triumphs at the end of *De Profundis* revels defiantly in his exclusion from society, his marginality as homosexual pariah. Thus, Wilde rejects the artificial society that has condemned him and looks to nature for comfort and consolation:

> Society, as we have constituted it, will have no place for me, has none to offer; but Nature, whose sweet rains fall on unjust and just alike, will have clefts in the rocks where I may hide and secret valleys in whose silence I may weep undisturbed. She will hang the night with stars so that I may walk abroad in the darkness without stumbling, and send the wind over my footprints so that none may track me to my hurt: she will cleanse me in great waters, and with bitter herbs make me whole.

This passage, with its defiant assertion of Wilde's status as a child of nature, its criticism of a shallow society, its yearning for a kind of Arcadian retreat, its faint but deliberate echoes of Ecclesiastes, and its self-dramatization that approaches parody, is at once slyly comic and deeply

moving, expressing in little the complex comic tone of the whole, where
tragedy and comedy not only coexist but also deepen each other. Perhaps
the very last sentences of the letter—when Wilde tells Douglas that "You
came to me to learn the Pleasure of Life and the Pleasure of Art. Perhaps I
am chosen to teach you something much more wonderful, the meaning of
sorrow and beauty"—illustrate most clearly the ludic triumph that Wilde
achieves in *De Profundis,* where he moves from broken and embittered ac-
cuser to blessed exemplar. Even the apparent contradiction of Wilde's re-
creating a self impervious to the need for social approval in order to
vindicate himself in the eyes of society is a comic paradox that Wilde must
surely have intended.

In *De Profundis,* his greatest gay fiction, Wilde emerges as Saint Oscar,
the homintern martyr.[43] It is in this sense that Wilde is a symbolic figure. It
may be true, as W. H. Auden observed, that the Wilde scandal had a disastrous effect on the arts "because it allowed the philistine man to identify
himself with the decent man";[44] but it is also true, as John Cowper Powys
remarked, that Wilde consequently became "a sort of rallying cry to all
those writers and artists who suffer, in one degree or other, from the persecution of the mob."[45] For homosexuals, he became a martyr figure, a
haunting symbol of gay vulnerability and gay resistance. Responsible more
than anyone else for forming the popular stereotype of the homosexual as a
dandiacal wit who flaunts middle-class mores, he is also most responsible
for exemplifying the political realities of gay oppression. Imprisoned and
marginalized because of his homosexuality, he came to understand the need
for imagination—i.e., attentiveness to the ways in which individuals are
shaped by social assumptions. The viciousness of his persecution and the
extremity of his suffering made him a victim, but his transforming imagination taught him insight into the nature of his society and into himself, and
thereby translated his victimization into martyrdom. He is a symbolic figure not only because his imprisonment is the political reality that all subsequent considerations of homosexuality must confront, but also because his
defiance and his painfully earned self-realization are important lessons in
the struggle for gay liberation. After years of experimenting with poses and
masks, his ultimate creation of a complex and contradictory persona, one in
which his homosexuality is an integral component, is probably his greatest
literary and historical achievement.

In the gay fictions of Oscar Wilde may be seen many of the themes and
concerns that will dominate modern gay fiction generally. The preoccupation with self-realization, the opposition of the individual and society, the
yearning for an escape from moralistic strictures, the exploring of connections between Eros and art, the search for a gay golden age and for the
recovery of the past (often imagined as Arcadian or Hellenistic), and the
depiction of divided selves: these characteristic concerns of Wilde's fiction

are explored with different emphases and varying resolutions in the gay fiction that follows. Perhaps most significantly, the rejection of society in *De Profundis* establishes separatism (either real or metaphorical) as a possible response to homophobia and functions as a polar position in gay fiction's continuing debate about the possibility of accommodation with the dominant society, a position challenged by Willa Cather in her story "Paul's Case," for example.

But in Wilde's own career, the progress from titillating hints of decadent homosexuality in *The Picture of Dorian Gray* and the foiled coming-out story of "The Portrait of Mr. W. H." to the frank acceptance and defiant defense of homosexuality in *De Profundis* is also instructive. Forced out of the closet by his disastrous trials, Wilde finally develops a deep political insight into the nature of gay oppression and a unified vision in which homosexuality is an ineradicable element in the wholeness of his personality. He progresses from ambivalent texts divided against themselves to a work that, finally, unambiguously resolves the homosexual's problematic relationship to society by embracing the outsider's potential for social criticism. In *De Profundis* as well as in "The Portrait of Mr. W. H.," Wilde learns that "in such surrender there may be gain."

If the post-prison years of his life are not particularly edifying, at least Wilde remained faithful to the gain he finally achieved at so great a cost. In an 1898 letter to Ross defending his reconciliation with Douglas, he described his imprisonment for homosexuality as a political incarceration analogous to jailing a patriot.

A patriot put in prison for loving his country loves his country, and a poet in prison for loving boys loves boys. To have altered my life would have been to have admitted that Uranian love is ignoble. I hold it to be noble—more noble than other forms.[46]

3

"A Losing Game in the End": Willa Cather's "Paul's Case"

Willa Cather's homosexuality, for years a well-guarded but scarcely well-kept secret, is by now widely acknowledged. Sharon O'Brien's *Willa Cather: The Emerging Voice* sensitively traces Cather's personal and artistic development, her emergence from the male-identified male impersonator of her adolescence and youth into the mature woman writer who created the first strong female heroes in American literature. Central to this transformation were Cather's eventual liberation from her early internalized male aesthetic, after a long and difficult struggle, and her acceptance of her lesbianism, even as she recognized the need to conceal her sexual identity as "the thing not named." As O'Brien remarks, "Throughout her literary career, Cather was both the writer transforming the self in art and the lesbian writer at times forced to conceal 'unnatural' love by projecting herself into male disguises."[1]

What has not been sufficiently noted, however, is Cather's early contribution to gay male literature and to the debate about homosexuality sparked by the Wilde scandal. More particularly, "Pauls' Case," the acclaimed story that marks the beginning of Cather's artistic maturity after a prolonged period of apprenticeship, has not yet been placed in the context of its author's growing awareness of the limits of the masculine aesthetic that she originally espoused. Nor has the story's insight into the homosexual's plight in American society at the turn into the new century been adequately explored. In *Playing the Game*, Roger Austen briefly discusses "Paul's Case" as a depiction of a sensitive young man stifled by the drab ugliness of his environment and places the protagonist in an American literary tradition of "village sissies."[2] And more exhaustively, Larry Rubin argues that the title character of the story is "very probably homosexual by nature and temperament" and that "Cather is trying to show us the tragic consequences of the conflict between a sensitive and hence alienated temperament, on the one hand, and a narrowly 'moral,' bourgeois environment, on the other."[3] But both discussions tend to sentimentalize the protagonist's gayness and to reduce the story to a simple conflict between the individual and society. Neither study locates "Paul's Case" in the context of Cather's response to the aesthetic movement in general or to the Wilde scandal in particular. Consequently, they fail to grasp the complexity of Cather's story and of her perspective on homosexuality in it.

For the young Cather, Oscar Wilde was a profoundly disturbing figure. The target of a number of her early critical remarks published in the *Nebraska State Journal* and the Lincoln *Courier* (now conveniently collected in *The Kingdom of Art*[4]), he unmistakably challenged some of her most deeply cherished social and aesthetic notions and roused her to some of her most visceral expressions of contempt. Cather's attitude toward Wilde and the aesthetic movement in these early newspaper columns and reviews is unremittingly hostile. Regarding him as a poseur who betrayed his talent, she despises his "insincerity," his tendency to mock social conventions, his elevation of art at the expense of nature, and, most importantly, his "driveling effeminacy." Interestingly, her hostility to Wilde is expressed so vehemently—indeed, so excessively—as to make one suspect that he represented for her not merely an artistic creed with which she lacked sympathy, but a personal psychological threat. The early comments on Wilde are revealing of Cather's cast of mind in the mid-1890s, as contrasted with the period some ten years later when she wrote "Paul's Case," and they form an illuminating backdrop against which to explore the story.

In an 1894 review of Robert Hichens's "clever and inane" but insinuating satire on Wilde and his circle, *The Green Carnation*, Cather remarks that "It certainly ought to succeed in disgusting people with Mr. Wilde's epigrammatic school once and for all. It turns and twists those absurd mannerisms and phrases of Wilde's until they appear as ridiculous as they really are." That same year, in a review of *Lady Windermere's Fan*, she observes that Wilde's "philosophy is so contemptible, so inane, so puny that even with all its brilliant epigrams the club talk in the third act is wearisome," and that through the "little puppy Cecil Graham" (who, like the protagonist of "Paul's Case" and like Wilde himself, sports a carnation in his buttonhole) Wilde "vents all his unwholesome spleen and his pitiable smallness." She finds the play artificial and unbelievable, because its theme is motherhood, a thing "which a man of Mr. Wilde's ethics and school and life cannot even conceive." Cather's dislike for Wilde in these pieces and the personalizing of her repugnance go beyond measured criticism; clearly, she found his artificiality and iconoclasm—especially his challenge to sex-role conventions and to the hearty masculinity that she embraced at the time—deeply dispiriting. Her references to Wilde in terms of fraility (his "puny philosophy," his "little puppy" of a character, his "pitiable smallness") are particularly noteworthy. They indicate her contempt for any deviance from the masculine ideal that Wilde and his circle mocked and that she celebrated in her effusive praise of such writers as Rudyard Kipling, as well as in her commendation of football as a force that "curbs the growing tendencies toward effeminacy so prevalent in the eastern colleges."

In her 1895 columns following Wilde's imprisonment, Cather continues to denigrate him. She begins an essay on Swinburne by noting—almost gleefully—that "his brother in Apollo is picking oakum in prison"; and in a column bitterly denouncing the aesthetic movement, she extravagantly hails Wilde's downfall as prefiguring "the destruction of the most fatal and dangerous school of art that has ever voiced itself in the English tongue." She says, "We will have no more such plays as *Lady Windermere's Fan*, no more such stories as *The Portrait [sic] of Dorian Gray*," and adds: "We can do without them. They were full of insanity." She relishes the irony implicit in the "peculiar fact" that a movement that set such store in beauty "has ended by finding what was most grotesque, misshapen and unlovely." She accuses Wilde of "the begetter of all evil—insincerity," and in effect congratulates herself on being among the few who were not blinded by the cleverness of *Lady Windermere's Fan*, who "felt in it that falseness which makes the soul shudder and revolt." She explains the rise of the aesthetic school as a consequence "of the artificial way in which men and women are living. . . . Every century or so society decides to improve on nature. It becomes very superior and refined indeed, until right through its surface there breaks some ghastly eruption that makes it hide its face in shame." She finds the aesthetes' insistence that nature imitates art particularly galling. She concludes the essay by saluting the salubrious effects of Wilde's disgrace:

> We put on sackcloth and go back to our father's house and become again as little children. Then it is that human endeavor becomes bold and strong and that human art is charged with new life. For it is while we are in that child-like mood of penitence that nature opens her arms to us and God tells us the secrets of heaven.

In this conclusion, Cather at once embraces the triumph of the patriarchy, which is implicitly defined as "natural"—in effect, welcoming repression—and yet she acknowledges a "shame" that she shares with the aesthetes. This barely concealed acknowledgment of identification with the movement that she vilifies may account for the extremity of her invective here. The tensions and contradictions palpable in this column suggest how thoroughly disturbing Cather found the aesthetic movement's challenge to conventional notions of the relationship of art and nature, and to her own aesthetic of hypermasculinity.

In a reflection on Wilde published later in 1895, Cather accuses him of having wasted his talent and of sinning against the holy spirit in man by having "used the holiest things for ends the basest." "He might have been a poet of no mean order, he might have been one of the greatest living dramatists, he might have been almost anything," she writes, "but he preferred to be a harlequin," thus anticipating Wilde's own clownlike self-representation in *De Profundis*, but denying the holiness he was to associate with the Harlequin-figure there. Although she asserts that the sins of the body are small compared to the sins of the spirit, she nevertheless judges him "most deservedly" imprisoned. "Upon his head is heaped the deepest infamy and the darkest shame of his generation. Civilization shudders at his name, and there is absolutely no spot on earth where this man can live," she remarks with some satisfaction. Significantly, she herself shudders at the prospect of naming Wilde: she begins the article by quoting Wilde's "Hélas!" and remarking that "I did not know whether to give the name of the author of that lament or not, for he has made his name impossible"; and she ends it by quoting lines from Robert Browning's "The Lost Leader" that begin: "Blot out his name then." This difficulty with naming may well be the result of Wilde's association with "the Love that dare not speak its name" and with Cather's own preoccupation with her lesbianism, which she would later characterize as "the thing not named."[5] For her, Wilde is a dangerous figure, at once unmentionable yet unavoidably fascinating.

Cather's disparagement of Wilde in the 1890s is especially interesting insofar as it coexists with her own intense admiration for many French *fin de siècle* writers, including Verlaine. This coexistence indicates that her contempt for Wilde is not merely an expression of prudish conventionality, or a reflection of her Nebraska readership, or evidence of a principled objection to *fin de siècle* preoccupations with immoral or unconventional subject matter. The point is not that it is necessarily inconsistent to disparage Wilde and praise Verlaine, but that the excesses and terms of Cather's attacks on Wilde are inconsistent with the strategies by which she defends Verlaine. Unlike many turn-of-the-century critics who saw Wilde and Verlaine as equally dangerous figures, and who linked them in a common enterprise of decadence, Cather scorns the artificiality of the aesthetes but celebrates the blessed degeneracy of Verlaine. Even as she condemns Wilde's subversive credo as "puny," she find Verlaine's revolt against bourgeois values heroic (i.e., masculine). The conclusion to be drawn from this apparent inconsistency is that Cather's principal objection to Wilde is as much personal as it is literary. More accurately, it is a reaction against his "drivelling effeminacy," his subversive mockery of the masculine ideal, as well as a rejection of his elevation of the artificial and the precious at the expense of the natural and the ordinary. Only when Cather herself came to redefine the masculine aesthetic of her youth could she qualify her attitude toward Wilde and the aesthetes. In a very real—if not altogether obvious—sense, "Paul's Case" reflects this modification in her thinking about Wilde and his circle.

The sources of "Paul's Case" are probably many, not least among them Cather's own personal experience as teacher and dreamer. Many years after the story's composition, she claimed that the protagonist was inspired by a student in the Pittsburgh high school at which she taught and that her character's experiences in New York were based on her own feelings about the city.[6] But there is reason to think that the story owes a great deal to her evolving response to the Wilde scandal and to Wilde's role as a symbolic figure, particularly as a discredited aesthete and as a persecuted victim. The work was published in 1905, five years after Wilde's death and soon after the appearance of the first, abridged version of *De Profundis,* at a time when Wilde was once again very widely discussed in literary circles.[7] Most significantly, the protagonist is depicted in easily recognizable terms as a Wildean aesthete, a dandy who sports a carnation in his buttonhole and who found "a certain element of artificiality . . . necessary in beauty."[8] In addition, the story's indictment of the failure of imagination in American society parallels Wilde's stress on imagination in *De Profundis,* though Cather ironically implicates the Wildean aesthete in her indictment. Moreover, placed as it is as the final story in a collection of stories focusing on art and artists,[9] the work invites consideration as a meditation on aestheticism and on the connection between art and nature—the preoccupation of the aesthetes—as well as a consideration of the homosexual's problematic relationship to society.

Central to the full experience of the story is recognition of the fact of Paul's homosexuality, a "fact" that is nowhere stated openly. This lack of explicitness reflects both the difficulty of writing about homosexuality in 1905 and Cather's own preference for insinuation and implication. In her essay on the craft of fiction, "The Novel Démeublé," first published in 1922, Cather calls attention to the presence of absence in her work. "Whatever is felt upon the page without being specifically named there—that, one might say, is created," she remarks. "It is the inexplicable presence of the thing not named, of the overtone divined by the ear but not heard by it, the verbal mood, the emotional aura of the fact or the thing or the deed, that gives high quality to the novel or the drama, as well as to poetry itself."[10] The startling phrase "the thing not named" connotes experience that the author does not, or cannot, express openly. As O'Brien notes, "the most prominent absence and most unspoken love in her work are the emotional bonds between women that were central to her life."[11] In "Paul's Case," however, the thing not named is Paul's homosexuality, a presence made palpable not by direct statement but by numerous hints and a distinct emotional aura and verbal mood.

In his brief article, Larry Rubin details some of the most significant clues that the story offers of Paul's gayness, from the youth's slight physique and the "hysterical brilliancy" of his eyes that he uses "in a conscious, theatrical way, peculiarly offensive in a boy," to his dandified dress, his attraction to the young actor in Pittsburgh and the Yale freshman in New York, his fastidiousness and use of violet water, his nervousness and internalized fears.[12] In addition to the clues detected by Rubin, the very title of the story, with its medical and legal overtones, is suggestive, for in 1905 public discourse on homosexuality was couched almost exclusively in terms of criminality or psychopathology. The protagonist, the title implies, is a fitting subject for a psychological or criminal case history. The subtitle, "A Study in Temperament," is particularly telling insofar as it implies a psychological condition and insofar as "temperament" is practically a code word for sexual orientation. But most interesting of all, in light of Cather's reference to the importance of verbal mood in her strategy of revelation within concealment, is the *language* of "Paul's Case." Throughout the story, Cather repeatedly uses diction suggestive of homosexuality. Although in almost every instance the words are used with no specific allusion to homosexuality, the startling number and pervasiveness of such terms as *gay* (used four times), *fairy, faggot, fagged, queen, loitering, tormented, unnatural, haunted, different, perverted, secret love,* and so forth create a verbal ambience that subtly but persistently calls attention to the issue. However innocently used, these words and phrases appear too often to be merely coincidental. They function to help establish the overtone by which the ear divines homosexuality in the text. Through this linguistic device, Cather creates a verbal mood that subliminally signals homosexuality as an important aspect of her work, even as she avoids any direct reference to the subject.

In the story, which might be described as a case study of a young aesthete, Paul's homosexuality is most vividly symbolized as the unnamed fear that has haunted him for years. "Until now, he could not remember the time when he had not been dreading something," he reflects after he has stolen the money.

> Even when he was a little boy, it was always there—behind him, or before, or on either side. There had always been the shadowed corner, the dark place into which he dared not look, but from which something seemed always to be watching him—and Paul had done things that were not pretty to watch, he knew.

The symbol of his gayness, this "apprehensive dread" profoundly shapes Paul's fearful, defensively contemptuous response to life and helps to account for his disaffection from the values of his middle-class environment. It is also clearly linked to his aestheticism: his preference for the artificial rather than the natural and his immersion in art at the expense of life. Paul finds freedom from this pervasive fear only when he breaks decisively with his stifling life in Pittsburgh by stealing the money. Then he feels "a curious sense of relief, as though he had at last thrown down the gauntlet to the thing in the corner," Cather writes, describing the break with his past as a kind of symbolic coming out. But although homosexuality in "Paul's Case" is a metaphor for alienation, and helps explicate the protagonist's problematic relationship to his society, it is not offered as a sufficient explanation for the youth's tragedy. That is, the cause of Paul's unhappiness and suicide is not his homosexuality but his inability to integrate his homosexuality into real life. This inability is itself the result of the homophobia that pervades his society and which he himself internalizes.

The complexity of the story arises from its skillful narration. The omniscient third-person point of view enables Cather to enter her protagonist's consciousness, yet it also establishes a crucial distance from him. The narrator evinces and creates sympathy for Paul but never unambiguously endorses his perspective. The distance that Cather achieves by means of her strategy of concealment, dispassionate title, controlled narrative technique, and use of symbols is overlooked by the conventional readings of the story that explain Paul's tragedy as simply the result of an insensitive and uncaring society. But Cather withholds authorial judgment in the contest she presents between Paul and his environment, and informs the poignancy of Paul's brief and unhappy life with a peculiar kind of irony. She finally implicates both Bohemia and Presbyteria (to use her private terms for the dichotomy)[13] in the fate of her young aesthete, whose doom is conceived as a bitterly ironic tragedy of errors.

Complicating rather than reducing, Cather transforms the materials of an overly familiar tale of a tormented artist destroyed by philistines into a rich and complex story that admits of no simple schematization. Her case study of an alienated youth almost mechanically moving to his doom is enriched by an awareness, subtly and delicately conveyed, of missed opportunities that might have saved him. Paul is not merely the homosexual victim hounded to his suicide by a society that persecutes him. Paul's society, including especially his teachers and father, is indeed culpable; but the youth himself partakes of the lack of imagination that culminates in tragedy. Although the understated narration imparts a sense of inevitability to his fate, Paul himself bears a major responsibility for the waste that it represents. In part shaped by the Wilde scandal, the story in effect comments on Wilde's own fate as one that might have been prevented and as one for which he must share the blame. In considering the homosexual's relationship to society, it therefore rebuffs Wilde's blanket rejection of society in favor of a strategy of accommodationism.

As in Wilde's *De Profundis,* imagination is a key faculty in "Paul's Case." But in the story it is present by virtue of its almost complete absence, even as the work finally becomes itself an enactment of that imaginative sympathy of which its characters are revealed to be devoid. The lack of imagination on the part of Paul's father, teachers, and neighbors is obvious in their inability to understand the young man and in their simplistic attempts to help him, as well as in their indifference to art and beauty. The father confesses his "perplexity" regarding his son; the teachers, for all their myriad speculations, admit that "there was something about the boy which none of them understood." The inability of conventional society to understand, and to deal humanely with, those who are different is clearly attacked by the story and exposed as a crucial failure of imagination. This lack of imagination transforms well-intentioned teachers into vicious inquisitors when Paul appears before them to answer various misdemeanors in the story's brilliant opening scene. The teachers are not unkind by nature, but they lack the imagination to understand sympathetically Paul's temperament and consequently allow themselves to be goaded into actions that contradict their own values. What spurs them to their packlike behavior is not merely what Paul actually does, but his defiant attitude and dress. The reaction of the teachers to Paul parallels Cather's own excessive reaction to Wilde's mocking manner in the 1890's, and may reflect the author's mature reconsideration of her own earlier lack of imagination in not dealing charitably with Wilde in his disgrace.

A similar failure of imagination leads Paul's father to force the son to break off his relationship with his only friend, the young actor, and to bar him from the theater and concert hall, the scenes of his only pleasures. Instead of regarding Paul's interest in art and in the friend (and potential lover) as possible resources that might be developed to help his son, the father reacts simplistically and increases Paul's isolation and alienation. The father's unimaginative response to his son's difficulties may be said to precipitate (if not to explain) the catastrophe, for, as Paul reflects after stealing the money, "It had been wonderfully simple; when they had shut him out of the theatre and concert hall, when they had taken away his bone, the whole thing was virtually determined. The rest was a mere matter of opportunity."

But somewhat less obvious than the failures of those who might have helped him is Paul's own lack of imagination, in the sense that Wilde employs the term in De Profundis, as an awareness of the meaning of one's experience and of one's relationship to others and to society. Yet the power of the story—and its importance as an original contribution to the debate about homosexuality in the first decade of the twentieth century—pivots on this very issue, for it is the exercise of imagination that might have altered Paul's case and allowed him to find a niche in his society. Paul's failure to analyze his society and to perceive possibilities of accommodation within it are personal, though understandable, failures that contribute to his tragedy.

But Cather intimates that the failure of imagination may be endemic to aestheticism itself, at least insofar as it became increasingly remote from ordinary life. In this sense, "Paul's Case" subtly criticizes the defiant rejection of society that *De Profundis* enacts (and that was undoubtedly a widespread temptation among homosexuals in the wake of the Wilde scandal) and calls for the exercise of imagination as a means of healing the rift between the homosexual and society.

Despite Paul's immersion in art, he is severely deficient in imagination. Art for him is merely a stimulation of the senses and an escape from human engagement. Significantly, the art to which Paul is most attracted excludes both ordinary reality and human relationships. For example, in the picture gallery he finds Raffelli's studies of Paris streets and Venetian scenes exhilarating and he "loses himself" in a blue Rico seascape. In contrast, he jeers at the representations of human figures, such as Augustus and Venus de Milo. He is imaginative only in the limited sense of being able to alter mundane reality by fantasizing more exciting, romantic alternatives. Music, about which he is utterly indiscriminating, is simply the spark that ignites his escapist fantasies. In his music-induced reveries, he is able to transform the glamourless, matronly German opera singer—a woman "by no means in her first youth, and the mother of many children"—into a "veritable queen of romance." In the atmosphere of Pittsburgh's Carnegie Hall, he is even able to re-create himself temporarily, momentarily feeling "within him the possibility of doing or saying splendid, brilliant, poetic things." Similarly, the stage entrance is for Paul "the actual portal of romance." It is a "wishing carpet" that whisks him from the realities of "smoke-palled" Pittsburgh to the "blue-and-white Mediterranean shore bathed in perpetual sunshine."

Not surprisingly, after his orgies of romantic escapism, Paul feels increasingly disaffected with mundane existence and alienated from ordinary life. Returning to his Cordelia Street home after an evening at the opera or theater,

> he experienced all the physical depression which follows a debauch; the loathing of respectable beds, of common food, of a house penetrated by kitchen odours; a shuddering repulsion for the flavourless, colourless mass of everyday existence; a morbid desire for cool things and soft lights and fresh flowers.

As described here, Paul's depression is reminiscent of the neurasthenic morbidity associated with aestheticism and decadence, exemplified, for example, in Wilde's Dorian Gray and Sir Henry Wotton. Significantly, despite his addiction to the stimulus of art, Paul is himself singularly uncreative. He is neither an artist, musician, writer, actor, or reader: "He felt no necessity to do any of these things; what he wanted was to see, to be in the atmosphere, float on the wave of it, to be carried out, blue league after blue league, away from everything."

What Paul lacks, of course, is imagination in the sense of *sympathy for others:* a capacity that is essential both for the creative artist and the successful human being. In the "physical aversion" he expresses toward his teachers, in his refusal to take others seriously or to consider the effect his behavior has on them, in his compulsive lying, and in his complete lack of remorse either for his petty cruelties or his betrayal of trust, Paul signals not merely his revolt against middle-class mores, but his contempt for life itself. It is noteworthy that he has almost no relationships with others. He is content to be a voyeur rather than a participant in life. Alone in New York, for example, he feels

> not in the least abashed or lonely. He had no especial desire to meet or to know any of these people; all he demanded was the right to look on and conjecture, to watch the pageant. The mere stage properties were all he contended for. Nor was he lonely later in the evening, in his loge at the Metropolitan.

His brief fling with the Yale freshman, "a wild San Francisco boy," ends with their "singularly cool" parting.[14] In his expensive hotel room, he insulates himself from the winter storm raging outside and from the exigencies of life itself, and is thereby subtly connected with the hothouse flowers he so admires, which he finds "somehow vastly more lovely and alluring that they blossomed thus unnaturally in the snow."

Paul's failure of imagination distorts his capacity to perceive clearly his relationship to society and to others. He assesses everyday reality as "but a sleep and a forgetting." He approaches his Cordelia Street neighborhood "with the nerveless sense of defeat." He thinks of his home as repulsive, with "his ugly sleeping chamber; the cold bathroom with the grimy zinc tub, the cracked mirror, the dripping spiggots [sic]; his father, at the top of the stairs, his hairy legs sticking out from his night-shirt, his feet thrust into carpet slippers." He rejects his middle-class origins and identifies with the wealthy, thinking of the inhabitants of the Waldorf as "his own people." But Paul's own values—epitomized in his belief in the omnipotence of wealth, in the fact "that money was everything, the wall that stood between all he loathed and all he wanted"—are actually not fundamentally different from the materialistic values of Cordelia Street, which also worships wealth and enjoys the "legends of the iron kings." Like his neighbors, he too relishes "the triumphs of these cash boys who had become famous," but unlike them "he had no mind for the cash-boy stage." Paralleling the tendencies of the aesthetes, including Wilde himself, to identify with upper-class and aristocratic society, Paul's rejection of Cordelia Street values is not based on any probing social analysis but is simply of a piece with his disdain for the ordinary and the everyday. His alienation from his own origins bespeaks both self-loathing and a failure to sympathize with the struggles of others.

Similarly, his interpretations of the motives of others are as inaccurate as his romanticization of the opera singer and the members of the acting company, more telling as projections of his disaffection than as reality. An important example of the morbidity of Paul's imagination, of its tendency to distort the motivations of those closest to him, is provided when he returns home from the concert near the beginning of the story. Fearful of facing "his father in his night-clothes at the top of the stairs," the young man spends the night in the basement. Unable to sleep, Paul creates various scenarios in which his father mistakes him for a burglar:

> Suppose his father had heard him getting in at the window and had come down and shot him for a burglar? Then, again, suppose his father had come down, pistol in hand, and he had cried out in time to save himself, and his father had been horrified to think how nearly he had killed him? Then, again, suppose a day should come when his father would remember that night, and wish there had been no warning cry to stay his hand? With this last supposition Paul entertained himself until daybreak.

The key word in this important passage is *entertained*. It indicates the extremity of Paul's alienation, his failure to take entirely seriously either his own life or his troubled relationship with his father, and it illustrates the youth's almost obsessive need to translate life into art, or at least into entertainment. This passage is also significant for its revelation of Paul's expectation that his father will reject him, that his father might well someday wish that he had killed his son. This assumption is an expression of Paul's "apprehensive dread," his fear that his father will discover his homosexuality. It reflects the homophobia he feels both in the larger society and within himself.

Rather than the unsympathetic ogre that Paul visualizes, his father is a concerned, though inept and unimaginative, parent, faced with a difficult situation, the full extent of which he fails to recognize. Mystified by his son's peculiar devotion to music and theater and disturbed by his problems in school, the father simplistically hopes that Paul will model himself after their much admired young neighbor who, "in order to curb his appetites and save the loss of time and strength that the sowing of wild oats might have entailed," took his boss's advice and "at twenty-one had married the first woman whom he could persuade to share his fortunes." Ambitious and hardworking, the father embodies the middle-class mores of his neighborhood, "where all the houses were exactly alike, and where business men of moderate means begot and reared large families of children, all of whom went to Sabbath-school and learned the shorter catechism, and were interested in arithmetic; all of whom were as exactly alike as their homes, and of a piece with the monotony in which they lived." These values, symbolized by the pictures of George Washington and John Calvin that hang in Paul's bedroom, are limited, for they presuppose a sameness to human nature that does not admit difference and they turn out to be ineffective in helping Paul. But the father's brief appearances in the story, his presence at the top of the stairs, his reluctant provision of car fare, his taking Paul out of school, and, most importantly, his reimbursement of Paul's theft and his trip to New York to retrieve his son, provide evidence not merely of the tyranny that Paul sees, but also of love and concern, however mistakenly and unimaginatively applied.

The failures of imagination that the story indicts are epitomized in the ineffective attempts of the father and his neighbors to help Paul after the theft and in Paul's rejection of these attempts. After the theft is discovered, the Pittsburgh newspapers report:

> The firm of Denny & Carson announced that the boy's father had refunded the full amount of the theft, and that they had no intention of prosecuting. The Cumberland minister had been interviewed, and expressed his hope of yet reclaiming the motherless lad, and his Sabbath-school teacher declared that she would spare no effort to that end. The rumour had reached Pittsburgh that the boy had been seen in a New York hotel, and his father had gone East to find him and bring him home.

Clearly, the response of the father and the community to Paul's crime is predicated on a stifling and narrow religiosity. It is unimaginative in its inability to conceive that Paul's needs may be other than those that can be satisfied by home and church. At the same time, it must be acknowledged that the response is unquestionably a generous and forgiving one. Paul, however, reacts to the newspaper report with horror. "It was to be worse than jail, even; the tepid waters of Cordelia Street were to close over him finally and forever," he thinks. "The grey monotony stretched before him in hopeless, unrelieved years; Sabbath-school, Young People's Meeting, the yellow-papered room, the damp dish-towels; it all rushed back upon him with a sickening vividness." Paul's failure of imagination is obvious here. Utterly oblivious to the generous concern expressed by his neighbors and exemplified by his father, he is as unable to imagine human sympathy on the part of others as he is to feel it himself.

The story is placed in perspective by its use of contrasting symbols associated with Paul and his environment. The very name Cordelia Street evokes Lear's daughter, whose death is as pathetic (and unnecessary) as Paul's.[15] Shakespeare's Cordelia functions in the story as a complex, double symbol, signifying at once the possibility of both individuality and community responsibility. On the one hand, she personifies individual integrity and fidelity to one's own vision, the refusal to sacrifice one's sense of self in order to make accommodation with the world. From this perspective, there is considerable irony in evoking Cordelia in connection with the monotonous and conformist neighborhood in which Paul lives, a place whose inhabitants seem unable to comprehend anything beyond their own narrow ken as they look over their multitude of squabbling children and smile "to see their own proclivities reproduced in their offspring." But, significantly, despite rejection by her father, in Shakespeare's tragedy Cordelia comes to personify not only individualism but also *agape*, an association that is strengthened in Cather's story by the framed motto, "Feed my Lambs," that Paul's mother had worked in red worsted and that hangs in Paul's bedroom. Signifying community and family loyalty, caring for others and helping bear their burdens, the symbols of *agape* underline the story's insistence on the importance of imagination in the sense of a capacity for human sympathy. Moreover, *agape* is certainly present, at least potentially, in the generosity and forgiveness of the neighborhood's reaction to Paul's escapade. More important, it haunts the story as an unstated presence that promises the possibility of integrating outcasts like Paul—and like Wilde and other homosexuals—into the community, and doing so without violating their individuality. The optimism implicit in the notion of *agape* inevitably challenges the pessimism of any social analysis—such as that in *De Profundis*—that would lead homosexuals to reject society or that would sanction society's persecution of gay people.

In contrast to the symbols of *agape* associated with Cordelia Street is the red carnation favored by Paul. A hothouse flower, unnaturally cultivated, and associated with Wilde, homosexuality, and aestheticism, the red carnation that Paul buries in the snow before leaping to his own death is a symbol of life's brevity and fragility and of the artificial mocking the natural. As Paul trudges through the snow, he notices that the flowers displayed in his coat have drooped, their red glory faded. He becomes sadly aware that all the flowers he had seen in the glass cases his first night in New York have similarly failed. "It was only one splendid breath they had, in spite of their brave mockery at the winter outside the glass," he acknowledges; and he concludes: "it was a losing game in the end, it seemed, this revolt against the homilies by which the world is run."

In this meditation, soon before Paul's "picture making mechanism was crushed" and he "dropped back into the immense design of things," Paul reaches a conclusion that contradicts his earlier confident assertion that his rebellion "had paid. . . . Ah, it had paid indeed!" In so doing, he enunciates one of the story's central points. The "brave mockery" undertaken by Paul (and by Wilde and the aesthetes) is a losing game in the end. In

"Paul's Case," Cather is not so much intent on either prosecuting Presbyteria or defending it from the assaults of Bohemia as on indicating the futility of the battle in the first place.

In "Paul's Case," Cather provides a case study of the Wildean aesthete. Her portrait of the young protagonist as a Romantic artist-manqué is, I think, intended as a comment on Wilde and the aesthetic movement, particularly on the movement's celebration of the artificial and mockery of the natural, its privileging of the precious at the expense of the ordinary, and its elevation of art above nature. She tends to explain this phenomenon in sociological terms and with a measure of controlled sympathy, as when she comments as follows:

> Perhaps it was because, in Paul's world, the natural nearly always wore the guise of ugliness, that a certain element of artificiality seemed to him necessary in beauty. Perhaps it was because his experience of life elsewhere was so full of Sabbath-school picnics, petty economies, wholesome advice as to how to succeed in life, and the unescapable odours of cooking, that he found this existence so alluring, these smartly-clad men and women so attractive, that he was so moved by these starry apple orchards that bloomed perennially under the lime-light.

In her unflattering depiction of American middle-class life, Cather provides a context that makes aestheticism understandable and attractive. At the same time, however, she exposes the unreality on which aestheticism is based, and condemns it for its disdainful rejection of mundane life and human relationships. She convicts, in turn, both Presbyteria and Bohemia for failures of imagination—the one for its dullness and conformity, the other for its lack of generosity in divining the motives of ordinary people. But insofar as the story evinces a more humane and sympathetic response to Wilde as victim than Cather was able to muster in 1895, "Paul's Case" is also interesting as evidence of the personal growth its author attained in the following decade, when she progressed from embracing the masculine ideal to apprehending the need for diversity and acceptance of others. Her story, indicting the failure of sympathy, actually enacts that imaginative response, the lack of which it exposes in its characters.

In depicting the futility of the aesthetes' "revolt against the homilies by which the world is run," Cather aims not so much to endorse those homilies as to indicate the loss involved in the "brave mockery" of them. But it is meaningful that she shares neither Wilde's pessimism nor his blanket rejection of society. In her tempered optimism, she clings to faith in the possibility of imagination and in the ideal of *agape* as antidotes to alienation and anomie. Moreover, she implies that the solution to the homosexual dilemma in an unaccepting society lies in integration rather than separation and in self-acceptance rather than self-hatred. The homophobia that Paul senses in the larger society is exacerbated by his internalized homophobia. His perception distorted by his fears, he fails to realize the possibilities for accommodation within his society and is thus doomed to his unhappy fate. His symbolic coming out, his defiant throwing down the gauntlet "to the thing in the corner," is not an acceptance but a rejection, and it leads not to liberation but to death. In her contribution to the debate about homosexuality in the wake of the Wilde scandal, Cather places on society and the homosexual alike the burden of imaginative sympathy, indicting the stifling conformity of American middle-class values even as she characterizes the homosexual's contemptuous rejection of society as "a losing game in the end."

As a gay fiction, "Paul's Case" is complex and resonant. By means of its masterful narration, it achieves an unusual balance of perspective. It vividly depicts what at first glance may seem to be the almost inevitable fate of gay people in an unsympathetic, nonpluralistic society, only to deconstruct this pessimistic assessment by subtly implying alternatives to alienation and suicide and envisioning possibilities implicit in those homilies by which the world is run. Embodied most fully in the notions of *agape* and imagination, these possibilities arise from a social analysis quite different from that offered by Wilde and the aesthetes: one that seeks accommodation rather than rejection, compromise rather than confrontation. Cather's accommodationism demands a generosity of spirit and a breadth of vision on the part of society and the homosexual alike.

Obviously, most gay people have had to practice various degrees of accommodationism, ranging from the social invisibility of relationships to the self-denial and hyprocrisy of the "closet." Even in the face of severe repression, very few could afford to reject society altogether, however painful and expensive the price of accommodation. Thus, Cather's humane plea for an imaginative accommodationism—one that insists on individuality and self-acceptance—is apt to strike most readers as at once more attractive and far more realistic than Wilde's bitter rejection of a persecuting society. Not surprisingly, the overwhelming issue in gay fiction is the relationship of the individual to society, and in exploring that issue most gay fictions search for some way to accommodate the conflicting needs of the homosexual and the demands of a conformist society. Cather's accommodationist concern in "Paul's Case" is, thus, shared by most of the gay fictions that follow. Nevertheless, it is important to stress that Cather's social analysis is subject to question. The very reticence of the story, its inability to name homosexuality openly, may to some extent compromise its authority as a gay fiction, even as this same silence eloquently testifies to the homophobia of its time. Moreover, based as it is on appeals to concepts as inevitably vague as *agape* and imagination, Cather's accommodationism is severely limited as a practical response to homophobia. And, finally, one may justly complain that in placing equal burdens on an alienated adolescent and an entire society Cather comes dangerously close to blaming the victim.

Although Cather's social analysis in "Paul's Case" is questionable, the story is nevertheless an important gay fiction. By subtly deconstructing its own plot, "Paul's Case" not only itself enacts an imaginative response but demands that its readers do so as well, both in the process of interpretation and in relating to others in the world beyond the boundaries of fiction. For all its reticence and indirectness, the story is actually surprisingly engaged. A work of unusual power that evokes genuine pathos, Cather's first major achievement is both a moving tale and a thoughtful contribution to the debate about homosexuality sparked by the Wilde scandal, an event that also affected the work of another important writer, E. M. Forster.

4

"The Flesh Educating the Spirit": E. M. Forster's Gay Fictions

E. M. Forster is the most acclaimed gay writer in modern English literature. Although he always remained to some extent an Edwardian—a product, as he said, of "the fag-end of Victorian liberalism"[1]—he embodies more fully than any other imaginative writer of his generation a modern gay-liberation perspective. Born in 1879, he became aware of his own homosexuality in the climate of repression and self-consciousness that permeated English society in the aftermath of the Wilde scandal. As a student at King's College, Cambridge, where he matriculated in 1897, he fell in love with a fellow undergraduate, with whom he enjoyed kisses and embraces but probably not genital sexuality. Forster, in fact, was not to experience a fully satisfying sexual relationship of any duration until he was nearly forty, when he fell in love with an Egyptian tram conductor in Alexandria. His sexual frustration undoubtedly influenced his art almost as much as his homosexuality itself, accounting for the emphasis in the early work on the need for sexual fulfillment and wholeness of being.

Equally important to an understanding of Forster's work is the specific form in which his homosexuality manifested itself, particularly his erotic preference for foreigners and for men of the lower social classes. Reflecting an appreciation of the natural vitality he connected with working-class men and an ambivalence about his own overcivilized temperament, this preference helps account for his tendency to romanticize the lower classes and the "natural" men of his fiction and for his sensitivity to the injustices of the British class system at home and to the effects of British imperialism abroad. Perhaps because of his erotic preference for lower-class men, Forster was also deeply affected by the belief that homosexuality could serve a positive social function by helping to bridge the barriers that separate the classes from each other. This belief, which is reflected throughout Forster's fiction and surfaces most explicitly in *Maurice*, derives from the Whit-manesque ideal of comradeship as expressed in the early English gay liber-ation movement. Edward Carpenter, for example, defends homosexuality in just these terms, when he writes that "Eros is a great leveler. Perhaps the true Democracy rests, more firmly than anywhere else, on a sentiment which easily passes the bounds of class and caste, and unites in the closest affection in the most estranged ranks of society."[2]

Forster's acute consciousness of gay oppression, as epitomized in the per-secution of Wilde, haunted his imagination throughout his life, fueling his anger at social and political injustice and making him contemptuous of the conventions that separate individuals and impede instinct. When he was almost eighty-five years old, he noted in his diary, "how *annoyed* I am with Society for wasting my time by making homosexuality criminal. The subterfuges, the self-consciousness that might have been avoided."[3] But notwithstanding his difficulties in making a satisfactory sexual adjustment, and despite recent attempts to characterize his attitude toward homosexual-ity as guilt-ridden and self-loathing, the fact is that Forster never felt shame for his sexual orientation (though he experienced considerable anxiety about his sexual difficulties). When Leonard Woolf asked him whether he would like to be "converted" to heterosexuality, he replied without hesita-tion, "No."[4] What he did feel as a result of his homosexuality were a sense of wariness and vulnerability and that sensation of standing "at a slight angle to the universe" that he detected in the Greek poet C. P. Cavafy.[5] Forster's sensitivity to the homophobia of his age—as expressed in soci-ety's incessant attacks on the self-esteem of homosexuals—probably ac-counts for that tinge of sadness so characteristic of the Forsterian voice. It certainly made him aware of himself as an outsider.

The posthumous publication of *Maurice* in 1971 and of *The Life to Come and Other Stories* in 1972, as well as the revelations of P. N. Furbank's scrupulously honest biography, caused a decided decline in Forster's repu-tation and led to a number of patently homophobic attacks on him and his work. The attacks inspired by bigotry generally betray their own absur-dity, as, for example, when Cynthia Ozick asserts that Forster's homosexu-ality devalues his humanism.[6] But the belatedness of the publication of Forster's gay fictions has had a more insidious consequence: the tendency among critics to isolate the explicitly gay fiction from the justly celebrated novels and stories published in Forster's lifetime. Such a division is artifi-cial, however, suggested by the publication history of the works and their external dramatic situations but not by the fiction itself, which embodies a consistent system of values centered on issues of self-realization, individu-alism, and responsiveness to life, nature, and the unseen. Moreover, what June Perry Levine identifies as the predominant pattern of Forster's posthumously published work—"the tame in pursuit of the savage, oscillating within a field of attraction and repulsion"—is one that may be seen in all his work.[7]

Forster's inability to publish explicitly gay fiction during most of his lifetime was frustrating. Indeed, he sometimes explained his failure to write novels during the final forty-six years of his life in terms of this frustration: as a homosexual, he said, he grew bored writing marriage fiction, and he could not publish his works on homosexual subjects. This explanation begs a number of questions, and should not be accepted at face value as the real reason Forster abandoned the writing of novels at the height of his career, but it does indicate the importance he attached both to his sexual identity and to his gay fiction. He seems initially to have turned to gay subjects during problematic moments in writing on publishable subjects. In 1911, for example, expressing his overweening "Weariness of the only subject that I both can and may treat—the love of men for women & vice versa,"[8] he abandoned a novel that was to have been called *Arctic Summer* and began writing homoerotic short stories. Similarly, in 1913, when his attempts to write an Indian novel faltered after a few chapters, he visited Edward Carpenter and conceived what was to become *Maurice*. He wrote the first draft of the work quickly and with a sense of exaltation. Although he knew that he could not publish it, he thought that having completed his novel of homosexual passion, his period of sterility would be over and he could turn to other work. But, as P. N. Furbank explains, "to his dismay he discovered that life had played a trick on him. To have written an unpublishable novel, he found, was no help at all towards producing a publishable one."[9] But if he undertook *Maurice* and his other early gay fictions largely for therapeutic purposes, that is not to say that he valued these works less than the published fiction. Indeed, his revisions of and tinkering with *Maurice* periodically occupied him for most of the rest of his life. The care that he spent on his unpublishable novel and the concern for it he frequently expressed to his close friends indicate the importance he attached to this work. And long after he had officially given up fiction writing—after the publication of *A Passage to India* in 1924 and *The Eternal Moment and Other Stories* (which collects tales, all of which were written before World War I) in 1928—he continued to write occasional stories on homosexual themes.

It has been argued that the stories and novels published in Forster's lifetime are better than the posthumously published ones precisely because the former contain rather than express directly their author's homosexual imagination, and that they required of the author interesting strategies of concealment, obliquity, and indirection unnecessary in the posthumously published fiction.[10] While it is true that the tension generated by the coexistence of heterosexual plot and homoerotic counterplot, of text and subtext, contributes to the energy of the justly famous fiction published during Forster's lifetime, it does not follow that the gay fiction is devoid of such power. Indeed, as the following discussion will demonstrate, the posthumously published work evinces the same qualities of intelligence and passion and partakes of the same complexities of technique and perspective that distinguish the more celebrated work. More specifically, *Maurice* deserves an honored place among Forster's novels—less ambitious than *Howards End* and *A Passage to India*, but equal in accomplishment to the minor masterpieces *Where Angels Fear to Thread, The Longest Journey,* and *A Room with a View*—and the posthumously published stories are among Forster's finest achievements in short fiction. Because Forster's homosexual fiction includes both his earliest and his latest work, and encompasses so wide a range of technique and perspective, it might even be said to be most fully representative of Forster's artistry. At the very least, it deserves full integration into his canon and serious recognition in its own right.

Although the gay fiction explored below was composed over a fifty-year period, it demonstrates both Forster's contemporaneousness and the extent to which he remained an Edwardian. In addition to the frustration he felt at not being able to explore homosexual issues openly in his fiction, Forster's decision not to continue publishing fiction was probably also influenced by the fact that the world he knew best had ended in 1914, with the beginning of the Great War. Even his final major fictional work—"The Other Boat," completed in 1958, when he was almost eighty-years-old—is set in the years just prior to World War I. Forster's conviction of belonging to an anachronistic tradition probably tended to inhibit his creative imagination, at least insofar as it came to publishing his work; and he even worried that, when published after his death, *Maurice* might be regarded as merely a quaint period piece. In 1932, he asked the young Christopher Isherwood, "Does it date?" and Isherwood wisely replied, "Why *shouldn't* it date?"[11] In fact, Forster's command of the Edwardian social scene, observed throughout his gay fiction, unifies and concretizes this diverse body of work, even as it also testifies to the timelessness of his insight into the pain and joy of growth and self-realization. For all their masterful settings in the concrete contexts of Edwardian England, Forster's gay fictions are remarkably contemporary in spirit.

Before turning to Forster's greatest gay fiction, *Maurice,* and a selection of the posthumously published short fiction, it may be instructive to examine briefly a gay fiction that he *did* publish. "The Curate's Friend," which originally appeared in *Putnam's* magazine in 1907 and was collected in *The Celestial Omnibus and Other Stories* in 1911, is a slight, fantastical tale of a young clergyman's encounter with a faun, an encounter that transforms his entire life, bringing him happiness and inner freedom. On first reading, it seems hardly more than an anecdote, yet concealed beneath its comic veneer is an account of homosexual recognition and acceptance that is undoubtedly autobiographical. The faun, a manifestation of the Greek spirit of life as localized in the Wiltshire downs, appears to Harry, the young curate, during a picnic. The other members of the party—his fiancée Emily, her mother, and another young man—cannot see the faun, but the curate can, for he possesses "a certain quality, for which truthfulness is too cold a name and animal spirits too coarse a one."[12] At first he is frightened, mistaking the faun for an evil spirit. But after the benign creature reassures him, Harry tests its powers by urging him to make Emily happy, supposing that the sprite will cause her to fall more deeply in love with him. Instead, however, the "great pagan figure" hovers above Emily and her young friend: "They, who had only intended a little cultural flirtation, resisted him as long as they could, but were gradually urged into each other's arms, and embraced with passion." The new lovers enact a rhapsodic ballet that is both comically absurd and strangely moving. Harry knows that he should be angry at this betrayal by his fiancée, but actually he is relieved and filled with joy. The faun tells him, "To the end of your life you will swear when you are cross and laugh when you are happy." Aided by his mythological friend, Harry goes on to a contented, useful, and natural life. He tries to share his joy with others, yet he can tell no one the source of his happiness:

> For if I breathed one word of that, my present life, so agreeable and profitable, would come to an end, my congregation would depart, and so should I, and instead of being an asset to my parish, I might find myself an expense to the nation.

The story is a playful but serious exercise in tentative self-disclosure. It conceals its true subject—which demands "lyrical and rhetorical treatment"—in the disguise of "the unworthy medium of a narrative." In the process, author and narrator jointly delude the reader "by declaring that this is a short story, suitable for reading in the train," thus recalling Gwendolyn Fairfax's comment about her diary in Wilde's *The Importance of Being Earnest:* "One should always have something sensational to read in the train."[13] The delusion is only apparent, however, for the allegory betrays as well as conceals its true subject: self-discovery and, more significantly, self-acceptance of homosexuality. Like the lovers, Harry too can sing, "In the great solitude I have found myself at last." As a result of his self-acceptance, he rises beyond such concepts as guilt and sin and conformity. He saves himself from a loveless marriage and learns to commune with nature. "That evening, for the first time," he remarks, "I heard the chalk downs singing to each other across the valleys." His happy life is shadowed by the prospect of prison should he reveal the secret of his transformation, but the clergyman's self-discovery is nonetheless rewarding. As part of the story's playful strategy of simultaneous disclosure and concealment, the prospect of prison is introduced ambiguously in order to permit a less explicitly homosexual reading, in which case the curate would be "an expense to the nation" by being confined in an insane asylum. But even this calculated ambiguity reveals as well as conceals, since by 1907 homosexuality was increasingly perceived as a mental-health as well as legal issue.

"The Curate's Friend" is unusual among Forster's early stories in that it records a character's awakening to happiness within society. Its spirit of accommodation seems closer to that implicitly recommended in Cather's "Paul's Case" than to the defiant militancy apparent in the rejection of society at the end of Wilde's *De Profundis*. But the story's opposition of nature and society, and its identification of homosexuality with naturalness and with the Greek spirit recall Wilde's perspective. And although Harry prospers in society, he fully understands the hollowness of his previous conformity, and he is constantly aware of the price society will exact should he reveal the homosexual root of his happiness. The story illustrates the great value of honesty to oneself, even as it also indicates the necessity for discretion—even hypocrisy—in a repressive society. "The Curate's Friend" documents the homosexual's dilemma in a homophobic society, torn as he or she is between the elemental, human need for self-affirmation and the undeniable dangers of disclosure. At the same time that it unveils Harry's strategy of accommodation, the story also betrays Forster's awareness in 1907 of his own precarious position in a society that rewarded him as author of two acclaimed novels but that was, nevertheless, prepared to punish him for the secret desires that animated his art. The prison door threatens to swing shut on the author as well as on the narrator of "The Curate's Friend."

This sense of the homosexual's vulnerability is also at the heart of *Maurice* and the other posthumously published gay fictions. But not written for publication in their author's lifetime, the posthumous novels and stories are more straightforward, less playful, less self-referential, and more obviously defiant than "The Curate's Friend." Like the early story, *Maurice* also has a happy ending, though one rooted not in accommodation but in a Wildean rejection of society, whereas the posthumously published stories frequently end in violence and death, recording the victimization of individuals by a repressive society. The gay fictions that Forster could not (or, at least, did not) publish in his own lifetime partake of the same satirical impulses and the same condemnations of class consciousness and philistinism that energize the published work, but they more openly express disaffection and alienation and less confidently seek reconciliation and connection. Written for a very select audience of friends, this body of work is not mediated by

the demands of a wide and diverse readership; consequently, it is probably
closer to Forster's unconscious imagination. Most significantly, sexual activity is at the fore of the fiction Forster did not publish. Whereas in the
published work, Forster's presiding deities are Pan, Demeter, and Orion,
the presiding spirit of the gay fictions is Priapus.[14] In the posthumously
published novels and stories, sexuality is at once more and less important
than in the work published during Forster's lifetime. Sexuality is celebrated
as an agent that expresses and intensifies love, and as an irreducibly essential dimension of human identity, but it is also demystified as life-enhancing
pleasure, valuable for its own sake.

Maurice was begun in September 1913, completed in July 1914, and periodically revised until 1960, when it reached its final state. These revisions
centered largely on increasing the prominence and credibility of Alec Scudder, who in the earliest draft was based more on Forster's idealized desire
for the working-class men he admired from afar rather than on any firsthand knowledge, and on making the ending more believable. In a fascinating "Terminal Note" drafted in 1960 and appended to the novel, Forster
describes the genesis of *Maurice* as the direct result of a visit to the social
pioneer and gay liberation activist Edward Carpenter: "It must have been
on my second or third visit to the shrine that the spark was kindled and he
and his comrade George Merrill combined to make a profound impression
on me and to touch a creative spring."[15] Inspired by Carpenter and his
working-class lover, Merrill, Forster wrote the novel guided by the conviction that a "happy ending was imperative." More than anything else, it was
this happy ending that made *Maurice* unpublishable. Since homosexuality
was illegal in England until 1967, the novel might have been construed as
recommending crime and hence have been subject to prosecution. But even
in manuscript, *Maurice* had a major literary influence, as an important
source for *Lady Chatterley's Lover*, whose author, D. H. Lawrence, had
read a typescript of Forster's work.[16] (Ironically, when *Maurice* was published, some reviewers dismissed it as a homosexualized *Lady Chatterley's
Lover*; more accurately, Lawrence's novel is a heterosexualized *Maurice*.)

Forster's most concentrated novel, *Maurice* dramatizes in deeply felt
human terms the most important recent conclusions of sexologists and psychologists—that homosexuality is a set of feelings, involving the connection and commitment one individual makes with another, and that such
feelings predate sexual expression, sometimes by years—while at the same
time placing this understanding in the concrete context of Edwardian
England.[17] The social setting is important, for *Maurice* also explores the
impact of self-awareness on social attitudes, and it is fundamentally a political novel. For Forster, individual growth is always measured in terms of
sharpened insight into the nature of convention and repression.

The first masterpiece of the early gay liberation movement, *Maurice* not only articulates the ideology of Uranianism, but also mirrors a significant debate within the movement. The two most important ideologues of Uranianism were John Addington Symonds and Edward Carpenter. Both disciples of Whitman, they preached the love of comrades in numerous poems, pamphlets, and books. Symonds and Carpenter equally deserve credit as pioneers in sexual reform, but their styles were quite different, and *Maurice* pivots on the contrast between them. Whereas Symonds tended to be evasive and apologetic, Carpenter was more open and visionary. Symonds implied the superiority of homosexuality to heterosexuality, finding the former more spiritual and less bound by material considerations; but Carpenter insisted on the equality of the two emotions, considering neither to be more, or less, spiritual than the other. And while Symonds isolated homosexual love as a private experience and minimized physical passion, Carpenter discreetly acknowledged the physical and linked homosexual emancipation with feminism, labor reform, and social democracy. For Carpenter, the homosexual experience provided an opportunity to question received ideas and to develop a radical critique of society itself.[18]

As Robert K. Martin has demonstrated, *Maurice* enacts a dialectic between these two main branches of Uranian thought.[19] The novel opposes not heterosexuality and homosexuality, but two versions of homosexuality, one associated with Symonds, the other with Carpenter. This dialectic is reflected in the very structure of the book, which divides into two parallel sections, the action of each half mirroring the other with significant differences. The first half (comprising Parts One and Two) is devoted to the Maurice–Clive relationship. It traces a false vision of "superior" homosexuality that is platonized and sublimated in the manner of Symonds. The second half of the novel (encompassing Parts Three and Four) is devoted to the Maurice–Alec alliance, and it tracks Maurice's salvation through a Carpenterian homosexuality that includes physical love and that leads Maurice to reject class barriers and social conventions. Maurice finally comes to embrace the political consequences of homosexuality and to adopt the radical perspective on society conferred by the outlaw status of the homosexual in 1913.

Appropriately, the most significant literary influence on Forster's novel is the work of Oscar Wilde. More specifically, *De Profundis* informs *Maurice* at every turn.[20] The frequent echoes of *De Profundis* serve to incorporate Wilde's work into the very texture of Forster's novel and help establish Wilde's martyrdom as the historical reality that all considerations of the social and political consequences of homosexuality must confront. Wilde's insistence in *De Profundis* on the transcendent value of self-realization and on the redemptive potentiality of suffering—its ability to transform perspective and to deepen character—shapes the development of Forster's hero. Moreover, Wilde's rejection of society and his expectation of solace in nature help explicate the retreat into the greenwood at the end of *Maurice*—a conclusion that has troubled many critics.

What is most impressive about *Maurice* is its superb artistry. Full appreciation of its subtlety depends on several readings. Indeed, *Maurice* demands the reader's engagement in a process of interpretation and reinterpretation. The "double structure" of the novel, in which the second half recapitulates the first with crucial differences, is complemented by an elusive narrative technique that combines the point of view of the focal character with frequent, though cryptic, authorial intrusions. The effect of this sophisticated technique is to force the reader to experience firsthand Maurice's bewilderment and pain and exhilaration and muddle, thus contributing to the book's peculiar poignancy. Only later, on rereading the first half in light of the second, is the reader able to place the early events of the novel in context, thereby correcting his or her original responses; and only through this process of reinterpretation can the reader detect irony in the narrator's apparent endorsement of a particular perspective. Much of the novel's pleasure resides in the subtle exposure of unexpected dimensions and unsuspected ironies.

In the "Terminal Note," Forster writes that in his hero

> I tried to create a character who was completely unlike myself or what I supposed myself to be: someone handsome, healthy, bodily attractive, mentally torpid, not a bad business man and rather a snob. Into this mixture I dropped an ingredient that puzzles him, wakes him up, torments him and finally saves him.

Like Lucy Honeychurch of *A Room with a View*, Maurice Hall is a very ordinary person who moves painfully from muddle to clarity, from conventionality to heroism. The journey of Forster's hero is from ignorance to truth, from dream to reality, from internal obscurity to the "light within," and from comfort to joy. The "vast curve" of Maurice's life includes a progress from an alliance in which spirit educates spirit to one in which the flesh educates the spirit and develops "the sluggish heart and the slack mind against their will."

The dominant imagery in the novel is that of light and darkness, ascent and descent, sleep and wakefulness. This imagery is crystallized in the recurrent metaphor of the "Valley of the Shadow of Life," surrounded by the lesser mountains of childhood and the greater ones of maturity. The metaphor itself—an ironic reversal of the biblical "valley of the shadow of death" (Psalms 23:4)—may have been suggested by Wilde's comment in *De Profundis* that "I have hills far steeper to climb, valleys much darker to pass through." In the "Valley of the Shadow of Life," Maurice Hall falls asleep, awakens, and finally scales the constricting mountains to emerge—after periodically slipping back into the abyss of the obscured "I"—into the full light of self-awareness. The emphasis throughout the novel on Maurice's torpor probably reflects Carlyle's description of life on earth as somnambulism, a state that underlines the difficulty of asking the crucial but unanswerable question, "Who am I; what is this ME."[21]

At the very center of *Maurice* is this paradoxical insight about the loneliness of the human condition: the achievement of self-knowledge depends on communion with another. "To ascend," Forster writes of his hero, "to stretch a hand up the mountainside until a hand catches it, was the end for which he had been born." Thus, Maurice's search for his own identity is necessarily bound up with his need for a friend. This need is expressed in the two dreams he has at school—which, Forster says, "interpret him." The first dream is of George, the garden boy, "just a common servant," whose name he whispers as a charm against his fear of the shadowy reflections in the looking glass. In the dream, George runs toward him, naked, bounding over obstacles. Just as the two meet, Maurice awakens, filled with disappointment. Maurice's attachment to his playmate is apparent when he bursts into tears, overwhelmed by "a great mass of sorrow," upon learning that George has left his mother's employment. Only later, after his encounter with Alec Scudder, whom he at first also regards as just a common servant, does Maurice realize "very well what he wanted with the garden boy." And only then is he able to accept without fear "the land through the looking-glass."

The second dream is one in which "Nothing happened. He scarcely saw a face, scarcely heard a voice say, 'That is your friend,' and then it was over, having filled him with beauty and taught him tenderness." This dream haunts the novel and establishes the ideal against which Maurice's struggles toward fulfillment are measured: "He could die for such a friend, he would allow such a friend to die for him; they would make any sacrifice for each other, and count the world nothing, neither death nor distance nor crossness could part them, because 'this is my friend.' " Maurice at first attempts to convince himself that the friend of his dream is Christ, then he thinks that perhaps the friend is a Greek god. He finally accepts the fact that "most probably he was just a man." He gradually comes to regard Clive Durham as the friend "who was more to him than all the world." But the dream achieves fleshly reality only in the person of Alec, whose name appropriately means "Help."[22] The morning after their first night together, Maurice asks the young man, "Did you ever dream you'd a friend, Alec? Nothing else but just 'my friend,' he trying to help you and you him. . . . Someone to last your whole life and you his." He finally recognizes Alec as "the longed-for dream."

Forster's vision in *Maurice* is a humanist one in which "man has been created to feel pain and loneliness without help from heaven." As in Matthew Arnold's "Dover Beach," the world of the novel is a land of dreams in which human love offers the only help for pain. This view of human isolation gives urgency to Maurice's plight and depth to his search for a communion of body and soul. The relationship with Clive, the development of which is one of the major achievements of the novel, is a necessary but preliminary step in Maurice's growth.

Significantly, Maurice meets Clive as a result of his interest in Risley, a self-proclaimed "child of light," or Uranian, modeled on Lytton Strachey. In *De Profundis*, Wilde describes the "child of light" as perpetually at war against the philistines and "their heavy inaccessibility to ideas, their dull respectability, their tedious orthodoxy, their worship of vulgar success, their entire preoccupation with the materialistic side of life, and their ridiculous estimate of themselves and their importance." Risley wages this battle in the luncheon party arranged by Mr. Cornwallis, and Maurice will later assume the same struggle. But Maurice's interest in Risley is a symptom of his loneliness. He is not attracted to the young Uranian, but he feels that "this queer fish" might help him, "might stretch him a helping hand." On his mission for help, Maurice discovers Clive in Risley's room and the two develop a friendship.

Maurice responds to Clive's sincere intellect and superior knowledge. Clive, on the other hand, "liked being thrown about by a powerful and handsome boy. It was delightful too when Hall stroked his hair . . . people in the room would fade: he leant back till his cheek brushed the flannel of the trousers and felt the warmth strike through." Soon Maurice's heart is lit with a fire "never to be quenched again, and one thing in him at last was real." Clive dominates Maurice intellectually, and the latter soon surrenders all his conventional religious opinions. The young men's debates about religion constitute a courting ritual. Maurice's pose as a theologian is simply a ploy to engage his friend's interest. He has no answer when Clive attacks his "tenth-hand" opinions, questioning whether it isn't improbable that genuine belief could be imparted by parents and guardians. "If there is [a belief for which you would die] won't it be part of your own flesh and spirit?" Clive asks, echoing Wilde's remark that belief "must be nothing external to me. Its symbols must be of my own creating. . . . If I may not find its secret within myself, I shall never find it: if I have not got it already, it will never come to me." These debates also provide the first concrete evidence of how Maurice's homosexuality can shape the curve of his life, saving him from a hollow existence fed on catchwords like that of his father, who "was becoming a pillar of Church and Society when he died." Forster adds: "other things being alike Maurice would have stiffened too."

Although Maurice loses the debates, "he thought that his Faith was a pawn well lost; for in capturing it Durham had exposed his heart." When the two embrace after their return to Cambridge from the long vacation, Clive declares his love, assuming that Maurice has understood the implications of the *Symposium*, which he had asked his friend to read. Maurice's shocked response—"a rotten notion really"—causes Clive to sever his links with the young man, suggesting in an icy note "that it would be a public convenience if they behaved as if nothing had happened." This break forces Maurice into a frenzy of self-examination:

> It worked inwards, till it touched the root whence body and soul both spring, the "I" that he had been trained to obscure, and, realized at last, doubled its power and grew super-human. . . . New worlds broke loose in him at this, and he saw from the vastness of the ruin what ecstasy he had lost, what a communion.

The pain of Clive's rejection and the introspection it provokes lead Maurice to an important step toward maturity. He determines not to "deceive himself so much." He accepts the fact that "He loved men and always had loved them. He longed to embrace them and mingle his being with theirs." He rejects the judgments of the world and determines no longer to be fed upon lies. He haunts the bridge leading to Clive's quarters; and one night, "savage, reckless, drenched with the rain, he saw in the first glimmer of dawn the window of Durham's room, and his heart leapt alive and shook him to pieces." Just as he springs into the room, he hears Clive call his name. Part One of the novel thus ends with Maurice's achievement of manhood and of communion.

Part Two of the book begins with the new dawn of the communion between Clive and Maurice and ends with the darkness of Clive's repudiation of their relationship. For two years the young Uranians enjoy "as much happiness as men under that star can expect." Their relationship is modeled on Clive's interpretation of the *Symposium:* "The love that Socrates bore Phaedo now lay within his reach, love passionate but temperate, such as only finer natures can understand." The elitism of Clive's assumptions here—and when he tells Maurice "I feel to you as Pippa to her fiancé, only far more nobly, far more deeply . . . a particular harmony of body and soul that I don't think women have ever guessed"—reflects his snobbishness and misogyny and the apologia of Symonds. The relationship is one in which Clive "educated Maurice, or rather his spirit educated Maurice's spirit." It is doomed to failure, as Forster hints early in the book when he describes the bridge leading to Clive's room as "not a real bridge: it only spanned a slight depression in the ground." Maurice's ascent from the Valley of the Shadow of Life requires a helping hand extended from greater heights than Clive has achieved. The Maurice–Clive relationship is limited, for it is based on distrust of the body and on a bookish—hence false— Hellenism.

Clive's distrust of the body and contempt for his sexuality are deeply rooted in his subconscious. They result from his having internalized the Christian prohibitions that he outwardly rejects, and they are reflected as well in his extreme reaction to Maurice's understandable shock at his declaration of love. Clive requests his friend not to mention his "criminal morbidity" to anyone and tells him, "It is a lasting grief to have insulted you." Clive's commitment even to the spiritualized homosexuality of the *Symposium* is so tenuous that his friend's conventional reaction breaks down his "whole response to life . . . and the sense of sin was reborn in its ruins." When Maurice protests his pain at Clive's rejection and declares, "I have always been like the Greeks and didn't know," Clive characterizes Maurice's pain as "only the Hell of disgust" and the avowal of homosexuality as "grotesque," thus revealing his own self-condemnation. Later, on the eve of his desperate journey to Greece, when he views his attachment to Maurice as unclean and longs for the forgetfulness of Lethe, Clive worries that "beyond the grave there may be Hell." For all his vaunted Hellenism, Clive's emotional life has been shaped by his early Christian conviction that homosexuality is an abomination.

Even on the apparently idyllic expedition into the Cambridgeshire countryside, Clive's distrust of the body is manifest. His refusal to undress in order to swim in the dyke is analogous to Mr. Beebe's failure to participate fully in the homoerotic bathing scene in *A Room with a View,* and similarly signifies self-repression. In contrast, Maurice disrobes, shouting "I must bathe properly." As Robert Martin has noted, this scene in its entirety is wryly ironic, concealing a note of warning beneath its surface of ecstatic prose. The lovers' reliance on a machine—"They became a cloud of dust, a stench, and a roar to the world," like the Wilcoxes in *Howards End*—signals an "opposition between nature and the products of an industrial society"[23] and establishes an important point of contrast between Maurice's false communion with Clive and his real one with Alec, who is consistently linked with nature and the natural.

Clive's self-imposed repression is equally apparent when he flushes crimson at Maurice's adulation on his first visit to Penge. "I think you're beautiful," Maurice tells him in the Blue Room, the color of which symbolizes the spiritual and cerebral nature of Clive's love.[24] "I love your voice and everything to do with you, down to your clothes or the room you are sitting in. I adore you." Clive responds tepidly, "Those things must be said once, or we should never know they were in each other's hearts," but insists that their love, "though including the body, should not gratify it." Clive insists upon the kind of restraint that Socrates urges in the *Phaedrus,* where male lovers are advised to restrict their passion to kisses, touches, and embraces. This arrangement initially satisfies Maurice, largely as a result of Clive's "hypnotic" power over him. But Maurice later comes to regret that he had

never fully possessed Clive even in their hour of passion and to reject his
friend's doctrine that the "less you had the more it was supposed to be."

The conflicting attitudes of the young men toward their sexuality are cast
into bold relief by their reactions to the moment they spend in bed together
on the eve of Clive's departure for Greece. Clive has already begun to develop heterosexual attractions and to regard his homosexual attachment as
something dirty and shameful. As an antidote to these feelings, he asks
Maurice if he may join him in bed. The encounter proves unsatisfactory to
each, but for tellingly opposed reasons:

> They lay side by side without touching. Presently Clive said, "It's no better
> here. I shall go." Maurice was not sorry, for he could not get to sleep either,
> though for a different reason, and he was afraid Clive might hear the drum-
> ming of his heart, and guess what it was.

Maurice is sexually excited by the closeness of his lover and fears that Clive
may disapprove; in contrast, Clive is confirmed in his disgust at the notion
of physical contact with his friend. Maurice and Clive's isolation from each
other here is strikingly underlined by the later scenes of bodily communion
between Maurice and Alec.

The limitations of the Maurice–Clive relationship are also evident in its
failure to provoke a searching analysis of their society and their roles in it.
The young men are aware of the hypocrisy around them, from Mr. Ducie's
embarrassment over his sex-lecture diagrams in the sand and Mr. Cornwallis's refusal to translate a "reference to the unspeakable vice of the
Greeks," to the Cambridge dons' deeming "it right to spoil a love affair
when they could" and the double standard of Dr. Barry. Yet the lovers fail
to question the fundamental assumptions of their society. Both are misogy-
nistic and utterly conformist, save for their Wednesdays and weekends spent
together. Although Clive professes to believe that fertility is not the goal of
love—"For love to end where it begins is far more beautiful, and Nature
knows it"—he does not challenge his family's expectations that he will
dutifully beget an heir for Penge. And although he thinks of himself as "a
bit of an outlaw," he acquiesces in the assumption that he will succeed his
late father as a Member of Parliament. The young men placidly step into
the niches that England has prepared for them, Clive as country squire and
Maurice as "suburban tyrant" and successful stockbroker. "Society received them, as she receives thousands like them," Forster writes, adding:
"Behind Society slumbered the Law. They had their last year at Cambridge
together, they travelled in Italy. Then the prison house closed. . . . Clive
was working for the bar, Maurice harnessed to an office."

This concept of society as a prison house probably reflects Wilde's comment in the letter to Robert Ross quoted in the preface to *De Profundis*—"I

know that on the day of my release I shall be merely passing from one prison into another"—as well as Wordsworth's idea in the "Intimations" ode that "Shades of the prison-house begin to close/ Upon the growing boy." Forster's adaptation of these views in the novel both exposes the shallowness of the Clive–Maurice relationship and anticipates the result of the social analysis occasioned by the Alec–Maurice liaison. That analysis will lead Maurice to reject the life of respectability for a life of freedom, to sacrifice a spurious safety for the struggle that "twists sentimentality and lust together into love."

Even Clive's Hellenism is conventional, distorting ancient ideals as thoroughly as does Maurice's Greek oration at Sunnington. Just as the oration wrenches Greek ideals toward exercise and bodily health in order to glorify war, so Clive distorts the Greek ideal of moderation into abstinence in order to justify his conventional distaste for sexuality—a distaste rooted in Christian rather than classical thought. Although Clive condemns the dean's suppression of references to Greek homosexuality on the grounds of "pure scholarship"—"The Greeks, or most of them, were that way inclined, and to omit it is to omit the mainstay of Athenian society"—his own classicism is equally partial. It ignores the Dionysian and overemphasizes the Apollonian. The "harmony of body and soul" that Clive proposes is purchased at the expense of the physical and the ecstatic. It represents comfort rather than joy; it is an example not of moderation but of disproportion.

Clive's devotion to an intellectualized classicism reflects the stupidity of his heart and constitutes a retreat from real life. His bookish Hellenism is similar to Rickie Elliot's literary pastoralism in *The Longest Journey*. In the earlier novel, Rickie's artificial idealization of the ancient Greeks blinds him to Stephen Wonham's natural absorption of the Greek spirit. Similarly, Clive's falsely romantic Hellenism causes him to ignore the Dionysian spirit latent in Maurice. This potential is suggested by the consuming "frenzy" Maurice experiences when he first falls in love with Clive. As Forster comments then, "A slow nature such as Maurice's appears insensitive, for it needs time even to feel. . . . Given time, it can know and impart ecstasy." The potential for Dionysian ecstasy is implicit as well in Maurice's "good head" for liquor and in his fur-clad appearance "like an immense animal." But Maurice's Dionysian potential is fully realized only after his communion with Alec, in which the flesh educates the spirit.

Precisely because Clive's Hellenism is artificial and disproportionate, it finds no sustenance in the Greek ruins—including the theater of Dionysus—that the young man visits in a "childish and violent" attempt to preserve his attraction toward Maurice. One of the novel's most revealing ironies is that Clive's tenuous classicism is so utterly routed by the faint stirrings of his incipient and unwilled heterosexuality. The elaborate intellectual edifice he constructs to justify his homosexual tendencies crumbles at the onset of his growing physical attraction toward the opposite sex. Clive defines himself exclusively in terms of his soul and denies his body, yet his change is a result of the body's "inscrutable" will, a "blind alteration of the life spirit" that resists rational explanation. Clive's conversion to heterosexuality vividly illustrates the power of the physical, even in someone who has struggled so long to repress it, "not realizing that the body is deeper than the soul."

Forster does not condemn Clive for his involuntary conversion to heterosexuality. After all, a central premise of the novel is that sexual preference is not a matter of choice. But Clive is exposed as shallow and hypocritical by the eagerness with which he embraces the "beautiful conventions" that earn social approval and also by the cruelty with which he denies the reality of Maurice's love for him in the pivotal confrontation scene that ends Part Two. This scene marks the termination of the long day of spiritual communion between Clive and Maurice and announces the dawn of "the full human day" that Clive believes the love of women promises him.

This promise, however, is belied by the evidence of the confrontation scene itself, which in a series of subtle contrasts reveals the insipidity of Clive's heterosexuality, while simultaneously implying the potential of Maurice's sexuality for stimulus and growth. Structurally, this scene is parallel to the encounter between Clive and Maurice that concludes the novel. Both confrontation scenes are set at night and in darkness. At the end of Part Two, however, Clive's way is lit by street lamps, while at the end of Part Four, Maurice's walk is guided by evening primroses; and the scene in Part Two takes place indoors, whereas the novel's final scene is out of doors. These differences signify the limitations of Clive's triumph here: its connection with the artificial and the societal. They also help explicate Maurice's fuller triumph at the end of the book, when he departs into "the darkness where he can be free."

Throughout the bleak final scene of Part Two, Forster explores the shallowness of Clive's passion and foreshadows the depth of Maurice's future commitment to Alec. For instance, as Clive awaits his friend's arrival, he appreciates the Hall women for the first time. But significantly, he finds them reminiscent "of the evening primroses that starred a deserted alley at Penge," the very place where Maurice will eventually encounter Alec and bid farewell to Clive. Clive is particularly attracted to Ada, whose voice is similar to Maurice's. He regards her as a "compromise between memory and desire," thus establishing a telling contrast with Maurice's earlier hope for a life without compromise and his later choice of such a life. The knowledge that he might arouse Ada's love lights Clive's heart "with temperate fire," thus recalling the fierce fire "never to be quenched again" that love had ignited in Maurice's breast and that finally will be sustained by Alec's matching ardor. Most pointed of all is the contrast between the appearances of the two young men when Maurice arrives, looking "like an immense animal in his fur coat," to find Clive bandaged like an accident victim, having happily "submitted his body to be bound" by the sisters. This contrast of animal vitality and voluntary repression cystallizes the differences between the former lovers and foreshadows their fates. Moreover, the scuffle between Maurice and Clive over the key to the Halls' drawing room anticipates Alec's later message to Maurice, "I have the key," a reference to the boathouse at Penge, where the lovers will meet at the end of the novel to begin their lives in the greenwood.

The immediate impact of the confrontation with Clive devastates Maurice. Clive not only affirms the reality of his heterosexuality, for which he cannot be blamed, but, more culpably, he also coldly rejects the legitimacy of his former attachment. "I was never like you," he tells Maurice. To deny one's experience is, in the words of Wilde's *De Profundis*, "to put a lie in the lips of one's life. It is no less than a denial of the soul." Clive's rejection of his past here exposes him as a hypocrite and casts into doubt the sincerity of the quality by which he defines himself, his soul. By characterizing romantic love between men as unreal, Clive also attacks the very basis of his friend's identity, for only through his love did Maurice become a "real" person.

The love affair terminates with an ugly scuffle and with Maurice sobbing, "What an ending . . . what an ugly ending." The repeated phrase alludes to Wilde's account of his despondency during his first year of imprisonment, when he "did nothing else, and can remember doing nothing else, but wring my hands in impotent despair, and say, 'What an ending, what an appalling ending!' " Significantly, however, the force of this allusion in *Maurice* is positive. It promises a new perspective, for Wilde—having grown as a result of his suffering—continues, "[N]ow I try to say to myself, and sometimes when I am not torturing myself do really and sincerely say, 'What a beginning, what a wonderful beginning!' " This allusion suggests the possibility that, like Wilde, Maurice too will profit from his pain.

On the surface, however, this appalling ending is bleak, leaving the former lovers enveloped in darkness, both literally and metaphorically. Maurice extinguishes the electric light and sits gloomily alone, while Clive goes out into the night, exchanging "the darkness within for that without." But Clive's promised dawn will culminate in a sexual relationship "veiled in night" and in a marriage marked by deception and ignorance; his deep-rooted distaste for "the reproductive and digestive functions" will continue to limit his communion with others. Maurice, on the other hand, will achieve wholeness of being; he will discover "the light within" and embrace the evening's external darkness as a refuge against ignorance and hypocrisy. The false climax at the end of Part Two thus ironically mirrors the triumphant climax of the novel itself. It is actually a new beginning.

Maurice's new beginning is painful indeed: he "returned in a few hours to the abyss where he had wandered as a boy." As a result of Clive's defection, his life is barren and empty. After abandoning the temptation to suicide, he continues a dreary existence for some time, "proving on how little the soul can exist." Forster poignantly conveys the pain of Maurice's grief, but central to the novel—as to *De Profundis*—is the meaningfulness of suffering. *Maurice* dramatizes Wilde's contention that suffering is not a mystery but a revelation: "One discerns things one never discerned before. One approaches the whole of history from a different standpoint." Thus, in his loneliness Maurice comes to a firmer understanding of his position in society: "He was an outlaw in disguise." Even in the depths of his despair, he fleetingly entertains the possibility that "among those who took to the greenwood in old time there had been two men like himself."

Maurice's regeneration begins with the stirrings of lust. On the very morning that he learns of Clive's engagement, he is awakened to desire. He glimpses the nude body of Dickie Barry, his young houseguest, whom he rouses from a late sleep. He discovers Dickie "with his limbs uncovered. He lay unashamed, embraced and penetrated by the sun. The lips were parted, the down on the upper was touched with gold, the hair broken into countless glories, the body was a delicate amber." This vision of Eros leads Maurice momentarily to abandon himself to joy and then to reproach himself bitterly. Significantly, Maurice faces his predicament with a new frankness: "His feeling for Dickie required a very primitive name. He would have sentimentalized once and called it adoration, but the habit of honesty had grown strong." Still, Maurice finds his newly awakened passion deeply troubling, and his resistance to his body's natural responses leads to a vicious assault on a railway passenger whose "disgusting and dishonorable old age" Maurice fears may prophesy his own. This resistance culminates in a desperate hope for punishment and cure. At the same time, however, Maurice's awakening to physical desire represents "the flesh educating the spirit." It promises the ultimate attainment of the "fresh mode of self-realization" that Wilde speaks of in *De Profundis:* "the mode of existence in which soul and body are one and indivisible: in which the outward is expressive of the inward." Even as Maurice resists the promptings of desire, his flesh continues to educate his spirit.

Maurice's progress toward wholeness is gradual but inexorable, complicated by his inner contradictions but never halted. For instance, in Part Three he would like to be "at one with society and the law," but he slowly begins to realize the corruption of both. His disastrous visit to Dr. Barry, in which he confesses himself "an unspeakable of the Oscar Wilde sort," is followed by his thrill of recognition when he reads a biography of Tchaikovsky. Although he grasps at the hope that hypnotism might cure him, he is nevertheless aware that "doctors are fools." Moreover, even as he pursues the cure, he knows the cost at which such normality will be bought. "If this new doctor could alter his being," he muses, "was it not his duty to go, though body and soul be violated?" When he does make an appointment with Mr. Lasker Jones, he bids "Farewell, beauty and warmth."

Maurice's internal contradictions are brilliantly juxtaposed on his visit to Penge, where "he seemed a bundle of voices . . . he could almost hear them quarreling inside him." At Penge he both pursues his appointment with the hypnotist and confirms "his spirit in its perversion," as Lasker Jones will later diagnose the result of his "sharing" with Alec. The visit to Penge also defines the distance Maurice has yet to travel in his quest for wholeness. His flesh can fully educate his spirit only when he escapes the influence of Clive, and he can free himself of Clive's influence only when "something greater" intervenes. Thus, it is fitting that Maurice's visit to Penge leads both to his disillusionment with Clive and to his discovery of Alec.

Penge itself functions as a double symbol in the novel, representing the duality within Maurice. As a dilapidated country house, it symbolizes the philistinism of the English upper middle classes; but located on the Wiltshire border, Penge is also part of the English countryside, embodying the solace of nature and the natural. Penge thus epitomizes the novel's contrast of the indoors and the outdoors, the values of society and those of nature, the life of respectability and the life of the earth.[25] It is the setting both of the Durhams' snobbery, in which Maurice initially joins, and of Alec's natural responsiveness to life, in which Maurice eventually participates. Its dichotomies may best be represented by Anne, whose maiden name—Woods—signifies a naturalness that her upper-middle-class upbringing has stifled through the deliberate inculcation of sexual ignorance. Interestingly, Anne functions as an unconscious agent of connection for Alec and Maurice, being responsible for Alec's employment at Penge and for drawing Maurice's attention to him at a pivotal moment. Presided over by Clive, "whose grievances against society had passed since his marriage," Penge is at once a citadel of oppression and a stimulus to Maurice's growth.

That stimulus is provided most forcefully by the under-gamekeeper, whom Maurice notices as he drives through the park to begin his visit at Penge. Throughout his stay, he is vaguely aware of Alec, though in his snobbishness Maurice denies full humanity to the lower classes. Maurice's class consciousness precludes an early union, but that is what each subconsciously desires. On his first two nights at Penge, Maurice gazes from his bedroom into the rainy night longing for a companion, only later to learn that Alec, filled with a similar yearning, had been waiting on the lawn for his call. Maurice first acknowledges Alec's individuality when he temporarily leaves Penge for his appointment in London. He offers Alec a tip and is outraged when the young man refuses it. Although Maurice's fierce reaction may seem petty, based as it is on a misinterpretation of Alec's independence as impertinence, it is actually more liberal than Archie London's condescending attitude that "When servants are rude one should merely ignore it."

As his carriage leaves Penge, Maurice looks out the window at the dog roses that border the lane and suddenly recognizes Alec:

Blossom after blossom crept past them, draggled by the ungenial year: some had cankered, others would never unfold: here and there beauty triumphed, but desperately, flickering in a world of gloom. Maurice looked into one after another, and though he did not care for flowers the failure irritated him. Scarcely anything was perfect. On one spray every flower was lopsided, the next swarmed with caterpillars or bulged with galls. The indifference of nature! And her incompetence! He leant out of the window to see whether she couldn't bring it off once, and stared straight into the bright brown eyes of a young man.

This recognition shocks Maurice into an awareness of Alec's beauty and anticipates the perfection of their eventual union. As James Malek remarks of the passage. "This initial association of Alec with nature and perfection leaves a lasting impression and colors our response to him throughout the remainder of the novel."[26] Placed immediately before Maurice's consultation with the hypnotist, the vision of Alec's perfection also renders ironic Lasker Jones's attempt to implant in Maurice's subconscious his own palely conventional aesthetic and erotic responses.

After his interview with the hypnotist, Maurice returns to Penge, convinced that "he wasn't the same; a rearrangement of his being had begun." But he is wrong to credit Lasker Jones with the alteration. The credit belongs to Alec, whom he encounters several times that momentous night in the darkness of the deserted alley starred with evening primroses. The change in Maurice is evident when he returns from a stroll outdoors with his head all yellow with pollen. The evening primrose pollen expresses Maurice's Dionysian potential, a potential implicit in his preoccupations as he strolls through the alley and encounters Alec:

Food and wine had heated him, and he thought with some inconsequence that even old Chapman had sown some wild oats . . . He wasn't Methusaleh— he'd a right to a fling. Oh those jolly scents, those bushes where you could hide, that sky as black as the bushes!

As he goes indoors, expecting to resume his life as "a respectable pillar of society who has never had the chance to misbehave," he bumps into Alec. The encounter sharpens Maurice's mind, making him consciously aware of the man as an individual, a "fine fellow," who "cleaned a gun, carried a suitcase, baled out a boat, emigrated—did something anyway, while gentlefolk squatted on chairs finding fault with his soul." Maurice attacks the clergyman Mr. Borenius's legalistic religion, telling him that "that may be your idea of religion but it isn't mine and it wasn't Christ's"—thus echoing Wilde's assertion that Christ "exposed with utter and relentless scorn" the "tedious formalisms so dear to the middle-class mind."

As Maurice goes to bed that night, his brain—wreathed with a "tangle of flowers and fruits"—works more actively than ever. He sees commonplace objects with a new clarity and he redefines darkness as something to be desired: "not the darkness of a house which coops up a man among furniture, but the darkness where he can be free." Conscious of the irony of having paid a hypnotist to imprison him in a "brown cube of such a room," Maurice drifts off to sleep, dimly aware of alternatives. "There was something better in life than this rubbish," he thinks half-asleep, "if only he could get to it—love—nobility—big spaces where passion clasped peace, spaces no science could reach, but they existed for ever, full of woods some of them, and arched with majestic sky and a friend . . . ." This dream of perfection, of harmony with nature and communion with another, achieves the promise of reality.

Maurice's sleepwalking cry "Come!" is answered by Alec, who scales a ladder into the Russet Room: "Someone he scarcely knew moved towards him and knelt beside him and whispered, 'Sir, was you calling out for me? . . . Sir, I know. . . . I know,' and touched him." This consummation, beautiful in its tenderness and simplicity, parallels the communion of Maurice and Clive at the end of Part One. But the sharing of Maurice and Alec in the Russet Room promises the fuller relationship for which both long, a union of body and soul, of the flesh educating the spirit.

Part Four of the novel chronicles the achievement of this promise and the completion of Maurice's journey toward self-realization. Beginning with the bright dawn of a new relationship and ending in the darkness of a confrontation scene, Part Four recapitulates Part Two. But whereas the dawn of Part Two is what Wilde describes as one of the "false dawns before the dawn itself," the new daybreak proves genuine. Similarly, the darkness in which Part Four concludes is the protective cover of the greenwood in which Alec and Maurice discover freedom, not the interior darkness of the earlier climax. And in the confrontation scene that ends the novel, Maurice triumphs unambiguously, having truly earned a new beginning.

Maurice's self-realization is accomplished as the result of a struggle between his real self and the obscured "I" of his social self. When he descends from the scene of communion with Alec "to take his place in society," his suburban gentleman's class-consciousness battles with his longing for fulfillment. His life disturbed "to its foundations," Maurice alternates between his conventional distaste for "social inferiors" and his desire for comradeship. As he and Alec play cricket together that morning, Maurice meditates on the possibilities of their union:

> They played for the sake of each other and their fragile relationship—if one fell, the other would follow. They intended no harm to the world, but so long as it attacked they must punish, they must stand wary, then hit with full strength, they must show that when two are gathered together majorities shall not triumph.

But this reverie of liberation is interrupted by the arrival of Clive, the apostle of class loyalty, to whom "intimacy with any social inferior was unthinkable." Suddenly sick with fear and shame, Maurice returns to his home, seeking security rather than joy.

But even as Maurice struggles against his deepest instincts, his flesh continues to educate his spirit. That night, his body yearns for Alec's: "He called it lustful, a word easily uttered, and opposed to it his work, his family, his friends, his position in society." But, Forster adds, "his body would not be convinced." In a childish and violent expedient analogous to Clive's trip to Greece, Maurice telephones Lasker Jones for another consultation. This time, however, he is unable to enter a trance. He leaves the hypnotist's office curiously relieved. Walking home, he observes the King and Queen passing through a park. He unthinkingly bares his head in a gesture of respect. Then he suddenly despises these symbols of society, seeing them as victims of the very values that oppress him. This insight gives him a new perspective: "It was as if the barrier that kept him from his fellows had taken another aspect. He was not afraid or ashamed anymore. After all, the forests and the night were on his side, not theirs." This new insight radically alters his previous image of himself wandering "beyond the barrier . . . the wrong words on his lips and the wrong desires in his heart, and his arms full of air." He realizes that "they, not he, were inside a ring fence," imprisoned by conventions.[27]

Maurice's acceptance of himself and his outlaw status here presages his final liberation. He gains new insight into the inequities and limitations of his society. He suggests to his aunt "that servants might be flesh and blood like ourselves." He questions the ethics of his profession, despising his clients' choice of comfort rather than joy, of "shelter everywhere and always, until the existence of earth and sky is forgotten, shelter from poverty and disease and violence and impoliteness; and consequently from joy." He determines himself to seek the "life of the earth" and to accept the struggle that may make possible the attainment of love. He evaluates his own past actions, concluding that he erred grievously in trying "to get the best of both worlds." In a society that criminalizes him and falsifies his experience, he must embrace his outlaw status and be true to himself. Thus, when he receives a threatening letter from Alec, containing many words, "some foul, many stupid, some gracious," he agrees to a meeting. "Both were outcasts," he thinks, "and if it came to a scrap must have it without benefit of society." Maurice's point here reflects Wilde's painfully earned confession from Reading Gaol: "The one disgraceful, unpardonable, and to all time contemptible action of my life was to allow myself to appeal to society for help and protection."

The meeting of Alec and Maurice in the British Museum is one of the most delightful scenes of the novel. Maurice quickly realizes that Alec's attempt at blackmail "was a blind—a practical joke almost—and concealed something real, that either desired." The extortion attempt is a reaction against Maurice's mistrust and condescension, a reflection of pain at having been neglected, and a sign of interest. As the two men spar, they are interrupted by Mr. Ducie, who, as always, gets "the facts just wrong" as he tries to remember Maurice's name. When Maurice tells the school master that his name is Scudder, the identification of the young men is complete. As Maurice will shortly realize, "In a way they were one person." Maurice succeeds here in winning Alec's love by approaching him as an equal: "Not as a hero, but as a comrade."[28] He "stood up to the bluster, and found childishness behind it, and behind that something else." By suffering, Maurice has learned to interpret the suffering of others. He has absorbed Wilde's lesson that "behind sorrow there is always a soul."

Forster's account of the lovers' communion in the hotel—the mixture of "tenderness and toughness" in their sharing—beautifully affirms Maurice's success in grasping the lessons that the flesh teaches the spirit. Tellingly, the night of passion in a "casual refuge" that protects them momentarily "from their enemies" is made possible by Alec's insistence that Maurice cancel the formal dinner party "of the sort that brought work to his firm." The cost of the joyful night thus anticipates the price of "the safety in darkness" that the escape to the greenwood will exact. That retreat requires mutual sacrifice, as Alec acknowledges when he protests that Maurice's vaguely formulated plan "Wouldn't work. . . . Ruin of us both, can't you see, you same as myself." But balanced against the loss of the young men's careers, family ties, and respectability is the prospect of being numbered among those few who, according to Wilde, "ever 'possess their souls' before they die." When Alec fails to appear for the departure of the *Normannia*, he surrenders his security and distinguishes himself from "the timorous millions who own stuffy little boxes but never their own souls." The mutual sacrifices of the lovers give the lie to Mr. Borenius's assumption that "love between two men must be ignoble," and their compensation is one familiar in Forster's novels: "They must live outside class, without relations or money; they must work and stick to each other till death. But England belonged to them. That, besides companionship, was their reward."

After Maurice's confrontation with Clive in the deserted alley at Penge, "where evening primroses gleamed, and embossed with faint yellow the walls of night," Maurice and Alec depart for the greenwood. The final chapter recounts Maurice's repudiation of Clive's influence—"the closing of a book that would never be read again." This ending is a necessary preliminary to the self-confessed outlaw's new beginning with Alec. When Maurice disappears into the night, having elected a life "without twilight or compromise," he leaves behind only "a little pile of the petals of the evening primrose, which mourned from the ground like an expiring fire."

Symbolic of the fire that Clive's love originally inspired within Maurice's breast, the dying petals signify the death of Maurice's love for him and the enormity of Clive's loss in failing to appreciate his friend's potential for Dionysian ecstasy. Ironically, however, although Maurice wrestles free of Clive's influence, the country squire who smugly denied the reality of homosexual love will never escape the memory of his incomplete passion. Maurice will continue to haunt him all the rest of his days, mocking his timidity and rebuking his hypocrisy:

> To the end of his life Clive was not sure of the exact moment of departure, and with the approach of old age he grew uncertain whether the moment had yet occurred. The Blue Room would glimmer, ferns undulate. Out of some external Cambridge his friend began beckoning to him, clothed in the sun, and shaking out the scents and sound of the May term.

Clive's fate is aptly summed in Wilde's description of men who desire to be something separate from themselves, such as a Member of Parliament. Such a person, Wilde writes, "invariably succeeds in being what he wants to be. That is his punishment. Those who want a mask have to wear it."

Maurice and Alec's retreat into the greenwood has frequently been scorned by critics as sentimental and unconvincing. Actually, however, the ending is neither. Alec and Maurice have earned their happiness through suffering and sacrifice; and despite their differences in background and education, they are well matched. There is nothing sentimental in the notion of hard-won happiness earned through mutual trust and support. This happiness is bought at a high price, but their willingness to pay such a toll is what finally enables Maurice and Alec to transcend the artificial barriers that separate them. Still, the ending is flawed. "The problem" as James Malek explains, "is that Forster succeeds more completely on the general level than on the particular. There is no doubt about the value or rightness of the lovers' decision. Nor, on the level of the particular, do we doubt their ability to follow through, but we have not been prepared for the specific form it might take, nor is it easy to imagine since Maurice has talked of it in very general terms."[29] The vagueness of the lovers' future life together probably reflects a compromise between Forster's original vision of two men roaming the greenwood and his postwar realization that "Our greenwood ended catastrophically and inevitably," as he remarks in the "Terminal Note." Although the escape into the "big spaces . . . arched with majestic sky and a friend" is too vaguely formulated and too broadly generalized, it is nevertheless essential to the novel's vision.

The escape into an Arcadian greenwood expresses Forster's radical critique of his society while it also conveys his humanist faith in personal relationships. The ending of *Maurice* is influenced by the conclusion of *De Profundis,* the moving coda in which Wilde looks to nature for healing and wholeness. Like Wilde, Forster has no faith in reforming society. Even in the "Terminal Note" of 1960, he remains pessimistic about social reforms, remarking that "Since *Maurice* was written there has been a change in the public attitude here: the change from ignorance and terror to familiarity and contempt." In his novel "Dedicated to a Happier Year," he shows how the "four guardians of society—the schoolmaster, the doctor, the scientist and the priest"—all condemn the homosexual.[30] Thus, Maurice and Alec must utterly reject society, whose injustices they perceive as a result of their homosexuality. But unlike Wilde's, Forster's pessimism is tempered by a belief in personal relations. Hence Maurice and Alec together accept England's air and sky as their birthright, facing the world unafraid, showing that "when two are gathered together majorities shall not triumph." The escape into the greenwood thus simultaneously renders a summary judgment against society and endorses the possibility of the flesh educating the spirit, even in the midst of repression.

Critics have also frequently denigrated *Maurice* as an exercise in special pleading, accusing Forster of claiming that homosexuals have a privileged status, a "heightened sensibility and a more profound aesthetic understanding" than heterosexuals.[31] In fact, however, Forster makes no such claim. As Robert Martin observes, "The novel clearly rejects the idea of the superiority of homosexuality, an idea which is specifically Clive's and derived from Plato, while keeping the idea that homosexuality may provide the occasion for a growth in spiritual awareness."[32] Forster certainly accepts Wilde's premise that to "become a deeper man is the privilege of those who have suffered." This "privilege," however, is the result not of a quality innate in homosexuality, but of the oppression homosexuals endure in a world that rejects the legitimacy of their experience. Maurice's progress

from a homosexuality linked with Symonds and other apologists to a homosexuality associated with Carpenter is a progress from claims of superiority
to assertions of equality. Forster properly emphasizes the spiritual and political insight that the pain of exclusion may confer, but he does not endorse
the claim that homosexuality is in itself either superior or inferior to heterosexuality.

Maurice is a book of haunting beauty, tracing the painful journey of its
hero from bewilderment to self-realization. It is preeminently a political
novel, for Maurice's education through suffering culminates in a sweeping
indictment of his society, one that results directly from his awareness of the
political implications of the homosexual experience in a hostile world. At
the same time, however, the book transcends the political by affirming the
possibility of alleviating the loneliness endemic to the human condition.
The communion of flesh and spirit achieved by Alec and Maurice may isolate them from "the congregation of normal men," but it promises help in
a universe in which "man has been created to feel pain and loneliness without help from heaven."

Although Forster published no more fiction after *The Eternal Moment and
Other Stories* in 1928, he continued to write fiction, nearly all of it on
homosexual themes. *The Life to Come and Other Stories*, published in
1972, collects these late gay fictions, as well as some early work that Forster either judged unworthy of the collections he published during his lifetime or that he felt he could not publish because of its explicitly
homosexual content. Some of the early gay fictions, such as "Ansell" and
"Albergo Empedocle," anticipate *Maurice* in their focus on homosexuality's potential for saving individuals from the burdens of class and conventionality. But the late stories in *The Life to Come*, those written between
1922 and 1958, are particularly interesting. Although they have been dismissed as frivolous and even pornographic,[33] these gay fictions are among
Forster's finest tales—ironic, witty, resonant, and angry. And though they
have been condescendingly psychologized as their author's therapeutic attempt "to record his despair and to utter, via fictional indirection, his cry
for help,"[34] they actually express a healthy rage against the injustices of a
repressive society. The most important of these gay fictions—including
"The Life to Come," "Arthur Snatchfold," and "The Other Boat"—rank
among the finest stories Forster ever wrote.

"The Life to Come" weds satire and prophecy to tragedy and myth.
Written in 1922, it recounts the conversion to Christianity of a primitive
tribal chief, Vithobai, by a young English missionary named Paul Pinmay. Central to the conversion is a night of lovemaking shared by the two
men, which leads Vithobai to believe the missionary's message of love and
brings Pinmay to "an agony of grotesque remorse."[35] Following the profes-

sion of faith, Vithobai (renamed Barnabas, for the colleague of St. Paul who joined the latter's mission to convert the gentiles) and his tribe are systematically deceived and exploited as the guilt-stricken Pinmay abandons the gospel of love for the "gloomy severity of the Old Law." When the newly baptized Barnabas asks Paul to repeat their lovemaking in the forest, the hypocritical missionary tells him, "Not yet." For five years, Barnabas waits for his friend to come to him: "God continues to order me to love you. It is my life, whatever else I seem to do." But on the eve of his marriage to a medical missionary whose brother owns a mining concession that exploits and sickens Barnabas's tribe, Paul bluntly tells the docile and Westernized chief: "Never." The two men are reunited five years later, as Barnabas is dying. Reverting to his original religion, the failing man looks forward to real love after death and stabs the missionary through the heart: "love was conquered at last and he was again a king, he had sent a messenger before him to announce his arrival in the life to come, as a great chief should."

"The Life to Come" anticipates *A Passage to India* in its opposition of Eastern and Western values, in its concern with the cultural barriers that separate individuals, and in its depiction of Vithobai's longing for the friend who never comes. As in the novel, Christianity is tested from an Eastern perspective and found to be narrow and small in its denial of the fullness of experience. This denial results from Christianity's refusal to take literally the doctrine of love that it professes. Paul Pinmay is the story's representative of this dichotomous mode of thought, and he is tellingly named for St. Paul, who in I Corinthians both expounds a vision of *agape*, or universal love, and denounces erotic love, enunciating an antisexual doctrine that has been crucial in forming Western attitudes toward sexual expression in general and homosexuality in particular.[36] The names of Paul and Barnabas are particularly ironic in light of the fact that the historical personages argued against the need for gentile Christian converts to obey Jewish law (see Acts 15), while as a result of his guilt, Paul Pinmay insists that Barnabas and his tribe strictly observe the Old Law. "The Life to Come" satirizes Christian hypocrisy, exposing Christian complicity in imperialism as a failure of *agape* as well as of Eros, and suggests that the repression of Eros perverts the expression of *agape*.

But the story is not merely satirical. It implies an alternative to the repression and exploitation that it documents. Proceeding from a holy joke—Vithobai's literal belief in Pinmay's slogan, "God is love"—the tale imagines a theology in which Vithobai is actually a fool in Christ. In such a theology, the profane is also the sacred, the literal also the true. In such a theology, God is truly love in all senses of the word.

"The Life to Come" has frequently been criticized as both unbelievable—particularly the notion that Vithobai would harbor his desire for Pinmay for ten years—and inflated in diction. But the concretely detailed story is a parable, mythic in inspiration and implication, the events of which expand from local to universal significance. Questions as to the realistic credibility of Vithobai's devotion are thus beside the point. Blending Christian and classical mythology (particularly the myth of Pentheus and Dionysus, as recounted in Euripides' *The Bacchae*), the story becomes, in Judith Scherer Herz's words, a "kind of sacred parody in which Paul's final punishment is a grotesquely inverted *imitatio Christi*. You don't play games with the gods is the conclusion that both Euripidean and Christian readings provide."[37] The resonant diction—the biblical syntax and language—calls attention to itself in order both to parody Christian orthodoxy and to reconsecrate the language of sacred mystery. As Herz declares, "'The Life to Come' is a scriptural fiction."

"Arthur Snatchfold," written in 1928, also ranks among Forster's best stories. Distinguished by an extraordinary control of nuance, the tale pivots on a brief but fulfilling sexual exchange between Sir Richard Conway, a successful speculator in aluminum, and Arthur Snatchfold, a young milkman. A weekend guest at the country home of Trevor Donaldson, a business associate, Conway resigns himself to a dreary visit, elaborately orchestrated yet lacking real pleasure. But as he gazes at his host's "dull costly garden" one morning, he is awakened to an altogether more pleasing prospect by the sudden appearance of a young man walking confidently down the amphitheater: "besides being proper to the colour scheme he was a very proper youth. His shoulders were broad, his face sensuous and open, his eyes, screwed up against the light, promised good temper." Delighted when the young man salutes him without deference, Conway arranges to accost him the next morning in the estate's adjoining wood, where they sport in the bracken. After a fully satisfying sexual bout, the wealthy businessman offers his handsome partner a gift of money, not as payment but as a token of appreciation. "The affair had been trivial and crude," the narrator explains, "and yet both had behaved perfectly."

The second half of the story is set some months later, in Conway's London club, where he is entertaining his former host, now a business rival. In the course of their conversation, Donaldson remarks on an "extraordinary case" in his village: "Indecency between males." Worried that the milkman might be in trouble, Conway presses Donaldson for details of the story. He finally learns to his horror that the youth was arrested shortly after their early-morning dalliance. Despite the promise of a reduced sentence for identifying his partner, the milkman bravely refused, claiming "it was someone from the hotel." Shaken by the fate of his anonymous lover and by the narrowness of his own escape, Conway asks for the name of the young man who saved him. He briefly flirts with the idea of confessing his own part in the affair but then realizes the futility of such a gesture of greatness:

"He would ruin himself and his daughters, he would delight his enemies, and he would not save his savior." The story ends with Conway writing into his notebook the name of his brief lover "who was going to prison to save him. . . . Arthur Snatchfold. He had only heard the name once, and he would never hear it again."

"Arthur Snatchfold" is a deeply moving story of great power. Unified by subtle rhythms and narrated with unfailing control, the tale—with superbly reined bitterness—indicts a stupid and cruel society that criminalizes harmless pleasure and distances individuals and classes from each other. The sexual encounter at the center is neither romanticized nor trivialized. One of "the smaller pleasures of life," the erotic exchange revitalizes and humanizes Conway. When both men are pleasantly satiated, it becomes "part of the past. It had fallen like a flower upon similar flowers"—a description that emphasizes the union's beauty and naturalness as well as brevity. The escapade has little significance beyond the considerable pleasure it provides the participants, yet it is distorted into a grave criminal offense by the barbarous prosecution of an engaging young man.

Arthur's defiant heroism in protecting his partner makes him a martyr to an unjust society. His loyalty contrasts with the disloyalty of the business world, as indicated by the shifting alliances of Conway and Donaldson. Arthur's martyrdom also reflects the larger social inequity of the class system. As Forster comments in the "Terminal Note" to *Maurice*, police actions against homosexuals mirror the class divisions that homosexuality can help bridge: "Clive on the bench will continue to sentence Alec in the dock. Maurice may get off." This unequal enforcement of unjust laws is suggested in the story when Arthur says, "We could get seven years for this, couldn't we?" and Conway replies, "Not seven years, still we'd get something nasty." The prosecution of either of them for their harmless activity is "Madness," as Conway remarks, but the class system affects even the dispensation of injustice. Although Arthur truly says, "we was each as bad as the other," their different social positions cause them to anticipate distinctly different fates at the hands of the law.

It is in this context of social injustice that Sir Richard Conway must be judged as he ponders a difficult moral dilemma at the story's conclusion. He is the tale's protagonist but not its hero, that designation belonging to Arthur, as the title suggests and his valor verifies. But Conway is by no means the villain that some critics think. J. I. M. Stewart, for instance, describes him as "a cold bisexual hedonist [who] seduces and thrusts money upon a young milkman," a description that is plainly inaccurate and that partakes of the very attitudes that the story attacks; and Wilfred Stone, who asserts on no convincing literary or biographical evidence that the "homosexual engagement stirred violent, and violently ambivalent, feelings in Forster," finds Conway "morally disgusting."[38] These reactions to Conway have no basis in the story and reveal a gross misunderstanding of For-

ster's attitude toward homosexuality and society. Forster reveals no ambivalence or guilt about his homosexuality. On the contrary, he is justly
indignant at the ignorance and cruelty of a society that criminalizes him.

Conway is, to be sure, a morally ambivalent character at the end of the
story as he decides against a futile gesture of greatness. Like Aziz in *A
Passage to India*, Conway believes that

> There is no harm in deceiving society as long as she does not find you out,
> because it is only when she finds you out that you have harmed her; she is not
> like a friend or God, who are injured by the mere existence of unfaithfulness.[39]

He is guilty only to the extent that he—"a decent human being"—is com-
plicitous in the society that condemns Arthur. Like the early Maurice and
other upper-middle-class homosexuals who are protected by the class system, Conway "may get off," but the threat of disgrace and punishment
remains very real. The point of the story is not to attack Conway for moral
cowardice in refusing to sacrifice himself and his family, but to expose the
cruelty of a repressive system. As James Malek remarks, a more important
issue than Conway's failure of greatness is the "spiritual bankruptcy of a
society that inappropriately turns little things into great ones in the name of
moral decency."[40] In its depiction of a homophobic society, the story illustrates the limits of accommodationism even for a successful and apparently
securely closeted businessman.

The longest of Forster's late gay fictions is "The Other Boat," which
evolved from a novel that he began in 1913 and soon abandoned. The first
section of the story was published in late 1948 in *The Listener* under the
title "Entrance to an Unwritten Novel" and in early 1949 in the *New York
Times Book Review* as "Cocoanut & Co.: Entrance to an Abandoned
Novel." Forster returned to the fragment in 1957 and completed the story in
1958. Despite this long and complicated evolution, "The Other Boat" is an
organic whole, betraying no signs of fragmentation or false starts. Indeed,
it is Forster's finest achievement in short fiction, the culmination of a lifelong preoccupation with the question of psychological wholeness.

The story recounts the struggle to fuse into wholeness the divided personality of Lionel March, a young army captain en route to India to marry
and begin a career in the colonial service. This struggle comes to a crisis in
his relationship with Cocoa, a "subtle, supple boy who belonged to no race
and always got what he wanted." The two first met as children on "the
other boat," one that had returned Lionel with his mother and siblings from
India, where they had been abandoned by his father, an army major who
"went native somewhere out East and got cashiered." In the interval between their reunion, Lionel has grown into a handsome soldier, "clean-cut,
athletic, good-looking without being conspicuous," the hero of "one of the
little desert wars that were becoming too rare." Cocoa, on the other hand,

has matured from "a silly idle useless unmanly little boy," as Mrs. March described him on the earlier voyage, into a sensuous, mysterious, wealthy, but classless and effeminate young man. Having nursed his desire for Lionel for years, Cocoa bribes the officials of the *Normannia* to allow Lionel to share his cabin, where he proceeds to awaken the young officer's repressed sexuality. Lionel is shocked by Cocoa's first advances, but as the ship enters the Mediterranean, "resistance weakened," and "in the Red Sea they slept together as a matter of course." Under Cocoa's tutelage, Lionel responds fully to a life of "luxury, gaiety, kindness, unusualness, and delicacy that did not exclude brutal pleasure."

As the *Normannia* nears Bombay, Lionel is forced to choose between his conventional tribal identity and the newly awakened self that has been aroused by his affair with Cocoa, or, in the terms of James Malek's Jungian analysis, between his persona and his shadow.[41] The story pivots on the question of identity. Just as Cocoa has two passports with conflicting information, so does Lionel repress his full identity on his passport, which drops half his name to avoid connection with his disgraced father. When Lionel playfully tells Cocoa, "you're no better than a monkey, and I suppose a monkey can't be expected to know his own name," the mysterious "twister" of no tribal affiliation at all replies: "Lion, he don't know nothing at all. Monkey's got to come along to tell a Lion he's alive." The story in effect dramatizes Lionel's tragically unsuccessful struggle to accept the wholeness of his personality, to become "alive" and thereby escape the death-in-life of his narrow companions and repressive mother.

Self-fashioning is a difficult task in "The Other Boat," for it is dependent on so many different factors, from genetic predispositions and environmental conditions to socially induced self-images and tribal pressures. Cocoa is painfully aware of this lesson when Lionel departs after their quarrel over the unlocked door to their cabin. "When you come back you will not be you," Cocoa says. He knows that Lionel is still dependent for self-definition on the social approval to which he himself is indifferent, as their conflicting attitudes toward the unbolted door indicate. Cocoa's fear that Lionel will be altered by the social mores of his peers is justified, for the prospect of wholeness frightens Lionel. He knows full well that the discovery of his interracial, homosexual relationship will mean the obliteration of his social identity, just as his father's illicit liaison earned him the social status of a nonperson. As Lionel surveys the English travelers aboard the ship, he thinks, "How decent and reliable they looked, the folk to whom he belonged! He had been born one of them, he had his work with them, he meant to marry into their caste. If he forfeited their companionship he would become nobody and nothing."

The achievement of wholeness is a heroic quest, one made especially difficult by the conflict between Lionel's secret love for Cocoa and his self-definition as a member of a racist society. The racism rampant on the *Normannia* militates against wholeness, forcing Lionel—whose "colour-prejudices were tribal rather than personal, and only worked when an observer was present"—into a duplicitous life, alternately enjoying sex with his "resident wog" in the magic circle of their cabin and shouting with laughter at racist jokes in the public rooms of the liner. This split in Lionel's personality is apparent when Colonel Arbuthnot remarks of the English sleeping section on the deck: "woe betide anything black that walks this way." Lionel initially replies, "Good night, sir," and then suddenly—unintentionally—blurts out, "Bloody rubbish, leave the kid alone," only finally to apologize to the colonel. These contradictory emotions reflect the conflicts within himself. Lionel's ripening but unwilled love for Cocoa Moraes is forbidden by the mores of his tribe and forces a crisis of identity.

Lionel's crisis is rooted in sexual as well as racial attitudes. Regarding homosexuality as "the worst thing in the world, the thing for which Tommies got given the maximum," his growing recognition of himself as a homosexual is deeply threatening to his sense of identity, especially his image of himself as a soldier. He has been reared to disdain all sexuality. "Hitherto he had been ashamed of being built like a brute," he reflects, relaxing in Cocoa's postcoital embrace: "his preceptors had condemned carnality or had dismissed it as a waste of time, and his mother had ignored its existence in him and all her children; being hers, they had to be pure." But Lionel is his father's son as well as his mother's, and this dual inheritance reflects the irreconcilable divisions in his personality. He has rejected his father as "cruel and remorseless and selfish and self-indulgent"—a description also appropriate to Cocoa, with whom he finds himself in love. But countering this love is his mother, in whose image Lionel has defined himself. The story's most forceful agent of repression and Cocoa's chief—and equally unscrupulous—rival for Lionel's soul, Mrs. March is a formidable figure. Whereas Cocoa represents personal fulfillment and dedication to the pleasure principle, Mrs. March embodies social conformity and adherence to the reality principle. A Freudian carnivore who devours her children, she is suggestive of the classical Fates,

> blindeyed in the midst of the enormous web she had spun—filaments drifting everywhere, she understood nothing and controlled everything. She had suffered too much and was too high-minded to be judged like other people, she was outside carnality and incapable of pardoning it.

Lionel knows that the thought of him "topping a dago" would kill her.

The story's violent conclusion represents the simultaneous triumph and defeat of both Cocoa and Mrs. March, as well as the tragic waste of Lionel.

In the murder-suicide, Lionel desperately attempts to fuse the divisions of his personality into a single whole. What results is an irrational merging that yokes the opposing parts together without unifying them. Provoked by Cocoa's presence in his bunk and by his bite that draws blood, Lionel simultaneously makes love to Cocoa and reenacts his wartime experience "in the desert fighting savages." This double action at once pays tribute to his forbidden love and to the socially approved brutality that helped shape his self-conception. He strangles his lover and then takes his own life: "naked and with the seeds of love on him he dived into the sea." Lionel's sad fate resolves the divisions between his social self and his real self without reconciling them, for both are unacceptable to him. Appropriately, when Cocoa's body is buried at sea, "It moved northwards—contrary to the prevailing current," and when Mrs. March learns of Lionel's death, "she never mentioned his name again." Unable to face either a life led contrary to prevailing currents or one without tribal identity, Lionel escapes both, a victim of his conflicting impulses. He lacks the heroism necessary to achieve wholeness.

The last story Forster completed, "The Other Boat" is distinguished by consummate artistry. Incorporating the same social criticism that animates all the late tales, it explores with new profundity the psychological effects of racism and homophobia. Beautifully textured and psychologically acute, the story is unparalleled in Forster's short fiction in the depth of its characterizations, the subtlety of its rhythms, the complexities of its contrasts, and the effectiveness of its symbols.

The gay fictions of *The Life to Come* also include three comic stories— "The Obelisk," "What Does It Matter? A Morality," and "The Classical Annex"—and Forster's only piece of historical fiction, "The Torque," as well as the haunting psychomachia, "Dr. Woolacott." These stories all scorn the oppressive morality that inhibits personal growth and distorts social health. They attack the antisexual attitudes that, paradoxically, exaggerate the importance of sex and pervert true morality into moralistic prohibitions. In so doing, the stories celebrate recreational sex as an important source of joy, accepting the pursuit of pleasure as a deeply human activity, even as they demystify sex. These priapic stories are at bottom anarchic, but they emphasize the power of sex to humanize and invigorate both individuals and societies, and they do so from a postmodernist perspective that refuses to justify sex in the name of love or refined emotions.

Much has been made of the fact that violence pervades Forster's gay fictions, and this has sometimes been simplistically adduced as evidence of his unhappiness with his own sexuality.[42] But violence is a trademark of Forster's fiction generally, however decorously presented in the fiction he published during his lifetime. It is typically offered as an element of the entirety of human experience, one that is denied only at the expense of wholeness. The brutality that surfaces in Forster's fiction is an antidote to the sterility associated with the cerebral and overcivilized, an aspect of the persistent attempts of the tame to pursue the savage and of the flesh to educate the spirit. For Forster, immersion in the physical is a necessary component of the quest for joy. Associating violence with masculine sexuality throughout his canon, he attempts to forge connections between the physical and the spiritual without denying either. In the stories written under the influence of Priapus, Forster pointedly contrasts the healthy violence of sexual expression with the repressive violence of state and church. In this contrast, there is evidence not of Forster's unhappiness with his sexuality but of his disdain for the conventions and his outrage at the injustices of his society. For all his image of soft-spoken gentility, Forster suffered acutely and personally the pain of homophobia, and this suffering is made manifest—sometimes violently so—in his gay fictions.

Vital protests against the heterosexual dictatorship, Forster's gay fictions make clear the fact that their author's passionate denunciations of social conventions, class distinctions, and militant Christianity stem, at least in part, from his awareness of himself as a homosexual. As a group, these gay fictions illustrate Forster's greatest gifts as a writer. Their fierce but rueful satire is comedy sharpened by pain; their prophetic strain is fantasy deepened by myth. Although they are concerned with gay issues and homosexual dilemmas, they are informed by the same concerns that shape all Forster's work: the quest for wholeness, the search for liberation, the exploration of the inner life, and the apprehension of the unseen. And although they are set in the Edwardian era, they reflect a contemporary understanding of the homosexual plight in a homophobic society. Long after the Edwardian period has vanished, Forster's gay fictions remain important contributions to the literature of gay liberation, illustrating the connections he sought to forge—not altogether successfully—between the rational and irrational, the public and private, the sexual and political. Informed both by the ideology of the early homosexual emancipation movement and by Forster's own unique vision, these gay fictions include the first gay liberation masterpiece and stories that both celebrate and demystify sexuality.

5

"The Cabin and the River": Gore Vidal's *The City and the Pillar*

The decade following World War II saw both the beginnings of a new homosexual emancipation movement and the emergence of a new, openly gay popular literature. In 1948, the first important American homophile group, the Mattachine Society, was proposed; the Kinsey report on *Sexual Behavior in the Human Male* startled the American public with its revelation that over one-third of the male population reported significant homosexual experience; and Gore Vidal's *The City and the Pillar* was published. By the end of this "crucial decade," homosexual themes and characters were, if not yet a staple of popular literature, at least no longer rare.[1]

In the literature of the period may be charted the transition of public opinion about homosexuality that Forster noted in 1960, the change from ignorance and terror to familiarity and contempt. But countering a host of novels which trivialized and sensationalized homosexuality was a small but considerable body of popular literature that took homosexuality seriously as a contemporary social issue and that sought to interpret homosexuality in ways other than stereotypically. Prime among the novels that challenged the widespread Anglo-American contempt for homosexuality and homosexuals is Vidal's pioneering work, which was one of the first explicitly gay fictions to reach a large audience. Emphasizing the normality of gay people, *The City and the Pillar* traces the coming-out process of a young man as ordinary and American as apple pie. Coming at the beginning of the postwar decade, the novel is an important and exemplary contribution to the emerging popular literature of homosexuality. Like many gay fictions that followed, it evokes central homosexual myths and reflects the social and sexual attitudes of its time even as it resists them.

In the Afterword to his 1965 revision of *The City and the Pillar*, Vidal explains the book's origin and his intention:

I wanted to take risks, to try something no American had done before. I decided to examine the homosexual underworld (which I knew less well than I pretended), and in the process show the "naturalness" of homosexual relations, as well as making the point that there is of course no such thing as a homosexual.[2]

Whatever Vidal's intent, the novel does not illustrate the latter point but rather its opposite, for despite the author's well-known belief in the natural bisexuality of the species and his frequent insistence that *homosexual* is an adjective rather than a noun (a position also held by Alfred Kinsey), the novel succeeds primarily as a *Bildungsroman* tracing its protagonist's gradual acceptance of a homosexual identity. While the book certainly provides numerous examples of bisexual behavior and rejects the notion of homosexuality as a rigid classification, its dénouement pivots on the inflexibility of sexual orientation, for the protagonist Jim Willard turns out to be exclusively homosexual and his idealized friend Bob Ford exclusively heterosexual, apart from his adolescent experimentation with Jim. Nor does the novel actually show the naturalness of homosexuality. Though it presents its gay hero as being ordinary to the point of blandness—thereby challenging the stereotype of the homosexual as effeminate and exotic—and though it depicts gay lovemaking as altogether natural, the novel nevertheless rather contradictorily conceives of homosexuality as an abnormal state demanding psychological explanation. For all its reformist zeal, it is, in this sense, clearly a document reflective of its era.

The City and the Pillar does, however, deftly accomplish what seems to have been one of Vidal's chief aims: it provides an unsensationalized portrait of the flourishing gay subcultures, first of Hollywood and New Orleans, then of New York, which is described as "a new Sodom" where gay people "could be unnoticed by the enemy and yet known to one another."[3] The novel thereby illustrates the vast range and diversity of homosexuals and presents to a wide audience the social dynamics, mores, and specialized language of a hidden or at least masked society. It challenges some widely held stereotypes and confirms others. Most refreshingly, while it recognizes the debilitating desperation that frequently characterizes the subculture, unlike many works of its era (including Mary Renault's *The Charioteer*, discussed in Chapter 7), it refrains from moralizing and from casting the gay underworld as the villain of the piece. The absence of a moralizing perspective not only distinguishes *The City and the Pillar* from contemporaneous popular literature on the subject, but it also facilitates the hard-edged irony that characterizes the book's style.

By presenting the gay subculture through the eyes of its naive hero, a native of small-town Virginia who must adjust to a new and strange world, the novel becomes a kind of Baedeker of the 1940s gay underground. In so doing, it captures well the coming-out experience as a time when a bewildering array of information is mastered and the individual passes gradually through various stages and levels of acceptance. Naturally athletic and apparently well adjusted, Jim Willard (whose profession as a tennis player may have been suggested by the 1946 scandal involving tennis great William "Big Bill" Tilden)[4] is at first an anomaly among the clique of gay bellboys with whom he associates in Hollywood. They are shallow, effeminate young men who all "desire to be wealthy and admired, to move in narcissistic splendor through the lives of others, to live forever grandly and not to die." But as he becomes more deeply involved, Jim discovers a complex society that includes, in addition to the stereotypical gay men and lesbians ("people so hunted that they have, at last, become totally perverse as a defense"), a much larger group of concealed homosexuals. As one character tells Jim, there are "thousands like ourselves. Perfectly normal men and women . . . ." Although the novel reflects its era in considering homosexuality as a psychological problem, it also confirms what Vidal wrote in the 1965 Afterword:

> When legal and social pressures against homosexuality are severe, homosexualists can become neurotic, in much the same way that Jews and Negroes do in a hostile environment. Yet a man who enjoys sensual relations with his own sex is not, by definition, neurotic.

Central points of the novel are that repression distorts the expression of homosexuality and creates a subculture that itself contributes to that distortion. Were homosexuality accepted by the larger society, the subculture would not be necessary or at least would be less distorting. The novel is especially sensitive to the heavy costs in emotional stability exacted by the homosexual's necessity to disguise his sexuality. For example, several characters angrily protest the need to mask their sexual orientation. "There should be no need to hide, to submerge in a big city; everything should he open and declared," Paul Sullivan remarks, as he doubtfully considers the possibility of coming out publicly. "We live a short life and it's hard enough to find love in the world without the added hazard of continual pretense," he adds. Similarly, near the end of the book, when visiting his Virginia home for the first time in years, Jim Willard grows impatient of the heterosexual mask he must don for the visit and wonders "what would happen if he were to be honest and natural; if every man like himself were to be natural and honest." He concludes: "It would be the end of the submerged world and it would make a better beginning for others not yet born: to be born into a world where sex was natural and not fearsome, where men could love men naturally, the way they were meant to, as well as to love women naturally, the way they were meant to." But even as he contem-

plates the potential benefits of openness and a world liberated by truthfulness, Jim acknowledges that "it was a desperate thing to be an honest man
in his world, and he had not the courage to be that yet." The novel defines
freedom as not having to tell lies, but it also soberly recognizes that, for the
gay man or lesbian in 1948 America, freedom is far from a reality.

A frequent subject of discussion in Vidal's gay subculture is the question
of the origins of homosexuality, a subject also inevitably raised as part of
the coming-out process. Although the gay characters sometimes discuss in
long, frequently stilted speeches the etiology of homosexuality—often at-
tributing its prevalence in America to the baleful influence of women and
mothers, and sometimes contrasting one form of homosexuality allegedly
caused by the effeminizing of society with another supposedly more primitive and natural Teutonic form—the novel itself takes no stand on this issue. It merely repeats the various speculations of the day and in so doing
locates itself as very much a product of late-1940s America.

At one point, Sullivan, the novel's most articulate and best-educated
character, attributes Jim's homosexuality to the fear of women, a popular
psychological explanation of the period and one consonant with Jim's (and
the novel's) horror of effeminacy. But this charge is disputed when Jim
characteristically thinks of Bob Ford: "because of Bob everything Sullivan
said was false; his homosexuality was not the result of negation, of hatred
or fear of women; it came, rather, from a most affirmative love." Sullivan
may speak for Vidal when he echoes Freud and professes to believe that
homosexuality is a "normal stage in human development, sometimes arrested but not for that reason to be censured." He surely speaks for Vidal
when he proclaims that "the real dignity is the dignity of a man realizing
himself and functioning honestly according to his own nature." In the pre-
gay liberation world of the 1940s, when homosexuals were too frightened
to risk exposure, the only possibility of affirmation in the face of repression
was to "Live with dignity . . . and try to learn to love one another."

Perhaps the most revolutionary gesture of *The City and the Pillar* is its
suggestion that the homosexual experience itself is valuable: an insight that
is extremely rare among the popular treatments of the subject in the postwar
decade and that both hearkens back to the early emancipation movement
and looks forward to the "Gay is good" philosophy of the 1970s. The experience of being gay in an unaccepting society may foster neurosis, but it
may also lead to healthy introspection and valuable social criticism. Jim
Willard acknowledges this at two points in the novel. When he is in military service and observes the enormous pressure for conformity all about
him, he realizes that his life with homosexuals taught him an indispensable
lesson: "the importance of being one's self, to make as few compromises
with one's real nature as possible." Later, on his return home for Christmas
1942, he becomes conscious of the limitations of the "safe secure people

whose lives were running in a familiar pattern." He thinks: "There was no
basis for understanding here. They had never been so emotionally severed
from society that they were forced to analyze and understand emotion."
The point is the Forsterian one that the alienation suffered by gay people
affords them, at least potentially, important insights both into themselves
and into the society from which they stand apart, at a slight angle to the
universe. *The City and the Pillar* protests against the injustices suffered by
homosexuals, especially the repression that creates the need to disguise
love; it exposes the mendacity and ignorance of the larger society; and it
discovers within the homosexual experience the potential for heightened
self-knowledge and deepened social analysis.

Notwithstanding its undeniable importance as a pioneering exploration of
a gay milieu and as a documentary that demystifies homosexuality by
showing its (relative) ordinariness and prevalence, the novel has more than
sociological interest. Although Anaïs Nin complained that it was a "prosaic
and literal book,"[5] *The City and the Pillar* is actually evocative and resonant. Its power resides in the simplicity, subtlety, and apparent artlessness
with which it connects a contemporary gay odyssey with archetypal concerns. Indeed, the book may be described accurately as a "mythic novel,"[6]
and its achievement as a gay fiction has less to do with its depiction of
homosexuality per se than with its incorporation and examination of the
myths of love, especially those associated with homosexuality. These myths
help shape the experience of Vidal's homosexual Everyman, and the novel
itself becomes a reflection both of and on those myths. The mythic dimension enriches the book's flat, understated style, and imparts scope and significance to its account of an unremarkable young man's journey toward
self-knowledge. Although it is severely flawed by its melodramatic ending
(especially in the original version), *The City and the Pillar* is an ambitious
attempt to trace realistically a homosexual's awakening in a particular time
and place, while also locating this experience in the vast expanses and repetitive patterns of myth.

The title and bipartite structure of the novel rely on the central myth of
homosexuality in Judeo-Christian culture, the story of Sodom. The curious
tale of the destruction of the Cities of the Plain by fire and brimstone, as
recounted in Genesis 18 and 19, provides, of course, the foundation for the
religious and civil persecution of homosexuality.[7] In the biblical account,
two angels are accosted by the men of Sodom when they visit Lot. Even
Lot's offer of his virginal daughters fails to dissuade the Sodomites in their
desire for the angels. In consequence, the angels destroy not only Sodom
but also Gomorrah and all the plain, with everything growing there and
everyone living there, save only Lot and his family. As Lot and his wife
flee the burning cities, she lags behind and gazes backward toward the
plain and is turned into a pillar of salt, presumably for disobeying the an-

gels' warning not to look back. In Vidal's subversive interpretation of this perplexing myth, the emphasis is not on the destruction of Sodom, but on the pillar of salt. Even as the retributive plot may at first glance seem to confirm the dangers of homosexuality, the myth functions finally as a condemnation not of sodomy but of the false romanticization of the past.

The plot is structured into a bifurcated flashback, framed by opening and closing sections set in 1943. In the opening frame chapter, twenty-five-year-old Jim Willard sits in a Manhattan bar getting drunk and trying not to think about the past, although "he could only forget, for a while, how it began." The first large flashback section, entitled "The City," locates the source of Jim's current anguish in his sexual initiation at the age of seventeen, when he and his boyhood friend Bob Ford spontaneously make love in a cabin by a river in Virginia. Shortly afterward, Bob joins the merchant marine, and the two young men lose touch. The following year, Jim also sets out to sea, hoping to find his friend. Unable to make contact with Bob, he takes a job as cabin boy on a passenger ship that plies the waters between Alaska and Seattle. After an embarrassing inability to perform sexually with a young woman in Seattle, Jim abandons ship and drifts to Hollywood, where he gets a job as a tennis coach at a Beverly Hills hotel and begins consorting with the gay bellboys. He soon forms a liaison with Ronald Shaw, a handsome but immature movie star. When Jim is unable to respond to Shaw's increasing emotional demands, he leaves him for Paul Sullivan, a vaguely masochistic novelist. Jim and Paul visit New Orleans, where they encounter Maria Verlaine, a friend of Paul's who has a history of attraction toward younger gay men. The two men accompany her to her home in the Yucatán peninsula. Maria falls in love with Jim, but he is unable to consummate their relationship. With the outbreak of World War II, Jim and Sullivan enlist in the Army. Jim is sent to an Air Corps base in Colorado, where he becomes a physical-training instructor and fends off the unwanted attentions of a sergeant and unsuccessfully pursues a corporal. After hospitalization for a severe throat infection, Jim develops rheumatoid arthritis. As he awaits his medical discharge, he writes letters to Shaw, his mother, Sullivan, Maria, and Bob, in an attempt "to recapture his own past."

Part Two of the novel, entitled "The Pillar of Salt," opens with brief vignettes describing the varying effects of Jim's letters on each of the recipients. The letter to his mother arrives just as she is awaiting the death of Jim's father, while Bob Ford receives his letter on the day of his wedding. After his discharge, Jim moves to New York and again works as a tennis coach, finally using the money that he had saved while living with Shaw to buy part-ownership of a tennis court in Greenwich Village. He meets Shaw and Maria again, temporarily resumes his relationship with Sullivan, and then becomes increasingly involved in the world of gay bars and one-night stands. For Christmas of 1942, he returns to Virginia to visit his family and is reunited with Bob, now a father as well as a husband. The two agree to meet in New York soon. When Bob is next in the city, he and Jim go out on the town and then return to Bob's hotel room. Jim attempts to make love to his friend, only to be cruelly rebuffed. Fury takes the place of love and in the fight that ensues Jim strangles Bob, leaves the hotel, and enters the bar in which the novel opened, intending to drink "until the dream was completely over."

As is obvious from the plot summary, Vidal's bold reinterpretation of the Sodom myth provides the novel with an important structural principle. In the "City" portion of the book Jim completes a prolonged coming-out process, while in "The Pillar of Salt" he regresses in an attempt to relive the past, especially his initiation experience, so that "the circle of his life would be completed." Jim is not destroyed by Sodom. In fact, the section of the book entitled "The City" charts a period of growth. Jim's destruction results not from his acceptance of himself as a homosexual—his positive achievement in the novel—but from his fixation on the past, which finally turns him into a pillar of salt.

Vidal's seriously witty subversion of the Sodom myth is paradigmatic of his treatment of other myths in the book, both nationalistic and homoerotic. For example, he explodes that staple of American literature, the myth of innocence. In *The Apostate Angel*, Bernard F. Dick reads *The City and the Pillar* in light of Leslie Fiedler's *Love and Death in the American Novel* and concludes that Vidal's book demythologizes the American Wilderness novel, creating a homoerotic Eden that "ripens with purity and rots with experience." Dick is no doubt correct to perceive that in the idyllic scene of lovemaking by the river Vidal evokes the homoeroticism implicit in much classic American literature, including *Huckleberry Finn* and *The Last of the Mohicans;* but he is wrong to think that the intent of the book is merely to reveal "the awesome truth the myth concealed"[8] or to condemn experience. *The City and the Pillar* is more sophisticated than Dick's analysis recognizes. The book does expose American hypocrisy by making explicit the homoerotic source of an important romantic strain in American literature, usually expressed as an idealization of innocence and a fear of experience. But it is not so much interested in discovering this "awesome truth" as in depicting the dangerousness of such false idealization. What is condemned is not experience, but the fixation on innocence.

Moreover, the idyllic initiation scene that is to haunt Jim Willard throughout the novel evokes not merely the nationalistic myth of innocence but some crucial myths deeply embedded in the homosexual literary tradition. The pastoral setting, the bathing in the river, and the spontaneous sexual episode of the two boys constitute a tableau traditionally associated with homosexuality and may be traced to the *Idylls* of Theocritus. There is no more pervasive motif in gay literature than the homoerotic recognition scene involving an outdoor bathing episode. Its analogues include the eleventh section of Whitman's "Song of Myself," with its "Twenty-eight young men and all so friendly" dancing and laughing and bathing by the shore; numerous bathing scenes in late-nineteenth-century literature and visual art; and the similar episodes in Lawrence's *The White Peacock* and *Women in Love* and Forster's *A Room with a View* and *Maurice*.[9] The fact that the lovemaking is preceded by wrestling is suggestive, as Roger Austen and Stephen Adams have pointed out, of the Hylas ritual in classical literature, as interpreted by Rictor Norton.[10] This ritual derives from an archetypal initiation ceremony that was eventually transformed into romantic homosexual love, and it underlies literature as different as Pindar's *Odes* and the wrestling scenes in *Women in Love* and *Maurice*. The irony of Vidal's use of this ritual that displaces violence with sex is made apparent in its reversal in the novel's grim conclusion, where a sexual overture ushers in violence.

But most significant of all is Vidal's allusion to the originary myth of homosexuality offered by Aristophanes in Plato's *Symposium*.[11] According to this myth, there were originally three genders: man, woman, and androgyne. These creatures were round, each having four feet, four hands, two faces, and two sets of genitals. In anger, Zeus sliced each down the middle, thereby creating new beings. Men who love men are thus explained as slices of the original male, and they seek, like the other divided natures, completion by recovering their lost halves. This originary myth is clearly alluded to in Vidal's description of Jim's sexual initiation by the river: "their bodies came together and for Jim it was his first completion, his first discovery of a twin: the half he had been searching for." Throughout the novel, Jim is in quest of his lost half, in search of this sense of fulfillment, this assuasion of loneliness. Indeed, the words *complete, completely, completeness* and *completion* recur over and over again in the novel, underlining the quest for wholeness as its central theme. As Jim comes to realize, after he has experienced the novelty of gay life, what he really wants is "a companion, a brother . . . a mingling of his identity with an equal." Perhaps the most enduring of all gay fantasies, indeed all romantic desire, this quest for completeness through another is deeply rooted in homosexual myth and consciousness. But Vidal does not merely validate the archetypal search for a lost partner, he also indicates the dangers attendant upon such a quest, particularly its susceptibility to falsification.

Indeed, the hard edge of *The City and the Pillar* is the result of Vidal's exposure of the false idealization implicit in the very myth that motivates Jim and the other central characters, all of whom search for self-validation in a lost half that might make them whole. Even in the pastoral scene of sexual discovery, Vidal's wry irony is clear, at least in retrospect. The first clue comes in the different evaluations of the experience by Jim and Bob. While both participate with an equal awareness and both are "made complete" in the embrace, Jim's enthusiasm is pointedly not matched by Bob's. The older of the two assesses the experience as immature and unnatural: "That was awful kidstuff," Bob reflects, "I don't think it's right. . . . It's not natural." This assessment does not preclude his further participation in sex-play that weekend, but it contrasts with the enormous sense of release and self-discovery that characterizes Jim's response and it foreshadows the devastating conclusion.

Most crucially, however, Vidal undercuts the idyllic scene—and signals its potential danger—by connecting it with dreams. For Jim, the experience of making love with Bob is one in which "half forgotten dreams began to come alive." After the lovemaking, he gains courage "now that he had performed a dream." In one sense, by linking Jim's sexual response to early childhood dreams that are made real in experience, Vidal validates the psychological insight of Aristophanes' myth of homosexuality by locating the desire for a lost partner deep in Jim's subconscious. The linkage certainly helps make credible the central premise of the novel: that Jim believes that in the encounter with Bob he has discovered something basic to his identity. And it helps explain the persistence of Jim's memory of the initiation scene, which for him is a recognition scene as well, one in which inchoate desires are literally made flesh. But dreams are deeply ambiguous. They may signify psychological truth, yet they can also distort reality. This is exactly the double-edged way in which Vidal uses them in this scene (and throughout the novel). What begins as "a consummation in reality" becomes translated into a distorting dream that will haunt Jim's days and nights to come. By the end of the scene, Bob Ford becomes for Jim not a real person but "a conscious dream." In the circular shape of the novel's plot, Bob is a romantic "dream–lover" who will materialize in the harsh light of reality as a nightmarish demon.

Vidal's interest centers less on the contrast between innocence and experience than on the contrasts of past and present, dream and reality. Thus, he appropriates for his own purposes another myth associated with gay men and women: the Freudian diagnosis of homosexuality as arrested development, an explanation that is explicitly evoked by Sullivan. But even as he provides in Jim's disturbed relationships with his bullying father and close-binding mother evidence for a psychological case history, Vidal subverts the Freudian myth by making it characteristic not of homosexuality per se but of American romanticism in general. Jim Willard, Ronald Shaw, and Paul Sullivan can be seen as cases of arrested development not because they are gay, but because they so idealize the past and so manufacture illusions that they are unable either to live fully in the present or to accept the imperfections of reality. These personal characteristics, interestingly enough, are *national* characteristics, for as Vidal has frequently pointed out the United States itself routinely falsifies and romanticizes its past. Thus Vidal's subversion of the American myth of innocence is intimately connected with his subversion of the Freudian myth. That he intends the arrested emotional development of his characters not to be read as a symptom of homosexuality is clear from the fact that Maria Verlaine suffers from the same affliction. She too harbors illusions about love and "would not accept incompleteness." Unfulfilled by heterosexual men, she falls in love with younger gay men for with them "she enjoyed a greater illusion of completeness." All of the central characters are emotionally immature. Trapped by distorting dreams, haunted by their pasts, seeking the recovery of a lost wholeness, they live in a world of illusion.

Perhaps because they are so emotionally stunted, Vidal's characters are not very interesting. With the exception of Paul Sullivan, the minor characters are predictable and sketchily drawn. Ronald Shaw is a caricature of a movie star and Maria Verlaine an intriguing but not altogether convincing portrait of a cosmopolitan "fag hag." Only Jim Willard is affecting, and he commands sustained interest largely because he combines unexpected characteristics. Bland and ordinary, he nevertheless has an unusually well developed interior life. Himself paralyzed by romantic illusions, he is surprisingly perceptive about the illusions of others. For all the novel's treatment of him as a case history, he nevertheless preserves an essential mystery. As Robert Kiernan comments, Jim Willard is

> Everyman and yet he is *l'étranger*. . . . The net effect is paradoxical but appropriate, for it decrees that in the last analysis we cannot patronize Jim Willard, sympathize with him entirely, or even claim to understand him. Much more so than the typical character in fiction, Jim Willard simply *exists*, not as the subject of a statement, not as the illustration of a thesis, but simply as himself.[12]

Appropriate for the protagonist of a coming-out story—a genre whose narratives are always the same, yet always different—Jim Willard is at once a representative figure yet highly individualized.

The City and the Pillar in effect traces the successive stages through which Jim Willard passes in his coming to terms with himself as a homosexual, from his period of experimentation through his achievement of a gay identity. In this sense, the novel enacts a mythic quest for wholeness and self-acceptance. Thus, Jim may be regarded as a figure of mythic dimensions insofar as his coming-out story recapitulates the experience of millions of other American homosexuals of his era. But his journey of self-discovery is highly individual, for it is conducted in the constant shadow of his idealization of Bob Ford. The memory of a cabin and a brown river is a secret that grows inside Jim, interceding at crucial points to shape the contours of his life.

The effects of Jim's romanticization of Bob are apparent early in the novel as the young protagonist fumblingly gropes toward a grasp of his own identity. For example, when Anne, the girl he is fixed up with by his shipmate Collins, attempts to initiate a sexual encounter, he instinctively compares her with Bob. On this basis, he rejects her: "he thought of the cabin and the river and he knew it was not like this; it was not dirty like this; it was not unnatural like this. He didn't care now if he *was* different from other people." This incident is an important step in Jim's growth toward self-knowledge, his recognition that what might be natural for others is unnatural for him. When Collins labels him "queer" for his failure to respond to Anne, Jim must question himself and confront the puzzle of his differentness. But at this point in the book, his naive romanticism continues to limit the answers that he finds.

The limiting tendencies of Jim's romanticism are also apparent when he compares himself to his peers in Hollywood. Jim is at first shocked to discover that the unattractive, effeminate young men he works with not only had the same dreams he had "but practiced them fully when awake." This discovery leads him to "study himself in the mirror to see if there was any trace of the woman in his face or manner; he was pleased always that there was not." The popular association of homosexuality with effeminacy works to confuse Jim. Since he is not effeminate, then, he thinks, he must not be gay. Jim's disdain of effeminacy is shared by most of the characters in the novel; even the outrageous drag queens value conventional masculinity in others, if not in themselves. This emphasis on masculinity anticipates the masculinization of American homosexuals widely noticed in the 1970s and often attributed to the pride inspired by the gay liberation movement, but which began much earlier and was probably at least partly influenced by the World Wars.

In a pattern familiar in the coming-out process, Jim decides that he is unique. He believes his experience with Bob is utterly unlike that of his colleagues at the hotel, and he resists labeling it as homosexual. Yet he senses a connection between his dreams of Bob and the stories that the bellboys tell of their affairs with one another. He pretends that he associates with the bellboys only for "the pleasure of saying no" to their sexual advances. But for all his disclaimers of homosexual interest or of identification with the stereotypically gay young men, he nevertheless desires "to know more, to understand this twisted behavior, to understand himself." This desire for self-knowledge propels him to accept Ronald Shaw's sexual invitation.

Significantly, Jim is attracted to Shaw because he is masculine and he reminds him of Bob, "and that made it all right." Yet even as he finds himself responding sexually to the actor, he compares the sensation to "a different night, a more important time." He does not find lovemaking with Shaw the "complete" experience it had been with Bob, but he achieves physical satisfaction and a kind of emotional contentment. Still, the relationship is shadowed by the inevitable comparison: "He was alive and aware that the last two years had been gray and without color; now he could only remember having lived on the peaks of sensation: Bob and now Shaw; the second not so good as the first but still exciting and almost satisfying."

The affair with Shaw is an important but preliminary stage in Jim's development, one that he must necessarily outgrow. In his unequal pairing with Shaw, Jim plays the dual role of the beloved and the somewhat detached student of gay life. At first he is impressed by Shaw's success and single-mindedness, "the glamour of his legend," and his kindness. As the object of Shaw's affection, Jim has only to accept, not to give. But he quite rightly comes to doubt whether Shaw is really capable of the love about which he so incessantly talks, and he understandably becomes impatient with the actor's self-pity. Moreover, Jim finally bridles under the restraints of the role in which he has allowed himself to be cast. He comes to yearn for a more active, less passive involvement, one in which he gives as well as receives.

For the mother-fixated Shaw, Jim is simply another in a long series of conquests. Shaw

> chose the handsomest, most masculine boys he could find and he was never pleased with them: he resented it if they came to love him, came to disregard the legend, and he was hurt when they could not give him the warmth he wanted, the warmth his mother gave him as a child.

Trapped in an emotional double-bind, Shaw constantly complains of "incomplete love," yet he is incapable of responding to a complete one. And at this point in his life, Jim is equally incapable of love. He does not pretend to be in love with Shaw: "The idea of being in love with a man was still a ludicrous one; still seemed unnatural and rather hopeless: in every case except Bob's and that was different." He comes to realize that what he wants is not a father-figure but a brother, ideally a twin. Jim recognizes the illusionary nature of Shaw's obsession with an ideal love, but he fails to see that his romanticization of Bob is itself illusionary.

Jim's more nearly equal relationship with Paul Sullivan represents an advance in maturity and self-knowledge, and another stage in his progress toward achieving a gay identity. Jim realizes that "now he wanted to possess as well as be possessed." Sullivan's smile reminds him of Bob, and he responds to the writer's masculinity and seriousness. Through Sullivan's agency, he comes to acknowledge his homosexuality. Ironically enough, Sullivan is attracted to Jim largely because he thinks him primarily heterosexual. Like Shaw and many other homosexuals of the day (and like Jim himself), Sullivan places a premium on heterosexuality, yet he also contradictorily yearns for "a complete and reciprocated love." Deeply wounded by a guilty Catholic boyhood, the writer clings to his painful past as tenaciously as Jim treasures his happy memory of Bob. Sullivan "could no longer give himself completely to anyone." As a kind of masochistic pleasure, he deliberately contrives to wreck his own chances for happiness, as when he intentionally endangers his relationship with Jim by introducing him to Maria Verlaine.

Significantly, however, when Sullivan outlines several typical patterns of homosexual development, Jim secretly recognizes himself. Now he no longer thinks of himself as unique, but as "a man not unlike these others, varying only in degree from a basic pattern." Although he silently vows to "defeat this truth," he secretly acknowledges his kinship with the fraternity of men who love men. He desperately hopes that "should he ever have a woman, he would be normal," but, as Vidal adds laconically, "There was not much to base this hope on." Moreover, whereas before he has cherished his presumed heterosexuality, now he is hurt to the quick when he learns that Sullivan considers him incapable of tenderness with another man. "He felt he knew what love was better than anyone who had ever lived," Jim thinks to himself and immediately relates his capacity for love to his memory of Bob: "He doubted if anyone had felt as desperate and as lonely as he when Bob had left. Yes, he was capable of love with Bob and, perhaps, with someone who could affect him in the same way, another brother." Unfortunately, however, his domination by the memory of the cabin and the river will preclude his full response to anyone in real life.

Jim's failure to respond sexually to Maria Verlaine finally confirms the secret knowledge of his gay identity. Their relationship is a kind of love affair, an attempt to find that elusive completeness sought by each. But more than a love affair, the relationship is also, and primarily, Jim's desperate attempt to defeat the truth of his homosexuality. Without sex, the affair is painfully incomplete for both of them. Repelled by Maria's softness, Jim realizes that "he would never be one with her or any woman." Still not wishing to be labeled, however, he is angered when she asks him, "Do you mind it very much, being different?" Yet when she defines love as "the thing that makes you dissolve, that makes you come together," he thinks of Bob and silently agrees: "He knew what it was." Finally, when Sullivan tells him that Maria "could rescue you from this world," Jim replies, "Why should I be rescued ?" Here, for the first time in the novel, he accepts himself as a homosexual. He is no longer a tourist passing through the submerged world but one of its citizens.

Jim's acceptance of his homosexuality is verified by his increasingly frequent awareness of sexual attraction toward other men and by his pursuit of Ken Woodrow, the handsome corporal he lusts after in the Army. In his successive relationships with Shaw, Sullivan, and Maria, Jim had been the beloved, the pursued, the object of their passion. Now, suddenly, the positions are reversed, and Jim assumes yet another role on his journey toward maturity, that of would-be lover and seducer. He is infatuated with Ken: "He was unable to think of anything else; he could not concentrate on his work, such as it was. He could only daydream and make himself miserable." He is inexperienced in the art of seduction, however, and although he manages to get the corporal into bed with him, his sexual overture is repulsed. Ironically, however, the unattractive Sergeant Kerwinski, whom Jim had spurned, apparently succeeds in his pursuit of Ken. The point is that Jim does not yet know how to play the game. He has arrived at a gay identity, but he still has much to learn, not only about gay courting rituals but also about himself.

As an inevitable part of the coming-out process, Jim's acceptance prompts him to a period of intense introspection. During the long days he spends in the Army, he probes his past, trying "to understand himself and the circumstances that made him the way he was." His self-examination is motivated not by doubt, but by curiosity and by a growing sense of solidarity with other homosexuals. "He was not displeased with himself; he had no feeling of sorrow or remorse for the sort of man he was and doubtless would remain. He was curious, however, to know more of himself and of others like himself." What bothers him is not the fact of his homosexuality, but the stigma attached to it. He reviews his early life, his friendship with Bob, which began when he was fifteen, his experiences aboard ship, and his liaison with Shaw. And though he recognizes that Sullivan and Maria had been important in his life, he knows that he was happiest with Bob. The "City" section of the novel, thus, ends with Jim having finally achieved a gay identity. Significantly, and forebodingly, however, at the end of the section, rather than looking forward to the future, he is gazing backward on the past.

The smaller, second part of the novel, "The Pillar of Salt," contrives to bring Jim in contact with those who had been important to him in the past: Shaw, Sullivan, Maria, his mother, and, finally, Bob. But there is a conspicuously stagnant quality to this section. Jim works hard, maintains nonromantic friendships with his former lovers, and has a lot of sex, mainly of the one-night-stand variety. Tellingly, however, he participates in no meaningful relationship. He discovers that it is easier "to have sex with other men than to have friends; he found it difficult to get to know people in New York though easy to have sex with them." Although he is introduced to the party circuit of wealthy queens and willowy young men with "sensitive girlish faces," he dislikes it intensely. He had hoped that by moving in this circle, he could accept this society and be happy in it, but he realizes that

> he could not find what he wanted here; there was an overripe, over-civilized aura about this society. Everyone deliberately tried to destroy the last vestiges of the masculine within himself, and this Jim found to be the worst perversion of all, the only perversion; because very often these people allowed the tyranny of their own society to geld them completely.

Instead, he turns to the gay bars, "finding in them, at least, young men like himself who were still natural and not overly corrupt." Despite his sexual success, however, he remains unhappy. He realizes that "he would have to find Bob again before he could be contented and at ease."

In Jim's romantic imagination, he sees the reunion with Bob as the culmination of his long journey. He thinks that it will provide the security and completeness that he lacks. When he learns that Bob has married, Jim has a brief flash of conscious doubt. It occurs to him that "The dream he had been constructing for years might be false, a daydream with no reality in it." But he quickly dismisses the disturbing thought. "What had happened by the river had been too important, too large for either of them to forget," he insists. "Bob must *not* have changed and, therefore, he had not." He is even able to accommodate Bob's apparent heterosexuality into his fantasy. "It would make their affair more unusual for both of them, more binding," he reflects. His privileging of heterosexuality here is typical of attitudes held by everyone in the novel, especially including the gay characters; but Jim's attempt to have Bob at once heterosexual and yet involved in a homosexual affair is an act of willful illusionism even more desperate than his earlier pretenses of his own heterosexuality. This fantasy is worthy of Shaw or Sullivan, who similarly valued Jim's presumed heterosexuality, and indicates Jim's failure to grow beyond them. Even when he comes face-to-face with the newly domesticated Bob in Virginia, he convinces himself, despite overwhelming evidence to the contrary, that Bob had not changed. "He remembered many things," Jim reassures himself, "and he would not have forgotten that day by the river and its importance."

But for all Jim's rationalizations, he is nevertheless plagued by unconscious doubts. This is made clear in the nightmares he experiences when he becomes ill in the Army. At that time he dreams of "a menacing subtly distorted Bob, who would never come near him, who always retreated when he tried to touch him." In the nightmare, the river is not placid as it had been in reality and in memory, but "rushing over tall sharp rocks." Jim is in a boat crossing the river, "but the boat was always wrecked on the sharp rocks." In the disturbing dream, the journey is never completed. This nightmare is important not merely for its anticipation of the conclusion, but also as Vidal's counter to the conscious dream constructed by Jim. In its reflection of the subconscious, the unwilled nightmare is far more real than the lovingly evoked daydream. It expresses deeply repressed fears that Jim cannot acknowledge. The truth of the nightmare is verified in the grim reality of the book's violent ending.

The original conclusion is unconvincing and melodramatic, and seriously mars the novel. Disregarding the overwhelming evidence of Bob's inflexible heterosexuality and, more important, the unmistakable signs that the experience by the river had had little meaning for Bob's life, Jim obeys his heart rather than his head, only to be rejected by his friend as "nothing but a damned queer!" The unconvincing scene culminates not only in the end of Jim's love but also in his murder of Bob in sheer fury. After the violence abates, Jim kisses his dead friend and then seeks forgetfulness in drink. In the final pages of the novel the consequences of the death of the dream are sketched: "It had ended at last: that part of his life which had belonged to Bob and to all men who might have been his brothers and his lovers the way Bob had been, once, years before." Jim initially thinks that his period of homosexuality is over: "He was changed; if he was not changed he could not live for he had destroyed the most important part of his life, Bob and the legend." But he hears the roar of a brown river and "he knew that he could not change, that no dream ever ended except in a larger one and there was no larger one." The problem with Vidal's original conclusion is not merely that it is melodramatic and unbelievable. It is also as falsely romantic as the modes of thought that the novel criticizes with such cool clarity. The original ending betrays the novel's carefully cultivated stance of detached irony.

The conclusion of the 1965 revision is altogether more satisfying. Here, when Jim makes a pass at the sleeping Bob, the latter initiates the violence. A menacing Bob, his fists ready, attacks Jim, and Jim, overwhelmed by an equal mixture of rage and desire, responds by overpowering and, finally, raping his dream lover. When the violence is over, Jim wonders, "Was this all?" Disillusioned and rudely awakened to his own folly, he is forced to come to grips with the discrepancy between dream and reality. In the final pages he realizes that "The lover and brother was gone, replaced by a memory of bruised flesh, torn sheets, and violence." Most important of all, instead of belaboring the past, he looks to the future: "he would ship out again and travel in strange countries and meet new people." He determines to "Begin again." Not only is the revised conclusion less melodramatic, but its muted optimism is convincing and in harmony with the rest of the novel. In the revised version, the encounter with Bob—so unlike the reunion he dreamed of—is the final and crucial step in Jim's journey toward self-knowledge. It releases him to face the future free of the false romanticism that had chained him to the past. Jim now sees his life not as a circle to be closed, but as a line to be extended.

It is no accident that in both versions, the violence is initiated by Bob's labeling of Jim a "queer," the same epithet that Collins had hurled at him when he was unable to perform sexually with a woman in Seattle and that Jim had suppressed in his mind as "what Collins had called him." Robert Kiernan severely criticizes Jim for this sensitivity, remarking that "the absence of a more profound response to his homosexuality makes him seem vacuous, half formed, and insubstantial."[13] But one of the distinctions of *The City and the Pillar* is its recognition of the profound effect of stigma on individuals. The difficulties in the coming-out process have much less to do with acceptance of homosexual desire than with adjusting to the social stigma attached to homosexuality. Words and attitudes that may seem merely reflective of conventional prejudice, and therefore of little consequence, actually have the power to cut very deeply, perhaps especially those who romanticize their attachments. Rather than evidence of a childish or simplistic reaction to his homosexuality, Jim's sensitivity to the contempt concentrated in the word *queer*,[14] especially coming from someone he loves, is a poignant response to the psychic assaults gay people continue to face even after having accepted their homosexuality. This sensitivity may also be testimony to the continuing and perhaps ineradicable legacy of internalized homophobia borne by gay people who have matured in an anti-gay society.

The City and the Pillar is a significant contribution to the literature of homosexuality in the crucial postwar decade. Although marred by a melodramatic conclusion, the novel presents an accurate and unsensationalized portrait of the gay subculture of the 1940s, and provides the best account of the coming-out experience of its time. The flat, nonmoralistic narrative of a young man's journey toward a gay identity is given mythic dimension even as it becomes the occasion for a trenchant critique of the false romanticism that traps its characters at various levels of arrested development. A remarkable achievement for a twenty-one-year-old author, *The City and the Pillar* is at once a penetrating study of self-deception and an unsentimental analysis of homosexual life in the 1940s. As a gay fiction, it achieved a legendary status in the 1950s and 1960s and exerted significant influence on the gay fictions that followed.

The City and the Pillar is especially distinguished for its social approach to the question of homosexuality. Although it is couched in the form of a coming-out story, it is also a "problem novel" that recognizes the homosexual's dilemma as a socially significant issue. Placing the plight of its ordinary young protagonist within a broad context of American values, it both reflects and challenges the sexual attitudes of its time. Not surprisingly, its approach to the question of the homosexual's relationship to society is clearly and unquestioningly accommodationist, yet Vidal's accommodationism is in no sense bought at the expense of individuality or gay self-esteem. Driven by its thesis that homosexuality is a normal variation of human behavior, Vidal's flatly written, unapologetic gay fiction is daring simply because it so calmly reveals a simple but profound truth about human sexuality and so unsentimentally depicts the struggle toward affirmation in a hypocritical and falsely romantic society. While exposing the mendacity and ignorance of the larger American society, *The City and the Pillar* suggests that the homosexual experience is valuable in its own right. Written before the virulent homophobic backlash of the 1950s, the novel somewhat underestimates the extent and ferocity of homophobia in American society and fails to probe very deeply its sources and causes. Thus, despite its melodramatic conclusion, the novel is essentially optimistic, sustained by a belief in its own power to help reshape social attitudes.

6

"The Charm of the Defeated": The Early Fiction of Truman Capote and Tennessee Williams

The milestone year 1948 saw not only the germination of the Mattachine Society and the publication of the Kinsey Report and *The City and the Pillar*, but also the appearance of Truman Capote's *Other Voices, Other Rooms* and Tennessee Williams's *One Arm and Other Stories*. If the burden of *The City and the Pillar* was to illustrate the basic "normality" of homosexuality, presenting its protagonist as an ordinary, wholesome young man struggling toward acceptance of his gay identity in a disapproving society, Capote and Williams adopted an altogether different strategy. Rather than insisting on the ordinariness of gay people, the Southern writers reveled in the extraordinariness of their exotic—often freakish—characters. In the gay fictions of Williams and Capote, a wide range of extreme character types—including sissy boys, mannish women, transvestites, "dirty old men," flamboyant queens, and male hustlers—coexist with other unconventional, obviously or obscurely wounded characters in a gallery of the dispossessed. For Williams and Capote, homosexuality is less a social problem than a manifestation of love's essential irrationality. As Cousin Randolph in *Other Voices, Other Rooms* remarks

> "The brain may take advice but not the heart, and love, having no geography, knows no boundaries: weight and sink it deep, no matter, it will rise and find the surface: and why not? Any love is natural and beautiful that lies in a person's nature; only hypocrites would hold a man responsible for what he loves."[1]

The animating theme of the early fiction of Williams and Capote is the universal human need for love, a theme explored most deeply by their fellow Southerner Carson McCullers, whose influence on them is palpable. Though McCullers's works frequently feature gay characters, they are not specifically gay fictions but generalized allegories of love and loneliness in which homosexual yearning is treated with the same dignity and rendered with the same pathos as any other form of love. In the world of Carson McCullers, to be alive is to be spiritually isolated, to be human is to be incomplete. Especially in her two greatest works, her haunting first novel, *The Heart Is a Lonely Hunter* (1940), which features a deeply affecting portrait of a deaf mute's love for a half-witted fellow mute, and *The Ballad of the Sad Cafe* (1943), in which the Amazonian lesbian Miss Amelia unaccountably falls in love with the hunchbacked homosexual dwarf, Cousin Lymon (who is smitten with the uncouth convict Marvin Macy, who in turn loves Miss Amelia), as well as in the flawed Lawrentian anatomy of repression, *Reflections in a Golden Eye* (1941), McCullers uses homosexuality as a symbol of isolation and alienation. But rather than attaching stigma or moral opprobrium to homosexuality, she envelops it within the web of her encompassing sympathy. Like the physical defects, race consciousness, sexual obsessions, or other qualities that separate all her characters from the conventional world, homosexuality in these novels is at one with loneliness.

In McCullers's work, loneliness and isolation result not from homosexuality per se but from the nature of love, which is based not on mutuality of feeling but on a stubborn inequality of emotion. As the narrator of *The Ballad of the Sad Cafe* explains,

> There are the lover and the beloved, but these two come from different countries. Often the beloved is only a stimulus for all the stored-up love which has lain quiet within the lover for a long time hitherto. And somehow every lover knows this. He feels in his soul that his love is a solitary thing. He comes to know a new, strange loneliness and it is this knowledge that makes him suffer. . . . Let it be added here that the lover about whom we are speaking need not necessarily be a young man saving for a wedding ring—this lover can be man, woman, child, or indeed any human creature on this earth. Now the beloved can also be of any description. The most outlandish people can be the stimulus for love.[2]

McCullers's great accomplishment is to evoke enormous compassion for her "outlandish" characters and to make them emblematic of a universal spiritual hunger. If they are finally defeated in their quests, this has less to do with their outlandishness than with the inexplicable economy of love itself.

Truman Capote creates in *Other Voices, Other Rooms* a world of Gothic romance reminiscent of *The Ballad of the Sad Cafe*, but one that lacks the philosophical seriousness and sure vision of McCullers's work. An initiation story, *Other Voices, Other Rooms* chronicles the movement toward acceptance of his homosexual nature by Joel Harrison Knox, a precocious thirteen-year-old "too pretty, too delicate" to be a " 'real' boy." Despite moments of effective magic realism, the novel's hothouse atmosphere, melodramatic plot turns, heavy-handed symbolism, overripe prose, and bizarre characters (nearly all of whom are sexually ambivalent in some way) finally overwhelm its basically simple story. Moreover, its stereotypically negative depiction of homosexuality works against the narrative thread that culminates in Joel's recognition of his gayness. The result is a muddle: the novel's positive theme of progress toward self-knowledge is contradicted by its subliminal message that homosexuality is a retreat from real life into a ghostly death-in-life existence.

In *Other Voices, Other Rooms,* Capote presents homosexuality as simply one among many grotesqueries. Because sexual ambivalence is so prevalent in the novel, even the most extreme manifestation of homosexuality, as epitomized in the person of Cousin Randolph, is made to seem, at first glance anyway, less aberrant than mildly eccentric. Compared with the ancient pygmy servant Jesus Fever, the toothless hermit Little Sunshine, and the midget Miss Wisteria (who is given to fondling young boys), the transvestite Randolph initially appears relatively normal. Soon after arriving at Skully's Landing, where he has come in search of his father, Joel gazes at the upper story of the decrepit mansion in which his father lies paralyzed and notices in the window of one of the other rooms a "queer lady . . . holding aside the curtains . . . smiling and nodding at him, as if in greeting or approval." He eventually learns that the "lady" is actually Randolph, and at the end of the novel, after this initiation into the world of literal and metaphorical freak shows, when the queer woman once again beckons to him from the upper room's window, "he knew that he must go." By following Cousin Randolph's summons, he accepts his place in the mysterious world of Skully's Landing and symbolically accepts his own homosexuality.

But this acceptance is disturbing rather than liberating, for the homosexuality that Joel finally embraces in *Other Voices, Other Rooms* is distinctly unappetizing and utterly unconvincing. As Stephen Adams rightly complains, "The journey, cementing the bond between Joel and Randolph, represents a ceremonious farewell not only to childhood innocence but also to dreams of becoming a man."[3] In the novel, homosexuality is a negation of masculinity, not simply because it involves effeminacy and transvestism but also, and most importantly, because it signifies passive resignation and despair. It is an "ugly room" that represents an escape from reality into the make-believe of Randolph's sentimental and self-indulgent fantasies. Rather than engaging life and challenging or at least defying the world's cruelty, Randolph relishes his victimization.

Capote contrives to make Randolph endearingly vulnerable and he explains his retreat into the death-in-life existence at Skully's Landing in terms that evoke pathos, but the effect is to confirm stereotypical notions of homosexuality as a deeply wounding experience without providing sufficient social context to test such notions or make them credible. For example, in the novel's most quoted passage, Randolph's account of his "doomed" love for Pepe Alvarez, which culminates in the paralysis of Joel's father as well as Randolph's self-imposed exile, homosexuality is unmistakably linked with death and homosexuals are seen merely as victims:

> "It was different this love of mine for Pepe, more intense than anything I felt for Dolores, and lonelier. But we are alone, darling child, terribly, isolated each from the other; so fierce is the world's ridicule we cannot speak or show our tenderness; for us death is stronger than life, it pulls like a wind through the dark, all our cries burlesqued in joyless laughter; and with the garbage of loneliness stuffed down us until our guts burst bleeding green, we go screaming around the world, dying in our rented rooms, nightmare hotels, eternal homes of the transient heart."

In this passage, Capote rings changes on McCullers's great theme of spiritual isolation and loneliness, and he captures the sense of alienation so central to homosexual identity. But unlike McCullers he reduces homosexuality to the status of an affliction and makes a causal connection between homosexuality and the death wish. Randolph's retreat to Skully's Landing is, in effect, a passive and ineffectual act of resignation, a flight from engagement with life, the antithesis of heroism. Thus, in *Other Voices, Other Rooms*, Joel's initiation is a cause more for sadness than for celebration. Joel has left the perplexities of childhood only to embrace Randolph's fearful and tormented life of fantasy.

Like Capote, Tennessee Williams also fills his fiction with grotesque characters and situations, and homosexuality in his work also often reeks of decadence. But Williams's gay fictions are altogether more various and more affirmative than *Other Voices, Other Rooms*. Whereas the youthful Capote's novel is sensationalistic to the point of raising questions as to whether it might not be a parody of Southern Gothic style, the gay fictions of *One Arm and Other Stories* (1948) and *Hard Candy and Other Stories* (1954) are never designed merely to shock, even when they contain undeniably shocking incidents, as in the infamous "Desire and the Black Masseur." Remarkably frank for the late 1940s and early 1950s,[4] these stories present homosexuality straightforwardly and unapologetically, and always seriously. Although they have been described as "sick" fiction,[5] they are actually strong and healthy contributions to the literature of compassion. Williams's gay fiction has attracted relatively little attention, except as

sources or preliminary sketches for his celebrated plays,[6] but the stories of
One Arm and *Hard Candy* are among the most significant gay fictions of
their time.

The title story of the first collection is the beautifully written and moving
tale of Oliver Winemiller, who had been the light heavyweight champion
boxer of the Pacific Fleet before he lost an arm in an automobile accident.
As a result of the mutilation, his life seems meaningless and he self-
destructively drifts into the underworld of male prostitution. One night,
"for no reason that was afterward sure to him,"[7] he murders a wealthy
man who had paid him to perform in a pornographic movie. He is eventually arrested, tried, and sentenced to die in the electric chair. While awaiting execution, he begins to receive letters from his former clients, and he
comes to understand that he has affected others. This realization helps re-
mold his nature and (somewhat cruelly) revives his interest in life. The day
before his execution, he is visited by a young Lutheran minister, whom
he attempts to seduce, hoping to repay the debt of feelings that he owes.
The minister flees the cell in horror, and Ollie goes to the electric chair
incomplete and unfulfilled, but desperately grasping the letters in the fork
of his thighs.

At the heart of "One Arm" is the transformation of Ollie from a cold
and detached icon of others' longing—a marmoreal figure who sleepwalks
through life, indifferently stirring the passionate imagination of others but
feeling nothing himself—into a fully responsive human being. As the story
opens, he is described as looking like "a broken statue of Apollo"; he has
"the coolness and impassivity of a stone figure." His mutilation left him a
psychic as well as a physical cripple, who cares for no one, least of all
himself. Once an athlete "wholly adequate to the physical world he grew
into," Ollie came to regard his splendid body as merely a commodity to be
bartered in a sexual exchange that had no meaning for him. By the end of
the story, however, he not only comes to understand the passion that he had
excited in others, but also to feel that passion himself. As he tells the minister, "For three whole years I went all over the country stirring up feelings
without feeling nothing myself. Now that's all changed and I have feelings,
too. I am lonely and bottled up the same as you are."

The instruments of Ollie's transformation are the letters that pour in from
across the country when his picture appears in newspapers in connection
with his trial and sentence. These messages from the men who had known
him as he plied his trade during his years of nomadic existence

> made allusions to the nights which he had spent with them, or the few hours
> which they almost invariably pronounced to be the richest of their entire expe-
> rience. There was something about him, they wrote, not only the physical
> thing, important as that was, which made him haunt their minds since.

What touched them so deeply about the large blond, one-armed ex-boxer was "the charm of the defeated," a wounded quality that only rarely co-exists with beauty and vitality. They glimpsed beneath the detachment and remoteness of the "unforgettable youth" to see a spiritual purity and inno-cence. For them, Oliver became a kind of secular saint, absolving them of guilt and soothing their sorrows.

At first these letters infuriate Ollie, but then they become his connection with the outside world of experience and interchange with others. He sleeps with them beneath his pillow and he finally begins to answer them in labo-rious but crudely eloquent and heartfelt replies. These responses are a des-perate attempt to discover meaning in his life and to establish communion with others. His sexual contacts "only meant money to me and a place to shack up for the night and liquor and food," he explains to his correspon-dents. "I never thought it could mean very much to them. Now all of these letters like yours have proven it did. I meant something very important to hundreds of people whose faces and names had slipped clean out of my mind as soon as I left them." He regrets that he treated some of his clients badly, and reflects that "If I had known then, I mean when I was outside, that such true feelings could even be found in strangers, I mean of the kind that I picked up for a living, I guess that I might have felt there was more to live for." Ironically, he comes to value himself and life just as he must face death.

The dramatic center of the story is the encounter with the young minister. A familiar character type in Williams's plays and stories, the minister is torn between the cavalier and puritan elements of his personality, between his strong but scarcely acknowledged sexual longings and his equally potent religious repression of those desires. Tellingly, he suffers "A little func-tional trouble of the heart," an affliction that has more to do with emo-tional than with physical problems. Drawn by the "virile but tender beauty" of Oliver's face in a newspaper photograph that contradicts the accompanying story of his violent behavior, the minister feels compelled by "an outside power" to offer the youth spiritual guidance. Although Oliver has refused to see the prison chaplain, the minister convinces the warden that his mission is divinely inspired.

But at his first glance at the prisoner's nearly nude body, the minister recalls a golden panther that he had been obsessed with in his adolescence and that had been the subject of deeply shameful erotic dreams. He sees in the condemned prisoner "the look of the golden panther again, the inno-cence in the danger," and the nature of his attraction to Oliver becomes obvious to us if not to himself. Although convinced that his compulsion to visit Oliver is supernatural, the minister is actually driven by sexual desire. He responds to "the charm of the defeated" even as he senses its danger to his own self-conception. Suffering from palpitations of his heart, torn between unfathomable desire and fearful guilt, the minister clumsily attempts to offer spiritual consolation, finally telling the skeptical youth, "Don't think of me as a man, but as a connection! . . . A wire that is plugged in your heart and charged with a message from God."

Although Oliver rejects the putative message from God, he does regard the minister as a "connection" even as he also thinks of him as a man. He attempts to seduce him as a means of establishing communion with the hundreds of men who had reached out to him with their feelings—which he now understands and shares. As he wipes the sweat from Oliver's perfectly formed body, and as Oliver seductively exposes his sculptural flanks, the minister panics in the face of temptation. Oliver recognizes the minister's repressed homosexuality, telling him, "I know your type. Everything is artistic or else it's religious, but that's all a bunch of bullshit and I don't buy it. All that you need's to be given a push on the head!" But just as Oliver is about to give that push, the minister calls out for the guard, who has to half carry him down the corridor.

Thus, Oliver dies "with all of his debts unpaid." The awakening of his emotional life is cruel, having come too late and in unpropitious circumstances to be acted upon. But the youth is comforted by the hundreds of letters that testify to his humanity, to the fact that his life has had meaning and significance. In his final hours, he reads the letters over and over, and he carries them with him into the death chamber "as a child takes a doll or a toy into a dentist's office to give the protection of the familiar and loved." Comforted by the fact that he has unknowingly affected the lives of others, he faces his death with surprising dignity.

It is no coincidence that Oliver's final visitor is a minister, for the story is permeated with religious imagery and allusions. For some of his correspondents, Oliver is said to have had "the curtained and abstract quality of the priest who listens without being visible to confessions of guilt." For others, "he became the archetype of the Saviour Upon The Cross who had taken upon himself the sins of their world to be washed and purified in his blood and passion." The beauty of his face in the newspaper photograph that so moves the minister is described as "of the sort that some painter of the Renaissance might have slyly attributed to a juvenile saint." As he replies to the letters, his brain "grew warmer and warmer with a sense of communion"; and Williams adds: "Coming prior to disaster, this change might have been a salvation." When autoerotic sensations bloom in him and he comes to share the passionate hunger of his former partners, the narrator comments: "Too late, this resurrection." The function of the religious imagery and allusions is to juxtapose conventional Christian belief, as embodied most fully in the self-denying minister, with a pagan humanism of which Oliver becomes exemplar, priest, and saint.

In contrast to the repression and denial of Christianity, the rites of this more primitive counterreligion are frankly sexual, for sexuality is the means of communion with others and of transcendence. In this theology, *agape* and Eros are not opposed but complementary. The "rainbows of the flesh" enable one to transcend the mundane world and to escape the prison of the self. They constitute an assertion of life in the face of death. Salvation and resurrection are not experiences to be savored after death but mysteries made possible in life through sexual sharing. Earthly existence is not "just a threshold to something Immense beyond," as the minister claims, but an opportunity to fulfill the spirit through the body. The point of the story is to celebrate the spiritual potential of ecstatic sexuality, and in doing so Oliver's awakened homosexuality is presented as salvific, an avenue for connection with others and a vehicle for transcendence. Among the many ironies of the story is that the minister, who is as painfully unfulfilled and as desperately in need of communion as Oliver, rejects the offer of grace and salvation implicit in the sexual overture.

Because of the minister's timidity and fearfulness, Oliver is denied the communion that he sought in his final days. Donated to a medical school, his body is dissected. "It seemed intended," Williams writes, "for some more august purpose, to stand in a gallery of antique sculpture, touched only by light through stillness and contemplation, for it had the nobility of some broken Apollo that no one was likely to carve so purely again." The story's rejection of the Christian doctrines that devalue earthly life in favor of a heavenly afterlife is made clear in the final sentence: "But death has never been much in the way of completion." The pathos of the story is rooted in the sad irony that Oliver's resurrection comes too late, yet the value of his salvation can be measured in the contrast between his description as a "broken Apollo" at the beginning and the end of the story. Initially, the epithet signifies his mutilation and coldness; ultimately, it emphasizes his pagan spirit and nobility. Central to this metamorphosis of signification in which Apollo is translated from a cold stone figure to a pagan god worthy of veneration is Oliver's altered regard of his sexuality.

"One Arm" is a compelling narrative, simply and straightforwardly told, but rich with suggestiveness. Crucial to the story's success is the portrait of Oliver Winemiller. One of Williams's "fugitive kind," Oliver awakens to the value of his life only when he is about to be deprived of it. But the heroism of his struggle gains him dignity and genuine pathos, particularly in contrast to the denials and rejections of the minister, who is unable to face the truth of his deepest nature and who is therefore far more crippled than Oliver. Its painful ironies notwithstanding, "One Arm" celebrates the power of sexuality—quite specifically including homosexuality—to express the spiritual and thereby to invest life with meaning.

The relationship of religion and sexuality is also explored in "Desire and the Black Masseur," Williams's most notorious short fiction. The story traces the history of Anthony Burns, a timorous, childlike little man who had from his beginnings "betrayed an instinct for being included in things that swallowed him up,"[8] and his involvement with a giant black masseur whom he meets in a bathhouse. Through his encounter with the masseur, Burns discovers his masochism: "The knowledge grew quickly between them of what Burns wanted, that he was in search of atonement, and the black masseur was the natural instrument of it." The beatings that the giant administers steadily increase in severity. During a session in which the masseur breaks Burns's leg and he is unable to stifle his outcry, their relationship is exposed, and the two men are expelled from the bathhouse. They continue their perverse communion in the masseur's quarters in the town's black section. During the Lenten season, against the backdrop of a neighboring church's religious frenzy, while the pastor exhorts his flock to suffer as Christ suffered, Burns is finally beaten to death by his lover and his body actually consumed. The masseur disposes of Burns's bones and moves to another city, where he patiently waits for another customer.

Although "Desire and the Black Masseur" has been severely attacked as a morbid and repulsive story,[9] it might be better seen as a seriously comic parable of socially and religiously induced guilt, a kind of macabre joke in which theological doctrines are parodied and the symbolic is reduced to the literal. The very extremism of the story indicates that it is not meant to be taken literally, though, paradoxically, the excesses actually result from a relentless literalism pursued to logical extremes—as when the early allusions to Burns's pleasure at being metaphorically swallowed up culminate in his being literally devoured. The account of Burns's discovery of masochistic pleasure is credible enough. After his surprise orgasm in the bathhouse, "when the little man grew more and more fiercely hot with his first true satisfaction," he and the masseur develop a symbiotic relationship: "The giant loved Burns, and Burns adored the giant." But as it proceeds to its logical conclusion of death and cannibalism, the story soon translates the sadomasochistic relationship onto a symbolic plane. That is, the story's relentless literalism actually facilitates its allegorical dimension even as it also functions to parody conventional religious symbolism. As the religious implications of the story become obvious, the horrific alliance between Anthony Burns and the black masseur is elevated to the plane of allegory, while the traditional religious doctrines of sacrifice and atonement are reduced to an absurdity.

"Desire and the Black Masseur" is, finally, less about the sadomasochistic attraction of Burns and the giant masseur than it is about human nature itself. What motivates Anthony Burns is his massive conviction of incompletion and imperfection, a conviction that he shares with everyone else, for it is basic to the human condition. But whereas this sense of incompletion is in most people "covered up or glossed over by some kind of makeshift arrangement" or expressed in art or in some form of socially sanctioned violence, such as war, Burns finds consolation in "the principle of atonement, the surrender of self to violent treatment by others with the idea of thereby clearing one's self of his guilt." In the black masseur, who "hated white bodies because they abused his pride," Burns finds his means of atonement. But their sadomasochistic ritual that culminates in cannibalism is finally revealed as a grim parody of the Christian communion, in which the body and blood of Christ are ingested as a symbol of at-one-ment with God, just as their Lenten passion recapitulates Christ's Passion.

The story is not simply the bizarre case history of an extreme masochist, but an allegory of the effects of guilt and feelings of unworthiness. It focuses on a perverse case history in order to make a larger point about human nature and sexuality and how they are manipulated by religious and social forces. Precisely because human pride is so often assaulted and wounded, people are driven to seek some sense of completion. While this need to compensate for the feeling of incompletion may have some beneficial results, it most frequently leads to violence and suffering. Christianity in the story is figured both as an expression of human inadequacy and a contributor to it, for in its doctrines of original sin and sacrificial redemption it has capitalized on the sense of imperfection innate to the human condition. "The sins of the world," Williams writes, "are really only its impartialities, its incompletions, and these are what sufferings must atone for." The analogy that the story makes between Burns's passion and the "fiery poem of the death on the cross" that so stirs the congregation in the church across the street from the death chamber is intended to place both the sadomasochistic ceremony and the doctrine of atonement in perspective as extreme expressions of a basic need rooted in human inadequacy.

The imperfection of humanity is a fact of existence that haunts the story. Suffering and violence are seen as "compensations for that which is not yet formed in human nature." The implication, of course, is that humankind might be evolving toward completion, that some "vast image out of *Spiritus Mundi*" is slouching toward Bethlehem to be born.[10] This evolutionary ethos is intimated in the conclusion, as the black masseur impassively awaits another client:

And meantime, slowly, with barely a thought of so doing, the earth's whole population twisted and writhed beneath the manipulation of night's black fingers and the white ones of day with skeletons splintered and flesh reduced to pulp, as out of this unlikely problem, the answer, perfection, was slowly evolved through torture.

In this view, the world is a massive torture chamber, a universe designed by the Marquis de Sade, as Edith Jelkes describes it in "The Night of the Iguana"; and the violent ceremony enacted by Anthony Burns and the masseur is symbolic of a universal process of guilt and atonement. But, unlikely as it may seem, the sufferings of the world may finally yield universal perfection, a vision that is itself a parody of Christian millenarianism.

"Desire and the Black Masseur" is less a gay fiction than a dark parable about human nature. Its concerns are more metaphysical than sexual. But it is noteworthy that the ritualized relationship of Anthony Burns and his black lover is presented straightforwardly as a paradigm of universal human desire, a sexual theater that enacts an ancient and continuing drama of guilt and expiation. Burns and the masseur are psychically wounded characters, but they are different from their fellows in degree, not in kind. Williams uses the strange bond between the two men as a stark mirror that exaggerates but does not distort the human condition itself, torn between sensual and spiritual impulses and desperately attempting to reconcile them. From this perspective, the sadomasochistic ceremony is less grotesque than an extreme reflection of modern man's intractable guilt and self-hatred. The mordant comedy of the story derives, in part, from Williams's use of a perverse homosexual relationship—so stigmatized by Christian moralists— as a symbol of universal atonement.

"Desire and the Black Masseur" is, as Benjamin Nelson notes, "masterfully wrought."[11] A stunning account of the effects of guilt on fragmented man, the story is a dark comedy that slyly satirizes Christianity and that boldly sketches a world wallowing in its own pain and suffering. It embodies that "Sense of the Awful" that Williams detected in McCullers's *Reflections in a Golden Eye* and described as "the desperate black root of nearly all significant modern art, from the *Guernica* of Picasso to the cartoons of Charles Addams."[12]

Two other stories in *One Arm* feature homosexuals prominently: "The Angel in the Alcove" and "The Night of the Iguana." "The Angel in the Alcove" is a loose, anecdotal account of a struggling writer's precarious existence in a New Orleans rooming house populated by a suspicious landlady and her deadbeat tenants, whom she denounces as "A bunch of rotten half breeds and drunks an' degenerates."[13] At its center is the homosexual encounter between the writer and a tubercular artist, witnessed and countenanced by a maternal apparition that appears in the alcove of the writer's attic room, a "tender and melancholy figure of an angel or some dim, elderly madonna." The homosexual incident functions as both a measure of the artist's desperate need for human contact and an emblem of the writer's compassionate acceptance. The force of the story is not to justify homosexuality but to condemn cruelty. Yet inasmuch as the work clearly contrasts the writer's acquiescence and the landlady's condemnation, it voices a defense of homosexuality—albeit one couched in negative terms. Love, even in the form of the artist's frantic "perversions of longing," is preferable to cruelty. Despite its slightness, "The Angel in the Alcove"—in its abhorrence of willful cruelty and its compassion for the wounded and the out-cast—states themes that are at the heart of Williams's vision.

"The Night of the Iguana" is the story of Miss Edith Jelkes, a thirty-year-old spinster artist recovering from a nervous breakdown at the Costa Verde, a resort hotel near Acapulco, and her siege of her fellow guests, two gay writers. Annoyed by the men's indifference to her, Miss Jelkes contrives to attract their attention in various ways, but succeeds only in making a fool of herself. When the son of the *patrona* captures an iguana and fastens it to the base of a column near Miss Jelkes's room, she rushes to the men to complain of the noise of the suffering animal and the cruelty of the Mexican boy. Using the iguana as a pretext, she moves into a room next to the writers' accommodations, "excitingly aware . . . that this would put her within close range of their nightly conversations, the mystery of which had tantalized her for weeks. Now she would be able to hear every word that passed between them unless they actually whispered in each other's ear!"[14] The next morning she overhears the two men making fun of her as they lie in bed together, and she confronts them. The younger of the writers accuses her of spying on them, but the older treats her more kindly. As a ferocious storm strikes, Miss Jelkes attempts to seduce the older man, then resists him when he responds by violently attempting to make love to her. He fails to achieve penetration but ejaculates on her stomach. Their erotic tussle interrupted by the return of the younger writer, she flees to her old room, discovers that the iguana has been released, and happily falls asleep, feeling the writer's sticky ejaculate that adhered "to the flesh of her belly as a light but persistent kiss."

"The Night of the Iguana" focuses on the difficulties of Miss Jelkes in coming to terms with life. Like many characters in Williams's stories and plays, she is torn between sensuality and repression. Her background is telling: "She belonged to an historical Southern family of great but now moribund vitality whose latter generations had tended to split into two antithetical types, one in which the libido was pathologically distended and another in which it would seem to be all but dried up." She herself is "not strictly one or the other of the two basic types, which made it all the more difficult for her to cultivate any interior poise." She is outwardly "such a dainty tea-pot that no one would guess that she could actually boil." In the story, she is at a crossroads in her life, terrified by the possible return of the neurasthenia that she has suffered in the past, baffled by the indifference of the men toward her, hungry for experience and desperate to attract the attentions of others, but frightened by sexuality. "Perhaps some day she would come out on a kind of triumphant plateau as an artist or as a person or even perhaps as both," Williams writes near the beginning of the story.

By the end of the tale it is clear that Miss Jelkes has triumphed in a way, and that the instruments of her triumph have been the gay lovers. The rope that binds the iguana—which represents her natural instincts that have been

reined in by repression—is cut, probably by the sensual younger writer, and
the animal scrambles into the bushes. As she drifts off to sleep after her
erotic encounter with the older writer, she thinks of the iguana and draws
the analogy between its release and her own: "And she was grateful, too,
for in some equally mysterious way the strangling rope of her loneliness
had also been severed by what had happened on this barren rock above the
moaning rivers." The "fierce little comedy" of sexuality that she enacts
with the writer is, by all reasonable standards, a dismal failure. Her "demon of virginity" fights off the man "more furiously than he attacked
her," and he is left sobbing as she flees the room, bearing the residue of his
semen. But as she lies in bed and touches the ejaculate with her fingers, she
reacts in an uncharacteristic way, signifying the change that has occurred:

> Her fingers approached it timidly. They expected to draw back with revulsion
> but were not so affected. They touched it curiously and even pityingly and did
> not draw back for a while. *Ah, Life,* she thought to herself and was about to
> smile at the originality of this thought when darkness lapped over the outward
> gaze of her mind.

But although the story ends with the triumph of Miss Jelkes, it also invests that triumph with considerable irony and implies that it may prove a
pyrrhic victory. She seems to have come to terms with life sufficiently to
transcend her squeamishness and accept with equanimity sexual facts that
she previously would have found repulsive, but she nevertheless remains a
virgin and, more significantly, she remains divided within, still not having
achieved interior poise. Her victory seems to consist chiefly in having broken down the older writer's indifference toward her and in proving that she
can arouse the sexual interest of even so difficult a challenge as a homosexual. The irony of her self-satisfaction at the end of the story arises from
the fact that she, who is "so humane and gentle by nature that even the
sufferings of a lizard could hurt her," is oblivious to the pain of her would-
be lover, who is left weeping and broken after the violent sexual encounter
that she initiated. For all her apparent delicacy of thought and feeling, Miss
Jelkes is remarkably insensitive. Moreover, in her self-absorption she fails
to respect the integrity of others, most notably the gay lovers.

The lovers in the story are sketchily presented, but it seems clear that
theirs is a turbulent relationship and that they both suffer sexual conflicts.
The younger writer has recently separated from his wife, and "Miss Jelkes
received the impression that he was terribly concerned over some problem
which the older man was trying to iron out for him." They seem to be
engaged in a perpetual argument, and their interactions suggest that they
enact the roles of a troubled youth and wise counselor. But if the older man
poses as wise counselor to the younger, there is reason to believe that he

suffers troubles of his own. This suspicion is verified when Miss Jelkes sees him without his dark glasses and notices that "his face looked older and the eyes, which she had not seen before, had a look that often goes with incurable illness." But the incurable "illness" from which the writer suffers is not a physical disease but homosexuality. He is unhappy with his sexual orientation and is as disturbed about sexuality as Miss Jelkes, though in a different way.

She intuits the writer's sexual disturbance when his unattractive but distinctive face reminds her of "a small chimpanzee she had once seen in the corner of his cage at a zoo, just sitting there staring between the bars, while all his fellows were hopping and spinning about on their noisy iron trapeze." Moved by the solitary chimpanzee's isolation and sadness, she had rushed off to buy him some peanuts, but when she returned to the cage, she discovered that the chimp had succumbed to the general impulse and joined the others on the trapeze, and now "not a one of them seemed a bit different from the others." The similarity that she perceives between the writer and the chimpanzee suggests that Miss Jelkes may be attracted to the writer both because of his apartness as a homosexual and because she subconsciously responds to the challenge of changing his sexual orientation. But this project is an exercise doomed to frustration, for if the writer becomes, like the chimpanzee, no different from the others, then the source of her attraction—which is rooted in her own ambivalence toward sexuality—will be destroyed. This process is the obverse of the privileging of heterosexuality by the gay characters of *The City and the Pillar,* whose yearning for love from heterosexual men is necessarily disappointed, for should the love be returned, the love object would then no longer be heterosexual.

That Miss Jelkes is subconsciously seeking to change the older writer's sexual orientation is clear in the seduction scene. She asks him whether the younger man is the right person for him. When he replies, "Mike is helpless and I am always attracted by helpless people," she then asks, "How about you? Don't you need somebody's help?" and then initiates the seduction. In effect, she offers herself as a means to help "cure" the writer's homosexuality, his "incurable illness." But Miss Jelkes's ambivalence about sexuality, and about the very sexual attraction that she so desperately needs to stir in the writer, is evident when he responds and she fiercely fights to preserve her much-vaunted virginity. Or rather, "Not she herself . . . but some demon of virginity that occupied her flesh fought off the assailant more furiously than he attacked her." What Miss Jelkes wants, of course, is not sex, but to be sexually desired. Hence, even as she needs to arouse the sexual ardor of the writer, she equally—and perhaps more fundamentally—needs to preserve her virginity.

In the sexual struggle, the writer's willed heterosexuality proves weaker than Miss Jelkes's "demon of virginity." His assault on Miss Jelkes is like the "giant white bird" of a storm that rages in the background, "lunging up and down on its terrestrial quarry," full of sound and fury, but finally signifying nothing. What Williams says of the storm is true of the writer's sexual huffing and puffing as well: "there is something frustrate in the attack. . . . It seemed to be one that came from a thwarted will. Otherwise surely the frame structure would have been smashed." For all the sudden violence that characterizes the attempt at lovemaking, it is half-hearted, defeated not only by the demon of virginity but by its own failure of desire. The writer's attempted rape is a kind of parody of Zeus's rape of Leda in the guise of a swan; but whereas the rape of Leda, at least in Yeats's "Leda and the Swan," may engender knowledge and power, the writer's attempted assault yields results even more ambiguous. Miss Jelkes achieves her goal of arousing him while preserving her virginity, but her victory is tarnished and severely limited, for it may have seriously harmed her momentary, if insufficiently ardent, lover and it leaves her as isolated and internally divided as ever.

In "The Night of the Iguana" the homosexual is both the sensual figure who severs "the strangling rope" of Miss Jelkes's loneliness and the challenge to her powers of attraction. From one perspective, the story identifies homosexuality with sexual inadequacy, for the writer's desire for Miss Jelkes is clearly insufficient to overcome her "demon of virginity," her own deep-seated sexual ambivalence. But from another, it may be seen as a powerful force that resists the willful attempts to alter it. Sexuality in the story is recognized as fluid and potentially malleable, but it is nevertheless deeply rooted in the psyche and resistant to casual manipulation. It is not "curable." While the writer is left weeping at the end of the story, clearly victimized by Miss Jelkes's apparent triumph, what may be destroyed is not necessarily himself, but only his dream of heterosexuality, his hope of being not a bit different from the other chimpanzees on the trapeze. In this view, his integrity remains intact, and the appearance of his lover at the end of the story, as Miss Jelkes slips away (realizing that "*I don't belong here*"), may signal hope for the two men's sexual adjustment. In any case, the irony of "The Night of the Iguana" redounds not on the older writer's sexual failure, but on Miss Jelkes and her ostensible victory.

In *Hard Candy and Other Stories*, Williams includes three gay fictions, "The Mysteries of the Joy Rio," "Hard Candy," and "Two on a Party." These tales embody the same values of compassion as those of *One Arm*, and they too focus on defeated individuals struggling against loneliness and isolation. Obsessed with time and death, the stories of *Hard Candy* are particularly interesting for their depictions of gay cruising rituals in a repressive preliberation era. The hunt in "Two on a Party" is wittily but hollowly romanticized as the pursuit of "the lyric quarry," while "The

Mysteries of the Joy Rio" and "Hard Candy" are concerned with "fleeting and furtive practices in dark places." But in all three stories, the attempt to make contact with others is depicted as a fundamentally human need, however pathetic or self-destructive its form might take. Williams's achievement in these stories is to invest "the sordid with the meaningful, even with a touch of the transcendent or compensatory."[15]

"The Mysteries of the Joy Rio" is the story of Pablo Gonzales, a watch repairer, who has inherited his tiny shop from "a very strange and fat man" named Emil Kroger, who had fallen in love with the graceful young Pablo and then died a slow and painful death.[16] Pablo has not only inherited the material possessions of his benefactor, but also Kroger's sound advice to take care when cruising the Joy Rio, a sadly derelict, third-rate movie theater that specializes in Westerns and other films "of the sort that have a special appeal to children and male adolescents." "Sometimes you will find it and other times you won't find it," Kroger has instructed him about the search for the alleviation of loneliness, "and the times you don't find it are the times when you have to be careful."

Soon after Kroger's death, Pablo loses his slim figure and youthful beauty, putting on weight "as a widow puts on dark garments." Now, twenty years later, after he has learned of his own approaching death from the same disease that killed his lover and after he has shrunk to an approximation of his former youthful grace, Gonzales pays a customary visit to the infamous theater. He unintentionally interrupts an usher in the midst of a tryst with his girlfriend, and then flees into the roped-off upper recesses of the Joy Rio. There Gonzales sees a dim figure beckoning him still further upward and calling him by the name of his youth, Pablo. He sinks into a seat in one of the boxes on the topmost tier and Kroger's ghost caresses him and whispers his old litany of advice: "don't ever be so afraid of being lonely that you forget to be careful. . . . Sometimes you will have it and sometimes you won't have it, so don't be anxious about it." As the ghost repeats the lecture, Gonzales "drifted away from everything but the wise old voice in his ear, even at last from that, but not till he was entirely comforted by it."

Despite its tawdry setting, "The Mysteries of the Joy Rio" is actually an extraordinarily moving love story. The unlikely relationship of Emil Kroger and Pablo Gonzales survives illness, death, bereavement, and loneliness finally to triumph in the fantastic conclusion. After years of searching for love in the dark glory of the Joy Rio's upper balconies, Kroger discovered young Pablo during a watchmaker's convention in Dallas. The fat older man experiences considerable anxiety about whether he can keep his beautiful young protégé, not realizing that "the incalculably precious bird flown into his nest was not one of sudden passage but rather the kind that prefers to keep a faithful commitment to a single place, the nest-building kind, and not only that, but the very-rare-indeed-kind that gives love back as generously as he takes it." During his illness, Kroger confesses his entire life to Pablo:

> It was his theory, the theory of most immoralists, that the soul becomes entirely burdened with lies that have to be told to the world in order to be permitted to live in the world, and that unless this burden is relieved by entire honesty with *some one* person, who is trusted and adored, the soul will finally collapse beneath its weight of falsity.

This truth-telling not only relieves Kroger, but it inspires in Pablo a matching ardor. Twenty years after Kroger's death, Pablo still loves him:

> If in his waking hours somebody to whom he would have to give a true answer had enquired of him, Pablo Gonzales, how much do you think about the dead Mr. Kroger, he probably would have shrugged and said, *Not much now. It's such a long time ago.* But if the question were asked him while he slept, the guileless heart of the sleeper would have responded, *Always, always!*

Pablo's love for Kroger prompts his grotesque exchange of personalities with his dead friend. Although he never becomes as obese as Kroger, he matures into a nondescript "plump and moonfaced little man" and soon adopts his friend's cruising routine at the Joy Rio, pursuing "a pleasure which was almost as unreal and basically unsatisfactory as an embrace in a dream." He comes to appreciate the practical wisdom of Kroger's advice as he searches for that one special person to whom he can be totally honest and yet be loved for who he is and not what he pretends to be. But if his life follows the basic pattern of his benefactor's, it differs in one significant respect: by the time he develops his friend's fatal disease, he has not yet found his own Pablo; instead, he is mired in the unfulfilling pattern, fraught with danger and guilt, that characterized Kroger's life before he met Pablo. In the fantastic conclusion, however, Gonzales returns to the persona of his youth, and he encounters in the ghost of his patron the same adoring and protective spirit that has sustained him throughout his life. He recognizes in Kroger that trusted and adored "*one* person" that Kroger had discovered in him twenty years previously.

"The Mysteries of the Joy Rio" is, to some extent, vitiated by its Gothic elements, which tend to undermine the tale's muted social protest and to emphasize the macabre and the grotesque. Nevertheless, the story is deeply affecting, primarily because its Gothicism does not entirely displace its rooting in a recognizable social reality. The social context is implicit in Kroger's complaint about the mendacity and hypocrisy necessary to live in the world, in the desperation that can transform the Dante-esque Joy Rio into Pablo Gonzales's "earthly heaven," in the randy usher's illiterate abuse—"morphodite," he sputters at Gonzales—when he is interrupted in his own furtive encounter, and in the fearfulness that marks Kroger's "romantically practical" litany of advice. This ancient lesson, repeated over and over "like a penitent counting prayer beads," romanticizes the brief and frantic liaisons in the Joy Rio as a quest for love, yet it also realistically recognizes the dangers in such activity and cautiously recommends the practice of stoic endurance. In "The Mysteries of the Joy Rio," homosexuals are depicted not simply as obsessive creatures of the night, but also as victims of a repressive and hypocritical society.

It is as a study of grief and loneliness that "The Mysteries of the Joy Rio" is most effective. The very success of Pablo's youthful alliance with Kroger makes his need for solace all the greater. Despite the repeated disappointments of the quest, the need for love persists. "You must always be able to go home alone without it," Kroger tells Pablo, for there will always be other opportunities to discover in the arid plain of the Joy Rio's dismal landscape "the solitary palm tree and its shadow and the spring beside it." Painfully alone after Kroger's death, Gonzales nevertheless continues the search. Fantastically, miraculously, his relentless pursuit is rewarded on his final pilgrimage, when he is soothed by the moist hot tremulous fingers and the wise old voice of Emil Kroger. A Gothic love story that celebrates domestic virtues even as it explores a subterranean world of furtive sexuality, "The Mysteries of the Joy Rio" captures the terrible pathos of human isolation and depicts the relationship of the unlikely lovers with surprising dignity.

"Hard Candy" is a later version of "The Mysteries of the Joy Rio."[17] In this tale, Williams dispenses with the Gothicism, but retains the setting of the disreputable movie theater and also concludes with the death of his protagonist. The story focuses on a seventy-year-old retired merchant named Mr. Krupper. Outwardly respectable but despised by his family—a group of unimaginative distant cousins—Krupper appears to be an ordinary old man. But the most vital part of his life is the secret part, finally revealed as his adventures in the upper balconies of the Joy Rio, where he uses hard candy from his cousins' sweetshop and a fistful of quarters to entice needy youths. On this particular occasion, he discovers in his box a beautiful young man who had wandered into the theater for no other reason than to catch a few hours' sleep. The youth accepts first the candy and then the coins, sealing the contract between them. Later that night, when the lights of the Joy Rio are brought up for the last time, Krupper's body is discovered. His ponderous frame wedged between two seats, he is on his knees, "as if he had expired in an attitude of prayer."[18]

"Hard Candy" is especially distinguished by its masterful narrative control, as it uncovers the hidden life of a "terrible old man," following him from the sweetshop to his final adventure in the Joy Rio. The sly indirection of the narrative, with its accumulation of apparently irrelevant details and the long delay before the central incident is introduced, functions to place the revelations of Krupper's secret predilections in context, and thereby to soften them in the way that sensational incidents in a life are qualified by the hundreds of other details that make up a long existence. "When I say that there was a certain mystery in the life of Mr. Krupper," Williams writes, "I am beginning to approach those things in the only way possible without a head-on violence that would disgust and destroy and which would actually falsify the story." Thus, although Williams maintains a detached irony toward Krupper, presenting him as a vaguely distasteful exhibit in a freak show, his narrative control makes possible the arousal of considerable sympathy for the old man, even as the mysteries of his nature are "made unpleasantly manifest to us."

Central to the story is the notion of mystery, though here the term signifies not the quasi-religious romanticism of the earlier version but the life below the life. The story is propelled by its awareness of the existence of subterranean and dark currents of character concealed behind masks of respectability. Despite his placid appearance, Mr. Krupper is not one of "the nice old men, the sweet old men and the clean old men of the world." He is "a bird of a different feather," the living embodiment of why children are cautioned not to take candy from strangers. But as Williams depicts him, he is no monster. More pathetic than threatening, he is a lonely creature as vulnerable as the youths he preys upon. Indeed, the unsavory old man rises to something of the heroic in his courtship of the beautiful young man, reminding himself to exercise control and not to hurry, "there's plenty of time, he's not going to go up in smoke like the dream that he looks!" Fully aware that he is "shameful and despicable even to those who tolerate his caresses, perhaps even more so to those than to the others who only see him," Krupper nevertheless pursues his quarry with steadfast determination. It is impossible not to admire his persistence or to wish him success.

Williams's great achievement in "Hard Candy" is to humanize a character who could easily be sensationalized or caricatured. Without sentimentalizing the activities in the Joy Rio, as he did in the earlier version of the story, Williams depicts the old man's adventures as far more exciting than anything in his outward life. In the process, Williams captures the thrill of the chase, conveying the cruising ritual as an engagement with life. As he shuffles away from the sweetshop, through the park filled with other old men fearfully preoccupied with death and terrified of change, Krupper comes alive and quickens his pace. As the narrator follows him to the Joy Rio, he chronicles the alterations that take place in the elderly protagonist, from the increasing attitude of expectancy that he exhibits as he boards the streetcar, through the "silly, squeamish kind of dissimulation" he practices by embarking from the streetcar a block away from his destination, to the heart-throbbing delight he feels when he lights a match and discovers the young man in his box:

> And then his heart, aged seventy and already strained from the recent exertion of the stairs, undergoes an alarming spasm, for never in this secret life of his, never in thirty years' attendance of matinees at the Joy Rio, has old Mr. Krupper discovered beside him, even now within contact, inspiring the dark with its warm animal fragrance, any dark youth of remotely equivalent beauty.

In the passage just quoted, and in several others, Williams nicely prepares for the dénouement in which Krupper dies of a heart attack, apparently—and appropriately—while fellating the beautiful youth. The old man's death is clearly from natural causes, but the poetic justice that allows him to die at the moment of his greatest conquest may imply a benevolence that extends even to "dirty old men" of heroic perseverance. The death is comic, as emphasized in the sentimental obituary and in the double entendre of the title and of the little cousin's exclamation, *"Just think, Papa, the old man choked to death on our hard candy!"* Yet the conclusion is more than merely comic, for in the angelic youth Krupper is rewarded with a more tangible manifestation of the gentle ghost that soothed Pablo Gonzales's final moments. Moreover, the death helps place in perspective Krupper's secret adventures as a heroic defiance of old age and the approach of death. Unlike the aimless existence of the other old men glimpsed in the story—who seem to be passively waiting for death—Krupper at least has maintained a stubborn commitment to life.

A lonely man, alienated from his meager family and apparently locked into a tepid and colorless routine, Krupper has led a divided life, his outward respectability cloaking a sordid half-life of dissoluteness. Despite the fact that his death is "given unusual prominence for the obituary of someone who had no public character and whose private character was so peculiarly low," his hidden life is never exposed. His secret remains alive only in the memories of those "anonymous persons who had enjoyed or profited from his company in the tiny box at the Joy Rio." Yet even this pathetic figure partakes of the charm of the defeated. For in sketching those adventures that "gave Mr. Krupper the certain air he had of being engaged in something far more momentous than the ordinary meanderings of an old man retired from business and without close family ties," Williams reveals the sad mysteries of the Joy Rio as the source of the old man's vitality. Like the heroes of the cowboy movies that blare from the silver screen as he performs his secret rites, Krupper fittingly dies in the saddle, with his boots on.

"Hard Candy" is not as affecting as "The Mysteries of the Joy Rio," but it is a greater artistic accomplishment. Narrated with superb control, "Hard Candy" avoids the sentimentality and Gothic trappings of the earlier story. Whereas the earlier tale tends to romanticize the mysteries of the Joy Rio, finding a strange beauty in the derelict theater and its sordid activities, and presenting it as a kind of cathedral of decadence, the later one strikes a more credible balance between romanticism and naturalism, depicting the theater and its denizens more realistically even as it also presents them with carefully controlled sympathy. The harder edge of "Hard Candy"—the result of its more naturalistic style—is appropriate to its altered focus. Although both stories feature lonely protagonists, their thematic concerns are quite different. The earlier tale is a gay love story, focusing on issues of love and grief, while "Hard Candy" is preoccupied with age and the defiance of death. Its dissolute protagonist achieves a kind of heroism precisely because he refuses to surrender to old age.

The fear of age is also an issue in "Two on a Party," Williams's brilliant account of the relationship of Cora and Billy, "a female lush and a fairy who travel together" on a merry-go-round of hard drinking and compulsive cruising, always hounded by the "one great terrible, worst of all enemies, which is the fork-tailed, cloven-hoofed, pitchfork-bearing devil of Time!"[19] The unusual couple meet at a Manhattan bar and soon decide to live together, discovering that in their common pursuit of the "lyric quarry" both are more successful together than either had been separately. They soon develop a deep respect for each other, and once even have sex together, an experience neither wishes to repeat. Their relationship is shadowed by their knowledge that eventually Billy will "get off the party," while Cora is destined to stay on it. Cora finally admits to herself that she is in love with Billy, but she shares this knowledge with no one, least of all him. The story ends with the two of them still on the party, "two birds flying together against the wind, nothing real but the party, and even that sort of dreamy."

Billy and Cora are two of Williams's most fascinating fictional characters, sharply etched and memorable. A self-described "queen," Billy is a thirty-five-year-old former English teacher and Hollywood hack writer, living on his savings, while Cora is an alcoholic remittance woman some ten years older.[20] They are both addicted to "butch trade," predominantly heterosexual young men, often in the military, who dabble in homosexual activity of a limited kind. But for all their frenetic pursuit of the lyric quarry and their continual round of one-night stands when the trade runs "as thick as spawning salmon" and the world is suddenly "lit up by a dozen big chandeliers," Billy and Cora are afflicted with a profound sadness that their campy wit, easy laughs, and brave defiance can never entirely conceal. They are lonely people, terrified of the ravages of time, desperate to prove over and over again their attractiveness. But their search for self-validation through sexual conquests is futile, for their self-doubt is an interior wound not susceptible to the healing embraces of anonymous young men. Indeed, Billy's apparently exclusive sexual attraction to nonreciprocating partners may be a psychological defense against the very nurturing he desires but subconsciously feels that he does not deserve, just as Cora's alcoholism may also reflect a deep self-loathing.

So obsessed with age are Billy and Cora that they forget that they are still fairly young and attractive people. For them, the future is a chilling prospect of ever-diminishing attractiveness, and time signifies nothing but loss. Already, Billy is sensitive about the steadily advancing baldness at the crown of his head, conscious that "there is no denying that the top of a queen's head is a conspicuous area on certain occasions which are not unimportant"; while Cora, whom Billy first thought of as an "old bag," is self-conscious about the fatty expansion of her breasts and buttocks. Their most frequent subject of debate is whether age does worse things to a queen or to a woman—an argument that Billy usually wins by default, "for Cora did not like gloomy topics of conversation so much as Billy liked them." But they both know that the "demon pursuer" Time draws nearer each day, "And knowing it, knowing that nightmarish fact, gave a wild sort of sweetness of despair to their two-ring circus."

What they share in addition to their terror of time is a deep sense of alienation. They are bound together by "a rare sort of moral anarchy, a really fearful shared hatred of everything that was restrictive and which they felt to be false in the society they lived in and against the grain of which they continually operated." Rejecting conventional standards and priding themselves on their outlaw status, they define themselves against conventional people, the "squares" whom they loathe and despise. Half the pleasure of their anarchic existence is in defying the squares: "except for that element, the thrill of something lawless, they probably would have gotten bored with cruising." The disapproval of their families, the wrangling with niggardly lawyers in control of funds, the contemptuous glares of middle-class couples as Billy and Cora drag their trade through hotel lobbies or engage in some flamboyant flaunting of their unconventionality, the police raids of gay bars, the possibility that "someone who looked like a Botticelli angel" might draw a knife or the law might suddenly swoop down on them: these provide the *frissons* that sustains Billy and Cora's interest in the prolonged party whose repetitiveness would otherwise soon stale and stultify.

Billy and Cora initially join forces simply because "they were mutually advantageous as a team for cruising the Broadway bars." But they stay together because their companionship alleviates their loneliness.[21] When a spiteful hotel clerk from Cora's hometown of Alexandria, Louisiana, threatens to write a damaging letter to her family, she decides that she must leave New York. At first, Billy assumes that they will go their separate ways, but then he realizes that he does not want to return to his status as a single:

> He discovered that solitary cruising had been lonely, that there were spiritual comforts as well as material advantages in their double arrangement. No matter how bad luck was, there was no longer such a thing as going home by himself to the horrors of a second- or third-class hotel bedroom.

Although their indefatigable pursuit of trade remains the mainstay of their relationship, at least on the surface, they are actually more securely bound by their shared alienation and their growing mutual respect. They shyly reveal to each other previously hidden aspects of their personalities—"the other things, the timid and tender values that can exist between people"— and they gradually develop "a respect for each other, not merely to like and enjoy, as neither had ever respected another person."

Their one complete sexual experience with each other is not satisfactory, perhaps because they are too self-consciously solicitous to respond spontaneously and naturally. What they feel for each other is affection, not desire. As Williams observes, "Sex has to be slightly selfish to have real excitement." They are faintly embarrassed by the experience and they try too hard to reassure each other that they enjoyed it to be convincing. But for all its failure of desire, the sexual sharing may nevertheless have added something to the intimacy of their relationship; "at least it had, as they put it, squared things away a bit." They agree not to repeat the experiment, for, as Billy remarks, echoing the wisdom of the "queen world" of the early 1950s, "Friends can't be lovers"—a sentiment that Cora endorses "with a note of sadness."

Cora's note of sadness as she resignedly accepts the fact that in their milieu friends cannot be lovers is especially poignant, for she soon must face the fact that she has fallen in love with Billy. This revelation comes to her on their adventure in the Florida Keys, after their flashy but defective 1947 Buick convertible predictably develops motor trouble. She flags down a stunning, blond-haired, golden-tanned motorcyclist, whose legs "could not have been better designed by the appreciative eyes and fingers of Michelangelo or Phidias or Rodin." Resorting "to the type of flirtation that even most queens would think common," Cora enlists the cyclist's aid by groping him and the three of them soon check into a motel across the street from the garage to which the Buick has been towed. As she rues her foolishness in pretending to understand automobiles and thereby wasting Billy's share of the purchase, financed from the reprint fees of a potboiler novel he had written several years before, she hears a whisper in her heart: *"I love him!"*

Cora's attitude toward the fact of her love for Billy is both characteristic of her basically secretive nature and illustrative of her fear of frightening him away. She resolves never again, as long as she is "on the party" with her beloved companion, to put into words her feelings for him. *"Le coeur a ses raisons que la raison ne connaît pas!"* she whispers to herself. But if she never tells him of her love, she soon demonstrates it. As she is contemplating the heart's unfathomable reasons, Billy attempts to seduce the cyclist, who turns out to be "bad trade" and quickly leaves Billy sprawled on the floor with a bloody mouth. Cora rushes to save her loved one by providing an instant diversion. She strips herself bare in ten seconds. As Billy escapes, Cora endures "the most undesired embrace that she can remember in all her long history of desired and undesired and sometimes only patiently borne embraces."

The story ends with Billy and Cora still on the party, still enjoying "the sweetness of their living together." Both of them are aware of lacunae in their lives when they look about them and see in their brightly lit existence "something like what you see through a powerful telescope trained upon the moon, flatly illuminated craters and treeless plains and a vacancy of light—much light, but an emptiness in it." Although they are still committed to the pursuit of the lyric quarry, much of the lyricism vanishes: "Trade ceased to have much distinction. One piece was fundamentally the same as another, and the nights were like waves rolling in and breaking and retreating again and leaving you washed up on the wet sands of the morning." What sustains them in the mornings after their repetitive nights is the fierce integrity of both their relationship and their anarchic morality, "a sense of being together no matter what comes, and the knowledge of not having struck nor lied nor stolen." The story's final tableau of Cora ordering room service in a husky, soft voice so as not to disturb Billy and then gently waking him with coffee captures the sweet solace of their togetherness.

But if "Two on a Party" ends on a note of shared happiness, it is nevertheless shadowed by the terrible knowledge that the party must end someday soon. "Meanwhile they are together. To Cora that's the one important thing left," Williams writes near the end of the story. But Cora knows that eventually Billy will get off the party, that he is "fundamentally a serious sort of a person" and that she is not. Billy's possibilities are symbolized in the portable typewriter that he drags about with him. In contrast, Cora has no alternative but to stay on the party. Williams compares the party to a fast-moving train, from which very few people have the courage to leap. The train only stops "when it crashes, the ticker wears out, a blood vessel bursts, the liver or kidneys quit working." Cora "was too tough to crack up any time soon, but she was not tough enough to make the clean break, the daring jump off, that Billy knew, or felt he knew, that he was still able to make when he was ready to make it." Although Billy and Cora, the fairy and the lush, the queen and the fag hag, have discovered in each other some alleviation of the massive loneliness that plagues them, there is little hope that their happiness will last. Either the party will crash soon or Billy will leap off the fast-moving train, leaving Cora to stay with it no matter where it takes her.

"Two on a Party" is a masterfully wrought narrative in which humor intensifies pathos and despair is leavened by a brave pluckiness. A valuable document of a certain kind of gay life in the early 1950s, the tale is, finally, a touching love story of two pals, bloodied by life but resolutely unbowed. The shared sexual compulsiveness that brings Billy and Cora together soon becomes little more than the pretext for their companionship, as they discover in each other the kindness and respect, the "timid and tender values," that give their life meaning. Defiant of social conventions and traditional morality, they live by their own anarchic moral code, and they rarely wallow in self-pity. If "Two on a Party" is a sad tale of social outcasts, plagued by self-doubt and self-loathing, it is also a tribute to the search for love and companionship in precincts far removed from polite society. For all their internal doubts and fears, Billy and Cora possess a full measure of "the charm of the defeated." Memorably written in a lively style that mimics the campy wit and underlying despair of its protagonists, "Two on a Party" is a compelling, sweetly sad story of an outrageous couple, a vagabond queen and an alcoholic fag hag, who find in each other relief from the horrors of loneliness and the fears of the future.

Peopled by a wide variety of social outcasts, from "dirty old men" to hustlers, from timid masochists to flamboyant queens, Williams's stories explore universal themes of loneliness and isolation that are poignantly localized and made concrete in the dilemmas of his characters. Williams's gay characters are often familiar types, but they are too fully individualized to be merely stereotypical. Even when they are obviously symbols of alienation and loneliness, they are particularized and made fully human. If they are frequently wounded by life and self-destructive, they are just as frequently in active contention. Often heroic in their persistence and commitment, they exhibit surprising strength and dignity. If they are sometimes frenzied creatures of the night, they are nearly always in pursuit of an ideal—whether it be love or beauty—and they are capable of tenderness. Although he employs a homophobic discourse that may reflect his own ambivalence toward homosexuality, Williams envelops his gay characters within an all-encompassing sympathy. And in so doing he achieves a pathos that is more than merely sentimental. By approaching his characters with compassion, he reveals in them "the charm of the defeated," a charm that relieves an emotional landscape that would otherwise be depressingly bleak and that renders them as something more than objects of pity. Williams's gay characters are too colorful and eccentric to serve as Everyman-figures or as exemplars of the mundanity of homosexuality. But by depicting them unapologetically as faithful representations of the human condition, he makes a major contribution to the gay literature of his day.

Distinguished by a romantic lyricism that creates, sometimes in the most unlikely places, a strange beauty, the gay fictions of *One Arm* and *Hard Candy* haunt the imagination. Williams is less interested in social context or political issues than in particular dilemmas, yet his stories reflect at least a limited social reality and document the cruelty and oppression suffered by gay people in mid-century America. Williams seldom questions the origins of homosexuality or charts the coming-out process, but his casual acceptance of homosexuality as a human condition and his serious regard for the plight of gay people and others at the margins of society are themselves political acts. His approach to the issue of homosexuality is less intellectual than emotional, based not on social analysis but on an intuitive sympathy for the dispossessed, a sympathy no doubt based in his own experience as sissy boy, alienated artist, and homosexual. Central to his vision is a wisdom that accepts the human in all its variety, that condemns only willful cruelty and mendacity, and that understands that the heart has reasons that the brain knows not of. Precisely because he views homosexuality as a fully human variation, he writes about it with a naturalness, a freedom from self-consciousness, that is highly unusual in the 1940s and 1950s. By emphasizing "the charm of the defeated," Williams expresses his own alliance with the victims of oppression, with those who have been defeated by life and yet have not given up. Impressive in their variety and affirmation, the gay fictions of Tennessee Williams are vital contributions to the literature of compassion.

7
"The Plain of Truth":
Mary Renault's *The Charioteer*

Unlike the fiction of Tennessee Williams or Truman Capote, Mary Renault's *The Charioteer* clearly reflects the specific social and political context in which it was written and published. Appearing in 1953, near the end of the postwar decade, it may more instructively be compared to Vidal's *The City and the Pillar,* which appeared at the beginning of the decade. Like Vidal's pioneering book, it too is a coming-out narrative informed by a Platonic myth, and it is also intent on arguing that at least some homosexuals are perfectly ordinary and well-adjusted individuals. A "homosexual problem novel" that presents a vivid sketch of the gay subculture, it also both confirms and challenges stereotypes. But the differences between the works are more telling than their similarities, reflecting both the different perspectives of their authors and the different times in which they were written. Whereas Vidal's novel is detached, nonmoralistic, and ironic, Renault's more circumspect book is none of these. An earnest attempt to illustrate the difficulties faced by the gay person in achieving dignity and self-respect in a nonaccepting society, *The Charioteer* tends to be apologetic and calculatingly accommodationist. Whereas *The City and the Pillar* confidently challenges the sexual attitudes of the 1940s, Renault's novel treads far more gingerly. Its social protest is muted and its vision is straitened by the 1950s sexual ideology that it reflects and only indirectly deconstructs.

Renault's early books, including *Promise of Love* (1939), *The Middle Mist* (1945), and *Return to Night* (1947), also feature an interest in homosexuality, but *The Charioteer* is a pivotal work in her development, marking the beginning of her mature achievement.[1] Offering a portrait of gay love as potentially elevated and dignified, and presenting homosexual protagonists notably free of stereotypical affectations, it is a book that meant much to many gay men and women in the 1950s and 1960s. But what is most surprising about *The Charioteer* from the vantage point of the waning years of the twentieth century is not its self-consciously compassionate approach to the "homosexual problem," but the depth of homophobia internalized by its gay characters and its utter disdain for the homosexual subculture that it depicts. In this regard, *The Charioteer* is far different from Renault's later historical fiction, in which she deftly and naturally integrates homosexual characters and situations in the world of ancient Greece.[2] The unconscious homophobia of *The Charioteer* results in part from a failure of vision, but it also reflects the extreme difficulties faced by writers who attempted to broach the issue of homosexuality in 1950s popular literature. At the same time that the novel mirrors 1950s homophobia, however, it also subverts that ideology, and in a peculiarly satisfying way. The context in which the book was written thus provides a gauge against which to measure its successes even as it also helps explain its failures.

A consequence of the increased visibility of homosexuality in American and British society during and following World War II was that in the 1950s homosexuals were more aggressively and systematically attacked than at any previous time in modern Anglo-American history.[3] The terms *sin, sickness,* and *crime* monopolized the discourse on homosexuality throughout the period, perhaps sparked by the revelations of the Kinsey report, whose statistics alerted moralists to a hitherto-unsuspected prevalence of homosexual activity. The developing consensus that homosexuals were immoral, emotionally unstable, and untrustworthy justified their punishment and stigmatization. The 1951 flight to the Soviet Union of British spies Guy Burgess and Donald Maclean may have helped fuel the emergence of homosexuals as the chief victims and scapegoats of the Cold War. "Sexual perverts" became a staple target of Senator Joseph McCarthy and his fellow cold-warriors, who spearheaded witch-hunts to purge homosexuals from the armed forces and federal employment. These efforts culminated in President Eisenhower's issuance in April 1953 of Executive Order 10450, which listed "sexual perversion" as sufficient and necessary grounds of disbarment from federal jobs.

Federal actions were matched by purges of state and local governments and by widespread harassment of homosexuals by the FBI and local police departments. In the United States and Britain throughout the 1950s, gays suffered from unpredictable and frequently brutal crackdowns, which resulted in the arrest and imprisonment of thousands of individuals. In England, the number of prosecutions for homosexual offenses increased dramatically in the early 1950s. Indeed, the widely publicized trials of several Members of Parliament, of newly knighted actor Sir John Gielgud, of the journalists Rupert Croft-Cooke and Peter Wildeblood, and especially of Lord Montagu of Beaulieu may have at least indirectly led to the appointment in 1954 of the Wolfenden Commission, whose unexpected 1957 recommendations to decriminalize consensual homosexual activities under certain limited conditions (while severely increasing penalties for prostitution) were not to be adopted until 1967.[4]

So pervasive was the popular consensus that homosexuals were decadent, corrupt, and depraved that such concepts inevitably infected the consciousness of gay men and women as well as heterosexuals. The self-doubt generated by such an atmosphere may well have been the most damaging and ubiquitous (and perhaps the cruelest) effect of the onslaught against gay people in the 1950s. The guilt and internalized self-hatred that many homosexuals felt made them blame themselves rather than their oppressors for their predicament, and led some to accept harassment and punishment as well deserved. Moreover, their absorption of society's nearly monolithic view of them as pathological and immoral precluded an effective political response. As John D'Emilio observes, "The dominant view of homoeroticism as sin, sickness, or crime accustomed homosexual men and women to seeing their situation as a personal problem, not a cause for political action."[5] Even activists in the tiny homophile movement seemed to acquiesce in the judgment of society that homosexuals were "almost invariably neurotic or psychotic" and should at least "*try* to get cured," as a prominent psychiatrist told a gathering of the Mattachine Society.[6] The gay-bashings of the 1950s no doubt warped the lives of numerous individuals, but the tendency to blame the victim was itself part and parcel of the problem. It is in this postwar context of greater familiarity with homosexuality but little real understanding that Renault's novel needs to be seen.

The Charioteer can best be understood as both a product of this context of anti-gay feeling and a response to it. The novel reflects the decade's received ideas about homosexuality in its adoption of the medical model to explain its major characters' gayness, in its depiction of gay society in general as populated almost exclusively by neurotic misfits, and in its inability to conceive of homosexuality as anything other than a personal failing. In documenting the book's homophobic assumptions and tactics, the point is not to hold Renault accountable to an anachronistic standard of political correctness, but to demonstrate how even a work obviously sympathetic to the homosexual plight nevertheless partakes of its era's pervasive anti-gay ideology. Renault's depiction of the gay subculture as a sordid collection of self-hating, irresponsible, and childish individuals may even reflect a limited social reality, but—lacking the balance and perspective of Vidal's depiction of the gay subculture in *The City and the Pillar—The Charioteer* is hardly "an abstract of homosexual life in England,"[7] as one critic describes it. Actually, it more accurately represents the preconceptions and fears of the larger society in the 1950s than the real lives of most gay people even then.

Set in the autumn of 1940, in the dimmest days of World War II, *The Charioteer* charts the development of Laurie Odell, a sensitive young man who has been wounded at Dunkirk. Confined to a military hospital, where he is treated for an injured leg, Laurie becomes involved with Andrew Raynes, a naive but courageous Quaker conscientious objector assigned to work at the institution. On a visit to Bridstow for treatment at a civilian hospital, Laurie is invited to a gay birthday party, where he is reunited with Ralph Lanyan, who had been his hero at public school and who was expelled for a homosexual relationship there.[8] Upon his expulsion, Ralph gave Laurie a copy of Plato's *Phaedrus*, a book that he has treasured ever since. Laurie is surprised to learn that Ralph, who has become a naval captain, saved his life at Dunkirk. The dashing officer has himself since been injured and consequently relieved of his ship's command. The two are appalled at the behavior of their fellow guests at the party, but obviously attracted to each other.

As the novel develops, Laurie finds himself torn between his attraction for the innocent Andrew, who is only dimly aware of his sexual nature, and the experienced Ralph, who envisions a relationship with Laurie as a means of escaping the sordid gay subculture. The book comes to a crisis when Bunny, a spiteful former lover of Ralph's, reveals Laurie's homosexuality to Andrew. Shocked by the lewdness with which the revelation is made, the young man violates his principles and strikes Bunny, who has introduced himself as Ralph. When Laurie learns of the incident, he convicts Ralph of the betrayal; breaks off his relationship with him; and seeks out Andrew in a bombed-out sector of London, where the young Quaker has fled. Andrew's spiritual advisor recommends that Laurie not confront the young man, and Laurie leaves his copy of the *Phaedrus* as a gift for him. When Laurie learns that Ralph was in fact innocent of the indiscretion, he rushes to his room, where they are reconciled.

As the title suggests, the novel pivots on Plato's myth of the tripartite soul, as recounted in the *Phaedrus*. According to Socrates, the soul may be imagined as a charioteer pulled by two horses, one good, the other vicious. The better of the two is noble, temperate, and sensible of shame, whereas the other is crooked, headstrong, and shameless. Socrates explains:

> Now when the charioteer beholds the vision of love, and has his whole soul warmed through sense, and is full of the ticklings of desire, the obedient steed, then as always under the government of shame, refrains from leaping on the beloved; but the other, heedless of the pricks and the blows of the whip, plunges and runs away, giving all manner of trouble to his companion and the charioteer, whom he forces to approach the beloved and to remember the joys of love.[9]

The book's central symbol, the *Phaedrus* informs *The Charioteer* at every turn, affirming the possibility of elevated love between men even as it also warns of the dangers of lust. The novel traces Laurie's attempts to reconcile the competing claims on his psyche of noble, chaste love (as associated with Andrew) and intemperate desire (as epitomized by the gay subculture). This reconciliation is finally achieved in the person of Ralph, but only after wrenching soul-searching.

But *The Charioteer* does not merely dramatize Plato's distinctions between elevated love and shameless appetite. It is always aware of the fact that Platonic idealism must be tempered by experience in the real world. As Ralph tells Laurie, upon presenting him the *Phaedrus*, "It doesn't exist anywhere in real life. . . . It's just a nice idea."[10] In the contemporary world, Christian prohibitions make the Platonic idea especially difficult to achieve. When Laurie leaves the copy of the *Phaedrus* for Andrew, even Dave, the novel's most sympathetic Christian, pointedly observes that "the most exalted paganism is paganism nonetheless." Despite such attitudes, the novel illustrates the arduous achievement in contemporary society of a worthwhile homosexual relationship based on a classical model of temperance. The myth of the charioteer illustrates the need for a balance of the sensual and the spiritual. It is not, as some critics of Renault's novel have apparently assumed, a recommendation for asceticism.

The classical locus is one among several means that Renault employs to elevate the triangular affair involving the young principals, thereby distinguishing it from stereotypical homosexual liaisons. But the classical resonance imparted by the haunting presence of the *Phaedrus* and references to ancient Greek ideals—including especially the army of lovers, as described by Phaedrus in the *Symposium*—also serves as a measure of the decadence of contemporary homosexual life. Although the novel is designed to urge compassionate acceptance for characters like Laurie, Andrew, and Ralph, whose romantic sensitivity, high-mindedness, and heroism finally come to strain credibility, it does so without overtly challenging the virulently anti-gay sexual ideology of the 1950s. Indeed, the novel tends to confirm stereotypical views of homosexuality even as it presents Laurie, Ralph, and Andrew as rare individual exceptions to these stereotypes. The compassion urged for the heroes of *The Charioteer* is bought at the expense of direct questioning of the decade's popular attitudes toward homosexuals and homosexuality.

In the postwar era, medicine achieved parity with religion and law in structuring the perception of homosexuality, and added to the view of gay people as immoral criminals the further idea that they were sick. The dominant medical explanation for homosexuality saw it as the result of abnormal relationships with parents, especially with close-binding or domineering mothers and absent or weak or bullying fathers.[11] This is the etiology of homosexuality that is implicit in *The Charioteer*, an explanation most fully developed in the case of Laurie, but implied for Ralph and Andrew as well, whose familial relationships are also disturbed. Ralph traces his homosexuality to his parents' reaction to his experimentations at the age of six with a seven-year-old neighbor girl. As he explains, "it was apparently the filthiest crime that had ever touched my mother's life. She found it quite hard to talk about, so by the time she'd done, I took away some dim idea that carnal knowledge of women would cause one's limbs to rot and fall off, like leprosy." Andrew, whose homosexuality is latent rather than overt—to use a distinction prominent in 1950s psychiatric literature—was orphaned at an early age. He was raised by his father's relatives, "one of those army families which every second or third generation throws off a sport." His decision to seek conscientious objector status leads to a rupture with his relatives and to his friendship with Dave, a Quaker friend of his parents who serves as his father-figure and spiritual guide.

If the family histories of Ralph and Andrew are only vaguely predictive of their gayness, Laurie's more clearly reflects the classic pattern. The opening chapter of the novel dramatizes the separation of Laurie's parents. His father banished from his life at the age of four, Laurie identifies with his mother, who "seemed to have declared in the clearest language that he was her only solace and the last refuge of her violated trust." "When I'm grown up, I'm going to marry you," the four-year-old tells her, flush "with a triumph too profound to recognize itself, that after all it was he whom she loved the best." His alcoholic father dies soon afterward, and the adolescent Laurie thinks of himself "as wholly his mother's child." A product of a broken home, Laurie is, according to the contemporary social and sexual ideology, *expected* to be neurotic. As Ralph says, "I must say, Spud, you're remarkably well balanced for the off-spring of divorce. Quite often being queer is the least of it."

The unnaturalness of the relationship of mother and son is further emphasized by the crisis over Mrs. Odell's decision to remarry. When he learns of his mother's plan, Laurie feels a sense of abandonment. He reflects that "He was marked for life . . . by the chain that had bound him to her." His great regret at the prospect of her marriage is that "She would never now, as once he had dreamed, say to him in the silent language of day-to-day, 'Tell me nothing; it is enough that no other woman will ever take you from me.' " Mrs. Odell explains to her distraught son that she had earlier turned down offers of marriage because "I didn't like the idea of giving you a stepfather when you were just at the difficult age. Now I'm not young any more; and next year, or the year after, when you want to get married, I should be all alone." Misinterpreting this confidence as meaning that his mother is marrying only for the sake of companionship, Laurie practically begs her not to proceed with the wedding, declaring in effect his own intentions toward her: "I don't want to get married. . . . I don't think I'll ever want to. It's just something I feel. If you don't want to go through with it . . . ." It is no coincidence that the first time Laurie goes to bed with Ralph is on his mother's wedding night.

Clearly, Renault offers the oedipal entanglement of Laurie and his mother as an explanation for the young man's homosexuality. Laurie's hero worship of Ralph at school and his fondness for childhood adventure stories are offered as manifestations of the stunted emotional and sexual development that results from his identification with his mother and his lack of a masculine role model. That Ralph functions as a father-figure for the young Laurie is made clear by the recurrent motif of torn papers, which Laurie notices on the occasions of his father's banishment from home and Ralph's expulsion from school and which symbolize loss and abandonment. The papers in Ralph's wastepaper basket "stirred in [Laurie's] mind some dimly remembered sense of dread," thus linking his sexual attraction for Ralph with his oedipal jealousy of his father. The relationship of Laurie and his mother is richly detailed in the novel, presented cumulatively in a series of understated and acute observations. Nonetheless, Renault's portrayal of Laurie's family situation in the stock psychiatric clichés of the 1950s is so obvious as to render trite and predictable what might have been an insightful study of the dynamics of mother–son bonding.

But in addition to providing the details of a clinical case history to explain her protagonist's gayness as symptomatic of disease, Renault also presents homosexuality as an emotional injury equivalent to physical disability. Indeed, Laurie's lameness is symbolic not only of his oedipal dependence (and, more positively, of his quest for self-knowledge) but also of his homosexuality itself. This is apparent when Laurie is unable to reply to Nurse Adrian's encouragement that his leg may improve:

> [H]e could only think of things too simple to say. "I shall always be different," he wanted to tell her; and some part of his mind expected that she would say "No," and everything would be changed. . . . "Different?" she would say, surprised. "But of course you're not."

Always conscious of "the solidarity that didn't include him," Laurie sees his sexual difference as more crippling than his physical disability. Ralph's injured hand is, similarly, the external manifestation of his psychic wound. For all their qualities of sensitivity and heroism, Renault's protagonists are portrayed as emotionally as well as physically crippled.

The concept of homosexuality as a disease goes hand in hand with the novel's insistent depiction of the gay subculture as deeply pathological. As he ushers Laurie into his building, which will be the site of the gay birthday party, the unstable Sandy Reid remarks, "It's a mausoleum"—a description whose appropriateness is justified by Renault's portrayal of the party guests as a species of the living dead and by Sandy's own melodramatic suicide attempt in a fit of jealous pique. Equally appropriate is the fact that Sandy's flat was formerly a nursery. Most of the homosexuals in *The Charioteer* are as childish as they are self-destructive. No wonder Laurie as he enters Sandy's building "could recall few doors which he had felt such reluctance to enter." Indeed, Laurie has been in flight from the gay subculture for years, having broken off his first homosexual flirtation— with a fellow undergraduate at Oxford—because of "the people he knew, awful people you'd never have believed." At the "queer party," a kind of gathering later defined as "something between a lonely hearts club and an amateur brothel," Laurie becomes aware of what it was he had been running away from: "They were specialists. . . . They had identified themselves with their limitations."

No one in the novel disputes the notion that homosexuality is a grave limitation. Ralph even sees it as a threat to human survival, pointedly remarking that "Even civilized people had better hang on to a few biological instincts. . . . Hell, can't we even face the simple fact that if our fathers had been like us, we wouldn't have been born?" A collection of "weasel-like" young men with high girlish voices and soft, self-pitying mouths, most of the homosexuals of this novel are depicted as silly, pretentious, irresponsible, corrupt, drunken, and vicious. They are described as ethical and moral "runts": "Souls with congenitally short necks and receding brows." When Bunny, the novel's gay villain, makes a pass at him, Laurie thinks, "What can you do about these people? The terrible thing is, there are such a lot of them. There are so many, they expect to meet each other wherever they go." Although he acknowledges an "upper crust" of famous homosexuals in history, Ralph insists that in the "vertical" gay society, "there isn't a bottom." "You've no conception, you haven't a clue how far down it goes," he tells Laurie.

The question of how great a limitation homosexuality proves to be depends entirely on the individual. "It's not what one is, it's what one does with it," Ralph says, enunciating the novel's individualistic ideal. Less optimistically, Laurie observes, "We sign the warrant for our own exile. . . . Self-pity and alibis come after." Since "normal" people have, at least according to Ralph, "learned to leave us in peace unless we make public exhibitions of ourselves," he rejects the idea that gays might have a grievance against society. "There wouldn't be the least justification for it," he fumes. Indeed, the only objection voiced to the precarious legal status of homosexuals is that "it gives the relatively balanced type, who makes some effort to become an integrated personality, a quite false sense of solidarity with advanced psychopaths whom, if they weren't all driven underground together, he wouldn't even meet." Not surprisingly, Ralph and Laurie, being of the "relatively balanced type," share no fellow feeling with other gays. They ridicule the need for a group identity, questioning the efficacy

of being roped "off with a lot of people you don't feel much in common
with, half of whom hate the other half anyway, and just keep together so
that they can lean up against each other for support."

The Charioteer is saturated with the anti-gay ideology of its time. Its gay
characters fairly reek of internalized homophobia and what passes for idealism is often only self-hatred. Laurie's own self-doubt finds explicit expression in his drug-induced delirium following the operation on his knee.
He thanks Nurse Adrian for her attention in a particularly revealing way. "I
don't deserve it, you know," he murmurs. "If you knew all about me, you
wouldn't be good to me like you are." Tellingly, the highest praise Laurie
can pay Ralph's friend Alec is the assurance that "you're more a doctor
than you're a queer." Similarly, Alec defines Ralph's admirable sense of
responsibility by means of a negative comparison with other homosexuals:
"About one queer in a thousand has the guts to accept that sort of responsibility, and he's the odd one." Even at the end of the novel, as the plot
culminates in Laurie's acceptance of his gayness and in his union with
Ralph, Renault is careful—perhaps for legal reasons—not to endorse homosexuality. The Socrates-like Dave counsels Laurie not to think of himself as
"typed and labelled" and encourages him to experiment with heterosexuality: "Some men could make shift, for a time at least, with any woman out
of about ninety per cent they meet. Don't fly to extremes the moment you
discover your own needs are more specialized." This advice echoes Ralph's
earlier injunction to Laurie: "You don't want to have written off half the
human race at your time of life." This curious injunction, which tortures
logic and common sense to allege that in loving a member of one sex one
somehow dismisses as unimportant all members of the other sex (a caveat
that apparently does not apply to exclusive heterosexuality), reveals the
privileged status granted heterosexuality even by Renault's homosexuals.

But to dismiss *The Charioteer* as merely homophobic is to distort the
novel and misrepresent its place in the literature of homosexuality, for despite its absorption of the popular cultural attitudes of its day, it is nevertheless earnestly dedicated to reforming some of those attitudes, at least in
regard to the "balanced type" of homosexual. Indeed, in its approach to
the "homosexual problem" it actually reflects the strategies of accommodation adopted by the small social and legal reform movements in England
and America in the 1950s. As D'Emilio writes of the men and women who
led the homophile movement in the United States,

> Although their involvement in gay organizations evinced courage in itself, they
> acquiesced too readily to the circumstances in which they found themselves.
> Convinced that America would not tolerate agitation for gay rights, they main-
> tained the lowest of profiles and advised their constituency against mounting
> any challenges to the status quo. In their effort to accommodate themselves to

a conservative political climate and a society antagonistic to homosexuality, they oftentimes abetted the attitudes and policies that stigmatized homosexuals and lesbians.[12]

This is precisely the case with Renault in *The Charioteer* as well. The movement's premium on respectability, its urging of homosexuals to adjust to a pattern of behavior presumably acceptable to society in general—and its acquiescence to religious, medical, and legal professionals as authorities who are qualified to dictate the nature of discourse about homosexuality—all parallel the strategies adopted by Renault, who determinedly presents Laurie, Ralph, and Andrew as rare respectable homosexuals, only slightly "bent," and willing and able to adjust to societal demands as articulated by the "authorities." What needs emphasis is the fact that, however benighted these strategies may seem now, they were intended as a positive response to the rampant homophobia of the 1950s.

Moreover, although it fails to challenge radically the sexual ideology of its day, *The Charioteer* nevertheless implicitly questions many of the received ideas that it seems to absorb. For instance, the picture it paints of the homosexual subculture is distinctly unpalatable, yet it also depicts almost all members of that subculture as loyal citizens effectively contributing to the national war effort. Even Bunny is engaged in work for the Navy and even Sandy Reid is capable of heroism, as illustrated by his brave and decisive action when the Bridstow hospital is bombed. There are reports of the deaths of gay servicemen and Ralph and Laurie have both been injured in military operations. The record of sacrifice and service compiled by Renault's gay characters is surely intended to respond to the Cold War clamor to purge the U.S. and British armed forces of homosexuals. And although Renault presents homosexuality as a psychic disorder, she nevertheless recognizes its naturalness—at least for some people—as is apparent when Ralph explains how he felt upon the expiration of his self-imposed two-year "sentence" of heterosexuality: "All I can remember thinking is 'Thank the Lord, back to normal at last.' " In addition, by sketching the infidelities of Madge Barker, the wife of Reg, Laurie's friend at the military hospital, Renault indicates that promiscuity is not the exclusive province of gay people. And by portraying Laurie's future stepfather, the Reverend Straike, as a distinctly unlikeable, pompous, and unimaginative prig, she illustrates the dangers of conformity and self-righteousness. Moreover, the individualistic ethos as embodied in the judgment "It's not what one is, it's what one does with it" may evince political naiveté but nonetheless contains the seeds of personal liberation.

Finally, Renault places the gay subculture's decadence in a historical context that helps explain its excesses. Despite Ralph's disclaimer of any grievance against society, for example, he acknowledges a societal contribution to the gay subculture's tawdriness and he identifies this baleful contribution as specifically Christian. "It's only since [homosexuality] has been made impossible that it's been made so damned easy," he remarks.

> "It's got like prohibition, with the bums and crooks making fortunes out of hooch, everyone who might have had a palate losing it, nobody caring how you hold your liquor, you've been smart enough if you can get it at all. You can't make good wine in a bathtub in the cellar, you need sun and rain and fresh air, you need a pride in the job you can tell the world about. Only you can live without drink if you have to, but you can't live without love."

Implicit in this impassioned speech is the awareness that homosexual love has been perverted by societal condemnation. That the condemnation is specifically Christian is indicated by contrast when Ralph observes, "The pagans did recognize our existence at least. They even allowed us a few standards and a bit of human dignity, just like real people." The ultimate achievement of a dignified homosexual relationship represents the recovery of Classical values in a hostile, Christian context.

Renault most effectively challenges the sexual ideology of the 1950s in the depiction of the triangular relationship of Andrew, Laurie, and Ralph. She does this most obviously (and least convincingly) by the accommodationist techniques discussed above: by separating her principals from stereotypical expectations, differentiating them from other gay people, and insisting on their high-mindedness and virtue, especially in contrast to the decadence of their fellow gays. More successfully, however, she also sketches them as individuals responding to human dilemmas that are exacerbated by the homosexual context but by no means confined to it. Thus, the relief from loneliness that Laurie and Andrew feel in each other's company transcends sexual categories. "It's all right when I'm with you," Andrew tells Laurie, "I don't have the feeling of being different then." Similarly, after speaking with Ralph, Laurie feels "less like a citizen of nowhere." The loneliness of the three men is aggravated by the societal condemnation of homosexuality, but it is an emotion endemic to the human condition itself. Moreover, the question of Laurie's acceptance of his gayness is expanded into a universal dilemma: the choice between innocence and experience. The ultimate embrace of experience, which includes a fully expressed homosexual relationship, is seen finally as inevitable. Most significantly, beneath the priggishness that pervades the novel lies a subtext that gradually emerges to assert the necessity of sexual expression as a component of self-knowledge—an ideal specifically pagan rather than Christian.

Laurie's journey toward maturity finally centers on his choice between two loves. He is attracted to Andrew's boyish innocence. He finds the young man's "austerity imposed on a latent sweetness . . . unbearably beautiful" and "he received infinite consolation and joy merely from the contemplation of [his] being." Appropriately, their courtship flowers in a pastoral "private Eden," the apple orchard where they share confidences and explore ideals. The vulnerability of innocence in the real world is symbolized by the intrusion of the religious fundamentalist Mrs. Chivers, who expels the young men from her garden when she discovers that Andrew is a pacifist. Driven from their private paradise, they meet across the stream in a beechwood copse they call Limbo, which Laurie defines as "A sort of eternal consolation prize." But if the young men's journey from the Edenic garden to Limbo to the real world involves the loss of innocence, it also entails the gain of experience.

For Laurie, in the first flush of his love for Andrew, the ideal of innocence is threatened not only by a cynical world, but also by eroticism itself. When Reg warns that Andrew may try to convert Laurie to pacifist principles, and cites the offense "Seducing His Majesty's troops from their allegiance," Laurie replies in a telling double entendre: "Don't worry, I guarantee that if any seducing goes on it'll be done by me." But in fact Laurie is so protective of Andrew's innocence, and so ambivalent about his own sexuality, that no seduction takes place. Only after Andrew complains of Laurie's protectiveness—"You oughtn't to think of me as a person whose head has to be stuck in a bag"—do the men share a moment of physical intimacy. They kiss and then, just "when Andrew was looking up with a kind of strangeness which was only the threshold of some feeling not yet formed," they are interrupted by a nurse, and Laurie returns to his ward feeling acutely self-conscious. Laurie's inhibited response to Andrew contrasts with the sexual magnetism he feels in the presence of Ralph.

Laurie's internalized homophobia contributes to the premium he places on Andrew's innocence. One of the young Quaker's attractions for Laurie is that he is so divorced from the threatening gay subculture. After describing gay society as a narrow, "closed shop," Laurie reflects: "It would never be like that with Andrew. . . . Talking in the hospital kitchen at night, they had felt special only in their happiness, and separate only in their human identities." Convinced that "It would spoil his life" should Andrew know of his homosexuality, Laurie conspires to keep him ignorant of his own feelings. Laurie's refusal to be frank with Andrew prompts Ralph's accusation:

> "[W]hat you're trying to do for him is to keep him like a mid-Victorian virgin in a world of illusion where he doesn't know he's alive. He mustn't be told he's a passenger when human decency's fighting for survival, in case it upsets his religion. He mustn't be told he's a queer, in case he has to do a bit of hard thinking and make up his mind. He mustn't know you're in love with him, in case he feels he can't go on having his cake and eating it."

Pointedly, Ralph adds: "If he amounts to anything, he won't really want to be let off being human"—a supposition that is verified in the event.

When Andrew is finally jolted into self-awareness by the malicious revelations of Bunny, he is of course deeply shocked. He regards homosexuality as sinful and his revulsion is compounded by guilt. As he says in his letter to Laurie explaining his violent reaction, "The thing you want to kill is really in yourself," and surely his application for dangerous ambulance work in London reflects an impulse toward self-punishment if not suicide. Most significantly, however, as he also says in his letter, "one can't refuse to know oneself."

Self-knowledge finally triumphs in *The Charioteer,* and its importance is apparent from the very beginning when Laurie—on the occasion of his parents' separation—knows "for the first time the burden, prison, and mystery of his own uniqueness." The novel is, after all, a *Bildungsroman* charting Laurie's growth toward self-knowledge, a pilgrimage inextricably linked to his quest for love and his acceptance of his sexuality. The connection between self-awareness and love is clear in the letter Laurie imagines writing to his mother soon after meeting Andrew: "I now know something about myself which I have been suspecting for years, if I had had the honesty to admit it. . . . I know now why I was born, why everything has happened to me ever; I know why I am lame, because it has brought me to the right place at the right time." But in the novel self-knowledge is epitomized most fully by Ralph, who "had been willing to lay on his pride the burden of self-knowledge, and carry it with his shoulders straight." Significantly, Ralph's self-knowledge includes his "curious innocence" and vulnerability as well as his vaunted self-discipline and strength. Though Ralph and Andrew are foils, they are actually more alike than they are different.

The union of Ralph and Laurie on which the book concludes reflects the triumph of self-knowledge and acceptance over illusion and fear. The achievement of their union is complicated by Laurie's love for Andrew's innocence and his romantic conception of life as "divided and irreconcilable, and the good so implacably the enemy of the best." But the extreme idealism that equates the "best" with ignorance and illusion actually twists the Classical virtues of moderation and proportion into a Christian prescription of abstinence. It is challenged by the reality of a mature love that combines self-knowledge and experience. Ralph may be mistaken in thinking of a love without physical bond "as something not quite real," but he is certainly correct to insist on the tangible value of his bond with Laurie. "You don't know how little there is in the world of what we can give each other," he tells Laurie. And central to their relationship is the sexual exchange that differentiates it from Laurie's romantic friendship with Andrew.

The sexual relationship functions to counter the apologetic tone of the novel and, ultimately, to subvert the 1950s sexual ideology. The sexual attraction of Ralph and Laurie is a reality that finally looms larger than both the homophobia of the general society and the self-hatred of the gay characters. Although his self-doubt and fear of the subculture in which Ralph has been living cause Laurie to hesitate in making a commitment, their lovemaking is an act of self-discovery for him. "It can be good to be given what you want; it can be better, in the end, never to have it proved to you that this was what you wanted," Laurie thinks ruefully after their first sexual experience, troubled by the knowledge "that he had moved to this with instinctive purpose, as animals move toward water over miles of bush." Despite his discomfiture with this insight about himself, however, he now at least recognizes his homosexual desire as a response utterly natural to himself, and he accepts the new knowledge as a part of his being: "If his wishes had not been fulfilled with such experienced intuition, he need never, perhaps, have been certain what they were. Now he knew, and must go on knowing."

The strength of the sexual bond is illustrated soon after Laurie returns to the civilian hospital following the night of lovemaking. Panicked by Ralph's plans for their future together, feeling torn by contradictory emotions, and (because of his infatuation for Andrew) unable to make the commitment he thinks Ralph deserves, Laurie determines to end the relationship. He persistently associates Ralph with the threatening gay subculture and unconsciously resents his dominance and control. In contrast, he feels needed and trusted by Andrew. But as Laurie enters Ralph's room to break off their affair, he discovers for the first time "the sensation of coming home again which is one of the more stable by-products of physical love." When he attempts to tell Ralph goodbye, his friend calls, "Come here, then. . . . Come and say goodbye to me," and Laurie falls into his arms, surrendering to the sexual response that contradicts his resolution of independence. The strength of the sexual attraction is felt equally by Ralph, who tells Laurie afterward, "When it came to the last I couldn't help myself, and that's a fact."

The mutuality of Ralph's and Laurie's need for each other is a crucial aspect of the novel. Ralph's assumption of authority and leadership at once attracts and repels Laurie. It reestablishes Ralph's status as schoolboy hero, but it also threatens Laurie's sense of autonomy, making him feel "young and amateurish again." The dilemma is crystallized when Laurie presents his fencing foil to Ralph:

> He felt in his own gesture the ancient symbol of the surrendered sword. His nature had suffered a self-discovery, a swing off its old center of balance, stranger to him and less foreseen than he had allowed Ralph to know. For a moment an instinctive hostility must have shown in his eyes.

At the heart of this problem is the Classical role-playing—that of lover or beloved—that each anticipates in a homosexual bond. Negotiation over these roles complicates their relationship almost as much as Laurie's infatuation with Andrew, who unconsciously accepts the role of beloved to Laurie's role of lover. Ralph, however, by insisting on the role of lover, transforms Laurie into the beloved. As Alec remarks, Ralph "would never let one do anything for him." But in the fencing scene, when he removes the glove from his mutilated hand, he exposes his vulnerability with important consequences: "There was something trustful and touching in this undefended surrender . . . ; it gave Laurie for the moment what he felt to be the most solid happiness he had known among so much contradictory emotion." Only when the men learn to be at once strong and vulnerable, both lover and beloved, can they transcend the role-playing and acknowledge mutual trust and need.

The lovers' mutual need is central to the end of the novel, at which point Laurie discovers not only that Ralph is guiltless of the betrayal, but also the depth of Ralph's dependence. Ralph's need is unfortunately dramatized by flirtation with suicide, that ultimate act of despair so often linked with homosexuality in popular literature. Nevertheless, the mutuality of their need is expressed in Laurie's acknowledgment that even if he had not learned the truth from Alec, "I should have come, anyway. I should have had to come back." In this statement, as in Ralph's earlier admission, "I couldn't help myself," Laurie recognizes both their mutual need and the inevitability of their union. In carefully developing this sense of inevitability, Renault manages to impart great power to Laurie's ultimate acceptance of Ralph as his lover, notwithstanding the melodramatic plot devices that force the novel to its conclusion.

Most importantly, the ending of *The Charioteer* is optimistic, and in its optimism it is subversive of the 1950s sexual ideology that would condemn homosexuals to unhappiness. Although one critic alleges the union of Ralph and Laurie on which the novel closes to be tragic—"both know their intimacy to be grounded in deprivation and despair"[13]—surely this is a misreading based on a crucial misunderstanding of the myth of the charioteer. The young men, against great odds, have forged a relationship with potential for growth. They have numbered themselves among the "army of lovers." Laurie has achieved self-knowledge and has learned that "a deep compassion has the nature of love, which keeps no balance sheet; we are no longer our own." From the beautiful coda, it is clear that in his relationship with Ralph, Laurie has at last achieved proportion, that balance of sensuality and spirituality idealized in Plato's myth:

Quietly as night shuts down the uncertain prospect of the road ahead, the wheels sink to stillness in the dust of the halting place, and the reins drop from the driver's loosened hands. Staying each his hunger on what pasture the place affords them, neither the white horse nor the black reproaches his fellow for drawing their master out of the way. They are far, both of them, from home, and lonely, and lengthened by their strife the way has been hard. Now their heads droop side by side till their long manes mingle; and when the voice of the charioteer falls silent they are reconciled in sleep.

The road ahead is uncertain, but the charioteer and the two steeds have arrived at what Socrates describes as "the plain of truth": "pasturage is found there, which is suited to the highest part of the soul."[14] At the end of the book, the division within Laurie's soul is healed. The horses are reconciled and the charioteer sleeps peacefully.

The Charioteer is not a great novel, but it is an important contribution to the literature of homosexuality in the 1950s, and both its limitations and its successes can best be understood in terms of this context. Its occasional preciousness of style, unconvincing characterization, and melodramatic plot solutions may all result from its self-consciousness in depicting homosexuality at a time of virulent opposition to homosexuals. It may well have been to avoid the problems she experienced in *The Charioteer* that Renault subsequently turned to historical settings, which allowed her to write of homosexual relationships with greater freedom and naturalness. All the same, however, *The Charioteer* deserves credit not merely for its compassionate acceptance of a few high-minded homosexuals but also for challenging, however timidly and tentatively, the popular assumptions it seems to adopt. Most interestingly, the novel tends to deconstruct the very ideology it reflects. Its insistence on the preeminent value of self-knowledge and its faith in the possibility of homosexual love even in the midst of repression transcend the limits of its context. Despite its apologetic tone and self-consciousness, the achievement of *The Charioteer* is finally to undermine its own calculatingly accommodationist approach to the "homosexual problem."

In their very different ways, *The City and the Pillar* and *The Charioteer* are each significant gay fictions. Vidal's unapologetic novel is more daring than Renault's, yet it is *The Charioteer* that provides a happy ending for its gay lovers. *The City and the Pillar* is ironic, unsentimental, sparely written, and coolly critical, but *The Charioteer* ultimately deconstructs its own earnest accommodationism. If *The City and the Pillar* is finally the stronger of the two gay fictions, it may well be because Vidal, writing at the beginning of the crucial postwar decade and more confident in his social analysis than Renault, is less fettered by the sexual and social ideology that impinges with such force on *The Charioteer*. But both works reflect their historical moment even as they subvert some of the widely held notions of their day and as they place their contemporary quests in the context of archetypal homosexual myths. Both gay fictions ultimately arrive at the "plain of truth."

8

"Looking at the Naked Sun": James Baldwin's *Giovanni's Room*

James Baldwin's first two novels, *Go Tell It on the Mountain* (1953) and *Giovanni's Room* (1956), explore, respectively, race and sexuality, the twin issues of identity that were to be the focus of his entire career. In his powerful and moving first book, Baldwin established himself as an incisive interpreter of the black experience in America; and in his second novel, he tackled forthrightly the issue of homosexuality that was understated and implicit in *Go Tell It on the Mountain*. In his subsequent novels, issues of racial and sexual identity are consistently linked. The Negro and the homosexual are both exposed as artificial concepts, social constructions designed to fulfill the needs of the white heterosexual majority. "People invent categories in order to feel safe," he once remarked. "White people invented black people to give white people identity. . . . Straight cats invent faggots so they can sleep with them without becoming faggots themselves."[1] The creation of these categories is an attempt to displace what he described as "the terror within."[2] In work after work, the effects of racism and homophobia are graphically illustrated. As Dorothy Lee has pointed out, in the later novels Baldwin's gay characters repeatedly serve as agents of transformation and as catalysts of social action. In the shape of his career, there is a distinct pattern of increasing attention to homosexuality's function as a means of redemption, both for individuals and for communities.[3]

Despite its articulation of some of Baldwin's most characteristic themes, however, *Giovanni's Room* is frequently seen as anomalous in the writer's canon, largely because its central characters are white; and it has consequently received much less critical attention than *Go Tell It on the Mountain*, *Another Country* (1962), and the acclaimed essays. Nevertheless, Baldwin's second novel is a central text both in his canon and in the American literature of homosexuality. The choice of a white American and an Italian as the focal characters and the decision to set the novel in Paris may

172

have resulted from the author's attempt to resist being pigeonholed as a writer capable of depicting only the black experience in America.[4] Ironically, however, despite the obvious differences between Baldwin's own life and background and those of his characters, *Giovanni's Room* has frequently been regarded as autobiographical, and the protagonist, David, seen as a disguised self-portrait of the artist.

While Baldwin undoubtedly draws on his own experience as an expatriate and homosexual, and while the Whitman quotation that he uses in the dedication of the book—"I am the man, I suffered, I was there"—may encourage identification of the author with his narrator, the work is hardly autobiographical. The equation of Baldwin with his characters is unfortunate insofar as it has been used as a pretext for dismissing the book and denigrating the author—as, most notoriously, in Eldridge Cleaver's disgraceful attack on Baldwin in which he equates homosexuality with baby rape.[5] Moreover, the autobiographical assumption is untenable because it obscures a crucially important theme in the novel that requires a typical, white American as protagonist: the clash of American and European values. Like all of Baldwin's work, *Giovanni's Room* is a critique of American attitudes and of the American inability to face facts and to express emotion honestly. The novel dramatizes some of the social observations that Baldwin repeats in his essays, including his analysis of the American longing for the recovery of innocence and the function of conformity as a means of avoiding self-questioning.

But although the artistic vision of *Giovanni's Room* necessitated a white American as protagonist, Baldwin may also have been partially motivated in his decision not to include black characters by a desire to distance himself from his controversial subject. And while the French setting is also artistically justified, it too may have been motivated in part by what Roger Austen describes as the "xenophobic view of homosexuality as being outlandish in the sense of foreign," a distancing tactic used by several writers of popular gay fiction in this period. As Austen comments, "By keeping his persona both white and just bisexually confused and by setting him in the midst of foreign rather than domestic depravity, Baldwin was able to confound the [homophobic critics like Alfred Kazin and John Aldridge] for quite awhile."[6]

The author also played it safe by creating sufficient ambiguity in the depiction of homosexuality to allow multiple interpretations. By telling the story through the first-person voice of a sexually confused, unreliable narrator, by depicting the homosexual milieu as unattractive and decadent, and by framing the story with the melodramatic plot devices of a murder and an execution, Baldwin permits an anti-gay interpretation. Homophobic readers hell-bent on distorting the novel into "as vividly negative [a picture of homosexuality] as any religious sermon might be"[7] can, by taking evidence out of context, build a shaky and dubious case—though to do so is to misunderstand the work. Like Renault's *The Charioteer, Giovanni's Room* is necessarily impacted by the homophobia of its time. It reflects in its ambiguities the homophobic tenor of the Eisenhower years even as it challenges those assumptions.

But if the novel's ambiguities may have functioned as a protective device for its author at the beginning of his career, those ambiguities are not included merely for that purpose. The ambivalences about homosexuality expressed in the novel both vividly reflect the social reality of the time and themselves constitute the core of the protagonist's inner conflict. *Giovanni's Room* is, preeminently, a novel of the divided and deceitful self. A powerful and poignant dramatization of ambivalence and of the consequences of ambivalence, it is a coming-out story in which the anti-hero wrestles with the terror within. Though marred by its melodramatic plot, the work is a beautifully written, searing, and unsentimental account of the tragic failure of integrity, a failure that is at once personal and social. *Giovanni's Room* exposes the moral cowardice of its indecisive protagonist, but it also places his betrayal in the larger context of a more generalized hostility to love, one found within both the homosexual and heterosexual worlds. As a gay fiction, it conveys the intense psychological suffering inflicted by homophobia, while also sketching the homosexual's potential role as a redemptive figure.

The novel opens with David, a young, blond American standing at a window in a great house in the south of France. Anticipating "the most terrible morning of my life,"[8] he contemplates his reflection in the window pane as he broods on the imminent execution of Giovanni, his former lover, a young Italian. In a series of flashbacks, David recounts his homosexual initiation as a teenager with his best friend, Joey, whom he subsequently rejected; his uneasy relationship with his father and Aunt Ellen, who had reared him after the death of his mother; his flight to Paris "to find myself"; his affair with Giovanni; and his escape from that relationship into an engagement with a young American woman, Hella Lincoln. The novel ends the morning after Giovanni's execution, with David aware finally that "the key to my salvation, which cannot save my body, is hidden in my flesh."

The structure of the novel into a bifurcated flashback is reminiscent of Vidal's *The City and the Pillar* and functions equally meaningfully. The flashback technique creates suspense, raising questions as to how David has arrived at his present state and why Giovanni is to be executed. These interconnected questions are at the very heart of the book, and the search for their answers both propels the narrative forward and establishes the terms by which David is to be judged. Moreover, the flashback is, as Robert F. Sayre observes, "a natural recourse for Baldwin. In all his work the source of self-knowledge is always a new compound of the present and the past. To understand one is to understand the other and thus to become aware of one's illusions."[9] In *Giovanni's Room* the retrospective structure emphasizes how the past creates the present and necessarily impinges on all the days and nights to follow. The narrator's guilt-ridden meditation on his personal history culminates in an epiphany that makes possible a hopeful future.

The two unequal divisions of the novel are also designed to reinforce theme and meaning, as John Shawcross explains:

> The first part, as it were, fits into the second. The first part explores largely the demands of traditional society and David's movement into a homosexual relationship. The second part explores the way in which the demands have been met before that relationship and are attempted to be continued afterward, with disastrous results for all concerned. The novel itself becomes a room in which there is another room: the inner room and being, the outer room and society.[10]

Thus, the book's very structure makes clear that the social and the personal, the public and the private are crucially interrelated. Despite the relentless focus on the protagonist's inner life, the novel's concerns are communal as well as idiosyncratic. Homosexuality in *Giovanni's Room* is not merely a private experience, for the social prohibitions against homosexuality are unavoidably internalized and they inexorably intrude even into Giovanni's closet-like retreat.

The social prohibitions against homosexuality—ranging from the "extreme disapprobation" with which the French regard "*les goûts particuliers*" to its criminalization by the United States—permeate the novel and variously but inevitably affect all its characters. These prohibitions are reflected in the decadence of Guillaume's bar (which is periodically raided by the police) and in the barely concealed despair of its patrons, the paunchy, bespectacled gentlemen with restlessly searching eyes, the "knife-blade lean, tight-trousered boys," and the improbably dressed *folles,* or transvestites, "screaming like parrots the details of their latest love affairs."

As depicted by Baldwin—and as filtered through the unsparing and clearly biased eyes of David, the first-person narrator—the gay subculture of early-1950s Paris is a loveless meat market devoid of affection, respect, and dignity. Its habitués seem doomed to suffering and pain, as epitomized by the sibylline warning of the grotesquely made-up "zombie" who clutches a crucifix as he warns David in the bar: "you shall burn in a very hot fire. . . . You will be very unhappy." The unfulfilling life of the gay characters in the book is defined most clearly, if also tendentiously, by David's taunting question to Jacques, "Is there really no other way for you but this? To kneel down forever before an army of boys for just five dirty minutes in the dark?'' As it turns out, however, the novel does suggest another way of life, but one that requires greater courage than David, for all his smug superiority, is at this point able to muster.

The effect of the social prohibitions is not only to create a desperate subculture that veers constantly on the verge of hysteria but also, perhaps even more damagingly, to promote an enormous quantity of self-loathing. Rather than feeling a sense of solidarity with other homosexuals, the gay characters in *Giovanni's Room* seek only companions to share their misery. The young and poor are simply prey to be used and discarded; the old and wealthy are merely objects of pity and scorn. As is the case with the privileging of heterosexuality in *The City and the Pillar*, the attraction of Baldwin's characters for heterosexuals has much less to do with sexual desire than with self-contempt, as is obvious, for example, in Jacques's vaunted affection for the ostensibly heterosexual David, which is actually "the desire, in fact, to be rid of me, to be able, soon, to despise me as he now despised that army of boys who had come, without love, to his bed." Self-loathing is reflected as well in the campy banter between Jacques and Guillaume, which "bubbled upward out of them like a fountain of black water." Self-contempt is present even in the epithets directed toward others, as when Giovanni refers to David, Jacques, and Guillaume "and all your disgusting band of fairies" and David describes the murdered Guillaume as "just a disgusting old fairy. That's *all* he was."

The gay subculture of *Giovanni's Room* is as sordid and unattractive as that in Renault's *The Charioteer*. Both authors differentiate their focal characters from their fellow gays, contrasting them with the decadent habitués of the gay scene in order to establish their relative normality and lack of corruption. But Baldwin is far less moralistic than Renault, much less concerned with issues of respectability, and even more skeptical of the romanticization of innocence. Consequently, for all the sensationalistic touches in his portrait, the gay subculture is depicted with much greater sophistication in his novel than in Renault's. The challenge that the gay *milieu* poses for the characters of *Giovanni's Room* is one that Baldwin noted in his 1954 essay "The Male Prison," where he observed that the homosexual can save himself only

by the most tremendous exertion of all his forces from falling into an underworld in which he never meets either men or women, where it is impossible to have either a lover or a friend, where the possibility of genuine human growth has ceased.[11]

Giovanni echoes this passage when he reproaches David as "a lover who is neither man nor woman, nothing that I can know or touch." As George E.

Kent notes, "The homosexual's problem [in *Giovanni's Room*] is shown to be the threat of being forced into the underworld, where bought love of the body, without transcendence, is simply productive of desperation."[12] But the trivialization of love that characterizes the homosexual subculture in the novel is by no means limited exclusively to it, as indicated by David's heartless exploitation of Sue and by Hella's reports of the widowed ladies in Spain, who prey on young men. In *Giovanni's Room* the homosexual underworld is less a symbol of depravity than a predictable product of homophobia, and its habitués are less villains than victims.

This context of external and internalized homophobia renders the problematical protagonist a victim as well. Appropriately framed by beginning and closing scenes of David in the great house staring at his reflection in the mirror, the narrative is a relentless self-inquisition and an unsparing confession. What David sees in his mirror is not a pretty picture, but Baldwin contrives to maintain sympathy for his narrator by revealing his attitudes as typical of his generation and background. David is held responsible for his actions, but the novel is aware that individual decisions are the products of elaborate social pressures. They are "at the mercy of more things than can be named." A painful exercise in unflinchingly "looking at the naked sun" after a long history of evading self-knowledge, the novel is David's attempt to understand himself and his persistent failures of intimacy. Central to that understanding is an honest recognition and, finally, acceptance of that aspect of his identity that he has so painfully denied at great cost not only to himself but to others: his homosexuality. Only with his acceptance of his homosexuality as an indivisible element of his identity will David be able to fulfill the promise of his name, which means "loving" in Hebrew.

As a coming-out story, the stages of David's awakening to his "insistent possibilities" are familiar enough, but, unlike Jim Willard of *The City and the Pillar*, he is not a homosexual Everyman. Like Jim, David is a bland and typical American scarcely distinguishable from others of his generation. But he is a more complex and more deeply divided character than Jim, and his suffering is more intense. As he describes himself early in the book, signaling both his complexity and his potential unreliability as a narrator, he is "too various to be trusted." He resists self-knowledge with a greater intensity and his coming to grips with his homosexuality is consequently a far more difficult and hurtful process than that experienced by Jim. Baldwin's acute consciousness of the power of homophobia to shape character and destroy lives helps make David's self-deceptions and betrayals comprehensible if not altogether forgivable.

The central betrayal of the novel is, of course, David's betrayal of Giovanni. But David's pattern of betrayal begins much earlier, with his rejection of Joey, which is simultaneously—and more fatefully—a rejection of himself as well. The spontaneous lovemaking with Joey, the sound of whose name suggests "joy," is an exhilarating but disturbing revelation that stirs heat and tenderness. It also occasions profound joy in mutual giving. "It seemed, then," David reflects, "that a lifetime would not be long enough for me to act with Joey the act of love." But that lifetime ends abruptly the next morning, for after joy comes fear and shame: "It was borne in on me: *But Joey is a boy.*" The very body that had inspired such tenderness now seems "the black opening of a cavern in which I would be tortured till madness came, in which I would lose my manhood." Suddenly afraid, David remembers all the ugly innuendos and homophobic slurs that are part of the psychic furniture of every adolescent who grows up in an anti-gay society: "A cavern opened in my mind, black, full of rumor, suggestion, of half-heard, half-forgotten, half-understood stories, full of dirty words. I thought I saw my future in that cavern." What had been an adventure of discovery becomes a black cavern in which the self is threatened with oblivion. David willfully and secretly decides to reject Joey. Not yet knowing the Forsterian lesson that the body is more powerful than the spirit, David determines "to allow no room in the universe for something which shamed and frightened me." He later comes to realize that his belief in his own willpower is itself but another act of self-deception.

The episode with Joey is significant not merely because it anticipates the later rejection of Giovanni, but also because it illustrates the pattern of David's entire life, which is a sequence of flights—not to find himself, as he supposes, but to escape knowledge of himself. The words *flight, flee, fly* recur over and over in the novel, establishing David's life as a series of evasions, of repeated attempts to avoid the confrontation with self that is like "looking at the naked sun." Thus, after he breaks off his friendship with Joey and treats him badly, David becomes terrified that the very fact that such a person as Joey could once have been his best friend might indicate something shocking about himself. It might be "proof of some horrifying taint in me," he fears. Characteristically, his solution is to flee the terror within by "not looking at the universe, by not looking at myself, by remaining . . . in constant motion."

David forgets Joey, takes up with a rougher, older crowd, and becomes secretive and cruel and increasingly self-destructive. Fearful that he cannot live up to his hard-drinking father's conventional ideal of red-blooded American manhood—"when I say a man," David's father tells his sister, "I don't mean a Sunday school teacher"—Butch, as David is tellingly nicknamed, retreats "in full flight." His inability to share himself with his father is paradigmatic of all his subsequent relationships. David's flight from intimacy leaves the older man—who escapes his own internal terror by recourse to alcohol—baffled and afraid, and himself lonely and alienated. Although David attempts to allay his recurrent doubts about his manhood by "wandering through . . . forests of desperate women," he occasionally, when drunk enough, indulges in one-sided homosexual encounters, one of which "involved a fairy who was later court-martialed" from the Army. "The panic his punishment caused in me," David admits, "was as close as I ever came to facing in myself the terrors I sometimes saw clouding another man's eyes." Utterly weary of a life of alcoholic binges and meaningless, emotionally unsatisfying heterosexual affairs, he departs for France ostensibly "to find myself," a phrase that, as he says, "betrays a nagging suspicion that something has been misplaced."

The self that David finally discovers in Paris turns out to be only the same self from which he has spent so much time in flight. There is, he ruefully confesses, "something fantastic" in having "run so far, so hard, across the ocean even, only to find myself brought up short once more before the bulldog in my own backyard." But in Baldwin's variation on the Jamesian formula of naive Americans in sophisticated Europe, Paris functions as the city he described in a 1954 essay appropriately entitled "A Question of Identity," in which

> everyone loses his head, and his morals, lives through at least one *histoire d'amour*, ceases, quite, to arrive anywhere on time, and thumbs his nose at the Puritans—the city, in brief, where all become drunken on the fine old air of freedom.[13]

In this more relaxed atmosphere, David feels safe to associate with homosexuals, though mainly to prove to himself that he is not one of them. Practicing "a tolerance which placed me, I believed, above suspicion," he is a tourist in *le milieu*, observing its inhabitants as though they were animals in a zoo. Always protective of his "*immaculate* manhood," he exudes a sense of heterosexual superiority and condescends to his companions. Nevertheless, when he accompanies Jacques to Guillaume's bar on the pivotal night that he falls in love with Giovanni, he is conscious of the fact that "people were taking bets about me," for once on a previous occasion, when very drunk, he had caused a minor sensation in the bar by flirting with a soldier. By the end of the evening, he is embarrassedly aware that "the tables had been turned; now I was in the zoo, and they were watching." As he feels an irresistible attraction toward Giovanni, he is self-conscious and ashamed, particularly since Jacques, to whom he had extended such condescending tolerance, is an amused witness to "the ferocious excitement which had burst in me like a storm."

Jacques, a Belgian-born American businessman, capable both of exceptional generosity and incredible stinginess, is an important character in the novel. A pathetic figure trapped in a futile quest for love with younger partners, whose favors have to be purchased, he partakes of the self-loathing and desperation characteristic of *le milieu*. He has, he tells David, "arrived at his present wretchedness by imperceptible degrees." He is implicated in the betrayal of Giovanni, but his hands, as David admits, "are certainly no bloodier than mine." In his undignified pursuit of an army of boys, Jacques is the living embodiment of David's internal terror, the actualization of that ugly future he had imagined the morning after his lovemaking with Joey. As David later comes to realize, "the contempt I felt for him involved my self-contempt." Perhaps this explains the younger man's failure of compassion toward the older, his inability to understand how loneliness leads to promiscuity and to see Jacques's life as less shameful than emblematic of the failure of love. As the Belgian says, encapsulating the premise of the entire novel, "*Somebody* . . . should have told us that not many people have ever died of love. But multitudes have perished, and are perishing every hour—and in the oddest places!—for the lack of it."

But if Jacques represents all that David dreads in himself, he also functions as a spokesman for a more positive alternative, the salvific potential that also resides within the young American. Jacques articulates the hopeful message that love can give meaning to sexual expression, transforming the "five dirty minutes in the dark" from something sordid into something beautiful. His advice to David on the brink of his affair with Giovanni establishes the terms against which the affair must be measured, and enunciates the positive potential implicit in homosexual love. Speaking from personal experience as a kind of negative exemplum, he envisions an alternative to the desperation of his own life. Conceding that a lot of his life is despicable, he insists that there are many ways of being despicable and that what is most despicable of all is "to be contemptuous of other people's pain"—the very sin of which David is repeatedly guilty.

In a discussion crucial to formulating the novel's attitude toward homosexuality and toward the David–Giovanni affair, Jacques explains that the reason his own encounters are shameful is not because of anything inherent in homosexuality but "Because there is no affection in them, and no joy." He urges David to avoid his own mistakes and not play it safe. "Confusion is a luxury which only the very, very young can possibly afford," he reminds David pointedly. He tells him to love Giovanni: "love him and let him love you. Do you really think anything else under heaven really matters?" He harbors no illusions about the prospect of a long-term relationship between men who "still have everywhere to go." But however brief the affair might be, Jacques cautions David not to think of the minutes he will share with Giovanni as dirty, for "if you think of them as dirty, then they *will* be dirty—they will be dirty because you will be giving nothing, you will be despising your flesh and his." He tells David that he can invest his time with Giovanni with beauty and meaning: "you can give each other something which will make both of you better—forever—if you will *not* be ashamed, if you will only *not* play it safe." He warns David that if he plays it safe long enough, "you will end up trapped in your own dirty body, forever and forever and forever—like me." Precisely because the young American is unable, or unwilling, to accept Jacques's advice, the affair with Giovanni is doomed.

The ambivalence David feels even as he responds most fully to the dark and leonine young man who is to become his lover both predicates the end of the affair and suggests its enormous potential. He is attracted to Giovanni's naturalness and charm and perceptively discerns beneath his beauty and bravado a touching vulnerability that he finds inexpressibly moving. Yet he is painfully divided. As he first feels drawn to Giovanni in Guillaume's bar, David desperately wishes he could find the strength "to turn and walk out—to have gone over to Montparnasse perhaps and picked up a girl. Any girl." Later, in Les Halles, he wants to reach out and comfort Giovanni, but at the same time he wants to flee once again. As he prepares to leave the bistro with the young Italian, he suddenly aches with a longing to go home, "home across the ocean, to things and people I knew and understood." As the young men finally enter Giovanni's tiny room, David thinks, "if I do not open the door at once and get out of here, I am lost. But I knew I could not open the door, I knew it was too late; soon it was too late to do anything but moan." As Giovanni pulls him into his bed, everything in David screams *No!*—"yet the sum of me sighed *Yes.*" Awakened to joy and amazement, yet dogged by fear and shame, David brings to Giovanni's room the warring elements of his personality: a capacity for homosexual tenderness coupled with the loathing of that very need.

The central symbol of the novel, Giovanni's womblike room is, at least initially, a safe refuge from the outside world's homophobia and hostility to love. Located far from the center of Paris and *le milieu*, the room is a private realm in which the young men can freely give themselves to each other. It is an emblem of the separateness of their love, its naturalness and purity. But it is also Giovanni's cluttered last retreat that houses the detritus of his wounded life. It is the place of his suffering and expiation, his "punishment and grief." And it is the increasingly claustrophobic space in which David is forced to face the truth of his own deepest nature, as the walls of the room close in on him. A maid's room where David plays the role of housewife while Giovanni goes off to earn their living, it is also the scene of the American's rebellion against unconventional sex roles, his revulsion at the thought of himself as less than a man. Rather than symbolizing "the sterility and self-destruction of homosexual love," as Colin MacInnes alleges, the room, as Stephen Adams observes, encapsulates all the complex facets of the Giovanni–David relationship[14] as it develops from the idyllic timelessness of its beginning in Part Two of the novel to the bitterness and despair of its ugly conclusion. It is the scene both of love's triumph and of its failure.

Foremost, the room is persistently and exclusively Giovanni's room, the place to which he fled from Italy and the place to which he is consigned when David abandons him. The disorder of the room represents Giovanni's "regurgitated life," his loneliness and alienation, his own inner terror. The great well of sorrow that lies beneath the hearty bravado with which he faces the external world is the legacy of a tragic past that is distilled and concentrated in the tiny enclosure. This is the baggage that he carries with him into the relationship with David, the counterpart of the American's ambivalence about homosexuality. At the birth of his gray, twisted, still-born child, Giovanni had cursed God and spat on a crucifix. In despair and as penance, he fled his wife and family and olive trees in Italy, where it was warm and sunny, for cold, damp Paris, "this city where surely God has punished me for all my sins and for spitting on His holy Son, and where I will surely die."

Like David's own flight to Paris, Giovanni's is also a rejection of life. "It was the day of my death," he tells David. "I wish it had been the day of my death." In Paris, however, he has been "saved," at least economically and temporarily, by his patron Guillaume. More significantly, his will to live has been awakened by David. As he tells the American on their initial meeting, "I have only just found out that I want to live." Giovanni's heroic but ineffectual struggle to remodel the room reflects his new commitment to life and to his relationship with David, who stands "between him and the dark." It is a brave attempt to transform the room from a bleak cave of despair into a bright haven of hope. As the scene of his lovemaking with David, the room signifies the possibility of Giovanni's rebirth. But as the place of his betrayal and abandonment by David, it also represents his consignment to the dark.

The Giovanni–David relationship offers both partners an opportunity to "say Yes to life," but this opportunity is ultimately rejected by David. He soon realizes why Giovanni fell in love with him and brought him to his room: "I was to destroy this room and give to Giovanni a new and better life. This life could only be my own, which in order to transform Giovanni's, must first become a part of Giovanni's room." But David is unable to share his life fully with anyone else. As he later admits, "Even at my most candid, even when I tried hardest to give myself to [Giovanni] as he gave himself to me, I was holding something back." Consequently, he never makes the room his own—it always remains Giovanni's. Unwilling to assume the burden of his lover's pain, David resents the Italian's dependence on him (even as he also encourages it, as indicated by his frequent references to Giovanni as "baby," an epithet that reflects his own need to believe in Giovanni's essentially childlike innocence). When Hella accepts his earlier offer of marriage, David feels relieved of his responsibility to Giovanni. "It seemed that the necessity for decision had been taken from my hands," the American rationalizes as he makes the choice to leave his sorrowful lover (whose name, significantly, means "God has given").

Cast in the role of Giovanni's savior, David becomes his betrayer. "Judas and the Savior had met in me," David thinks, when he gives his lover false assurances after he has already decided to leave him. The enormity of David's betrayal is emphasized by Giovanni's despair when he is humiliated and fired by Guillaume and turns to David for comfort and solace. "If you were not here," Giovanni tells his friend, "this would be the end of Giovanni. . . . I do not think I would be able to live if I had to be alone again." When Giovanni tearfully recounts his humiliation at the hands of his employer, David takes him into his arms, but at the same time also wonders "with an unwilling, unbelieving contempt, why I had ever thought him strong." David's contempt for his friend's suffering is thus related to his allegiance to conventional ideas of manly behavior, his unease with Giovanni's tears. In his rejection of Giovanni, and in his unwillingness (or inability) to bear his lover's burden, David proves himself, in Jacques's phrase, "really despicable." As Giovanni complains after the American leaves him, "It is cruel to have made me want to live only to make my death more bloody." The guilt that informs David's narrative is justified.

But David's betrayal of Giovanni is also comprehensible. The American's internalized homophobia is so great that the very source of his love for Giovanni engenders its opposite. Holding the Italian responsible for the same homosexual tendencies that make possible their love for each other, David comes to hate him with a hatred "which was as powerful as my love and which was nourished by the same roots." In a characteristic refusal to look at the naked sun, he blames Giovanni for having "awakened an itch" of homosexual desire.

In the first flush of David's love for the Italian, when the two men leave the room and sport childishly outdoors, an incident occurs that illustrates the complexity of the American's feelings of love and hate for Giovanni. At this very moment when David loves Giovanni with an intensity that causes him to flow toward his friend "as a river rushes when the ice breaks up," at this moment a stranger passes and David is astonished to find himself sexually attracted: "I invested him at once with Giovanni's beauty and what I felt for Giovanni I also felt for him." Giovanni notices David's reaction and laughs, finding it a natural response to beauty, but the American is badly shaken, his innocent idyll suddenly tainted by blatant sexual desire. "I felt sorrow and shame and panic and great bitterness," he reports. He regards his homosexuality as a "beast which Giovanni had awakened in me [that] would never go to sleep again." He wonders, "would I then, like all the others, find myself turning and following all kinds of boys down God knows what dark avenues, into what dark places?" David is similarly panic-stricken when he encounters a beautiful blond American sailor who, wearing his masculinity "as unequivocally as he wore his skin," recognizes David's homosexuality and gives him a contemptuously knowing look: "I knew that what the sailor had seen in my unguarded eyes was envy and desire: I had seen it often in Jacques' eyes and my reaction and the sailor's had been the same." Once again, David sees yawning before him a black cavern of homosexual desire in which lies an intolerable future. His fear of this dread future poisons his relationship with Giovanni, causing him to project his self-loathing onto the very person he loves.

The extremity of David's fear of homosexuality is presented as an aspect of his American identity, as is his related tendency to valorize innocence, which tellingly contrasts with Giovanni's untroubled acceptance of bisexual experience and his European sophistication about *la vie pratique*. As Stephen Adams notes,

> The Italian's frankness, warmth and uninhibited desires are set against the other's duplicity, reserve and feelings of guilt. These differences form part of a cultural dialectic, the Mediterranean temperament being pitted against the North American in a confrontation between pagan and puritan outlooks on life.[15]

When Giovanni protests that "We have not committed any crime," David responds revealingly, "it *is* a crime—in my country and, after all, I didn't grow up here, I grew up *there*." The contrast between David's and Giovanni's attitudes reflects Baldwin's contention that Americans are singularly hostile to homosexuality. "What always occurs to me is that people in other parts of the world have never had this peculiar kind of conflict," the writer observed in an interview. "The fact that Americans consider [homosexuality] a disease says more about them than it says about homosexuality."[16] In a very large measure, David's internalized homophobia is the product of American prejudice, and the novel's indictment of the world's hostility to love is specifically (though not exclusively) directed against American attitudes.

The American criminalization of homosexuality reinforces its connection in David's mind with the loss of innocence, a commodity that Giovanni has already sacrificed in his troubled past. In his 1961 essay, "The Black Boy Looks at the White Boy," Baldwin identifies the desperate need to preserve innocence as a characteristic of white Americans: "the things that most white people imagine that they can salvage from the storm of life is really, in sum, their innocence."[17] But the innocence so salvaged is merely naiveté. David's yearning for a recovery of innocence is at once (and relatedly) a verification of his status as a *vrai américain*—one who needs to pretend that suffering and death do not exist—and an expression of internalized homophobia. It is a way of saying No to life, denying its complexity and comprehensiveness.

The naiveté of David's desire to evade experience is apparent in his romantic nostalgia for the Garden of Eden. This symbol of innocence, and of its loss, is parodied in the description of *les folles* as barnyard animals, indicating the lack of innocence of the inhabitants of *le milieu*, which is anything but a paradise. More interestingly, the Garden of Eden is evoked in the ragged wallpaper in Giovanni's room, which depicts a man and woman walking together in a rose garden. From David's perspective, the wallpaper's idealized representation of heterosexuality underlines the unnaturalness of his relationship with Giovanni, but from another perspective the fading image of archaic lovers functions as a kind of blessing, verifying the essential innocence of David and Giovanni's idyll. From yet another vantage point, the image, in its sterility and irrelevance, its removal from the real life seething in the room, may be seen to mock David's yearning for a timeless, hermetically sealed, eternal spring of innocence. As a relic from a crumbling past, the representation rebukes David's attempt to arrest time and resist growth.

Most significantly, the myth of the Garden of Eden is explicitly invoked when David tells Jacques that Giovanni should have "stayed down there in that village of his in Italy and planted his olive trees and had a lot of children and beaten his wife." This romanticization of Giovanni's paradisal past is undercut when Jacques, the voice of experience, observes that "Nobody can stay in the garden of Eden." David sadly muses that one scarcely sees the garden before the flaming sword of expulsion descends. "Then, perhaps," he thinks,

> life only offers the choice of remembering the garden or forgetting it. Either, or: it takes strength to remember, it takes another kind of strength to forget, it takes a hero to do both . . . the world is mostly divided between madmen who remember and madmen who forget. Heroes are rare.

Giovanni attempts to forget the garden, David to remember it. Neither, at this point in the novel anyway, is a hero. But by the end of the book, when David abandons his illusions and both remembers the garden and forgets it, he accepts the world of experience and achieves a kind of heroism. Like Milton's Adam and Eve, he goes forward into a fallen world sustained by God's grace, exchanging internal terror for the possibility of creating a paradise within.

David's valorization of innocence and his evasion of experience are related to his obsession with cleanliness, including, most particularly, his
"*immaculate* manhood." Images of dirt and smell abound in the novel, and
they are connected with David's conviction that the world is dirty and that
sexual experience, especially homosexuality, is sordid. It is not coincidental
that his lovemaking with Joey begins in the shower, that afterward David
notices the sweat on Joey's body and the "sweet disorder" of the bed-
sheets, and that ultimately he describes the incident as remaining in his
mind "as still and as awful as a decomposing corpse." Similarly, David
first notices the clutter of Giovanni's room, gradually becomes uncomfort-
able with its disorder, and is finally repelled by its dirt. If Giovanni is also
in flight from a soiled world, at least he has a more mature acceptance of
the messiness of life and he does not consider homosexuality to be dirty per
se. When David reminds him that "People have very dirty words for this—
for this situation," Giovanni rebukes his attitude as immature. "I really do
not know how you have managed to live so long," he tells David, "People
are full of dirty words. The only time they do not use them . . . is when
they are describing something dirty."

In a passage crucial to understanding David's inability to share himself
with anyone else, Giovanni bitterly accuses the American of wanting "to be
clean. You think you came here covered with soap and you think you will
go out covered with soap—and you do not want to *stink*, not even for five
minutes in the meantime." This indictment of David's obsessive cleanliness
underlines his emotional isolation, his fear of contamination by involvement
with others. In its echo of David's characterization of Jacques's sexual encounters as "five dirty minutes in the dark," this passage also evokes Jacques's point that the lovers can make their lives beautiful if only they do not
regard their lovemaking as dirty, and his warning that by being ashamed
and playing it safe, David risks ending up trapped in his own dirty body.
Because of David's fear of "the stink of love," this is precisely his fate.

In "A Question of Identity," Baldwin writes that after experiencing the
cavalier freedom of Paris, Americans characteristically begin "to long for
the prison of home—home then becoming the place where questions are
not asked."[18] This is exactly the case with David and Hella in *Giovanni's
Room*. They both discover that "nothing is more unbearable, once one has
it, than freedom." Consequently, the prison of America's rigid sex-role expectations becomes attractive to them, representing safety and stability.
There is some truth, as it turns out, in Guillaume's cynical description of
David as "just an American boy . . . doing things in France which you
would not dare to do at home" and in his comment that "The Americans
always fly. They are not serious." Moreover, the American reluctance to
probe emotion very deeply offers David and Hella the prospect of welcome
relief from the incessant self-examination of their exile, a dispensation from
the demand that they look at the naked sun.

The American reluctance to ask questions is illustrated when David receives a letter from his father requesting him to return home. He notices that the question his father really wants to ask—"*Is it a woman, David?*"—is not in the letter. "He could not risk the question because he could not have endured an answer in the negative," David reflects. "An answer in the negative would have revealed what strangers we had become." Interestingly, the letter in which Hella announces her acceptance of David's proposal also provides a conventionally respectable answer to his father's unasked question. With Hella's return, David's life with Giovanni will be finished and, he thinks, his homosexuality will "be something that had happened to me once—it would be something that had happened to many men once." It will be consigned to the unexamined past. Appropriately longing for a place where questions are not asked, especially not of oneself, David flees Giovanni for the arms of Hella and the prison of home.

David and Hella eagerly embrace the straitjacket of traditional American sex-role conventions. After their self-confrontations in Paris—David with his homosexuality, Hella with her own sexual confusion and lack of artistic talent—the two expatriates long nostalgically for a "web of safety." But this safety is simply the security of conformity, in which the conventional sex roles reassure the participants of their sexual identity. Precisely because Hella and David find the prospect of looking at the naked sun—confronting directly the terror within them—so frightening, they find the unquestioned adherence to conventional sex roles comforting.

Indeed, the most threatening aspect of homosexuality for David is its implicit challenge to these conventions. Living in the maid's room causes him to doubt his masculinity, as he ludicrously casts himself in the role of a dependent female housewife. In asking Giovanni "What kind of life can two men have together, anyway," David reveals his inability to conceive of relationships except in terms of the conventional heterosexual paradigm of the 1950s. He accuses the Italian of wanting to emasculate him:

> "You want to go out and be the big laborer and bring home the money, and you want me to stay here and wash the dishes and cook the food and clean this miserable closet of a room and kiss you when you come in through that door and lie with you at night and be your little *girl*."

But this parody of conventional heterosexual relationships is clearly a projection of David's own insecurities, for, after all, he has financial resources sufficient to rescue both of them, if only he had the courage to make a commitment. Because of his having "absorbed the simplified, compartmentalized thinking of his background," as George Kent describes his habit of thought,[19] he consistently sees lovers in terms of their sex roles rather than as individuals. This contrasts with Giovanni, who talks about *who* he wants, not *what* he wants, reflecting Baldwin's own view that "It's impossible to go through life assuming that you know who you're going to fall in love with. You don't."[20] When David protests, "But I'm a man . . . a man! What do you think can *happen* between us?" Giovanni replies, "You know very well . . . what can happen between us." He adds insightfully: "It is for that reason you are leaving me."

David's doubts about his masculinity prompt him to a callous and characteristically selfish act, when he uses Sue to allay his anxiety about his ability to perform heterosexually. This ruthless experiment assures him that "what I had been afraid of had nothing to do with my body." But all that he really proves is his ability to make love "only with the body," a practice that compounds loneliness. Even as he labors to complete the "grisly act of love" with Sue, the image that fills his mind is not hers but Giovanni's. David hurts and bewilders Sue, making her feel exploited and rejected. Even he acknowledges that what he does with Giovanni "could not possibly be more immoral" than what he does to her.

As David walks home from Sue's room, confirmed in his heterosexuality, he entertains dreams so conformist as to be poignant:

> I wanted to be inside again, with the light and safety, with my manhood un-questioned, watching my woman put my children to bed at night. I wanted the same bed at night and the same arms and I wanted to rise in the morning knowing where I was. I wanted a woman to be for me a steady ground, like the earth itself, where I could always be renewed.

There is nothing intrinsically wrong with these dreams, but they are rendered hollow by David's motivations and by his selfish disregard for others. Juxtaposed with his abuse of Sue, this vision of heterosexual bliss is severely undercut, for it is based on exploitation. It confirms David's tendency to think in terms of sexual classifications rather than of individuals, and it reveals his profound lack of self-knowledge. The poignancy of the vision stems from the combination of its simplicity and the impossibility of his achieving it. He thinks, "It only demanded a short, hard strength for me to become myself again." But in his refusal to look at the naked sun, David has at this point in the novel only managed to evade knowledge of who he really is.

In a familiar pattern, David flees knowledge of himself for the respectability of heterosexual conformity, in this case as localized in the person of Hella Lincoln, whose surname ironically promises emancipation but whose Christian name intimates the underworld of guilt into which David will later lapse. The relationship of the two is fatally flawed from the very beginning, for it is based not on love but on fear. For each of them, marriage represents a means to escape self-knowledge. In flight from his homosexuality, David sees marriage as a way to preserve his *"immaculate manhood"* and to satisfy traditional sex-role expectations. He finds in Hella's body "the possibility of legitimate surrender"—a phrase that recalls his conception of homosexuality as criminal. In making love to her he hopes to exorcise his continuing desire for the young Italian, "whose body was burned into my mind, into my dreams." In Hella's bed, he seeks "to burn out . . . my image of Giovanni and the reality of his touch . . . to drive out fire with fire." Thus, David's desire for Hella is less active than reactive. Serving her up to his conventional father as *"just the little woman,"* he uses her almost as ruthlessly as he uses Sue.

But Hella's own attraction to David is similarly implicated in self-doubt and also represents a lack of courage. Her embrace of the 1950s conservative ideal of womanhood, her willingness to be David's "obedient and most loving servant," is less an affirmative choice than a retreat from her own sexual confusion and artistic failure. She is aware that the traditional sex-role expectations are unsatisfying. She expresses some reluctance to assume the role women are assigned in a conventional heterosexual relationship: "to be at the mercy of some gross, unshaven stranger before you can begin to be yourself." But because of her self-doubt and sexual confusion, she accepts the "humiliating necessity" to submit herself to masculine authority. "From now on," she explains revealingly, "I can have a wonderful time complaining about being a woman. But I won't be terrified that I'm *not* one." Having failed as an artist, Hella also doubts her talent and, even more damagingly, her self-worth. Although David sees her as the means by which he can make real his ideal of heterosexual contentment, Hella herself sees marriage and motherhood as merely her only option, her last retreat. "I'm not really the emancipated girl I try to be at all," she tells David. "I guess I just want a man to come home to me every night. I want to be able to sleep with a man without being afraid he's going to knock me up. Hell, I want to be knocked up. I want to start having babies. In a way, it's really all I'm good for." Self-contempt is by no means the exclusive province of Baldwin's gay characters. Hella's lack of self-esteem throws a new and different light on her comment, when she accepts David's proposal of marriage, "I've decided to let two try it. This business of loving me, I mean." She, too, is a victim of love's failure.

Forged as it is in desperation and self-doubt, and pursued in the shadow of betrayal, it is not surprising that the relationship of David and Hella soon sours. No more able to share himself with Hella than he was with Giovanni, David's relationship with her sinks beneath the terrible burden of his guilt and the undeniable reality of his homosexuality. When the scandal of Giovanni's arrest and conviction for the murder of Guillaume breaks, David and Hella flee to southern France and the "nightmare" of the great house begins. In this rented house, so much more spacious than the closet-like

maid's room that he shared with Giovanni, David feels even more imprisoned and claustrophobic. He cannot get Giovanni out of his mind; he learns
that "in fleeing from his body, I confirmed and perpetuated his body's
power over me." David's desperate attempts to exorcise him through furi-
ous lovemaking with Hella fails: "something was gone: the astonishment,
the power, and the joy were gone, the peace was gone."

Repeating his previous reactions to intimate relationships, David comes
to associate Hella with uncleanliness, complaining of the smell of her
washed underwear as it dries in the bathroom, much as he had complained
of the disorder of Giovanni's room. David's reaction is, of course, yet another expression of his fear of intimacy, his rejection of the "stink of
love."[21] This response to Hella indicates that David's revulsion against the
dirt of Giovanni's room had less to do with homosexuality than with an
aversion to sexual experience itself. Perhaps most tellingly, he comes to
find her body grotesque: "I sometimes watched her naked body move and
wished that it were harder and firmer, I was fantastically intimidated by her
breasts, and when I entered her I began to feel that I would never get out
alive." When Hella pleads for him to make love to her, "Just let me be a
woman, take me. It's what I want. It's *all* I want," David feels his body
recoil and draw away from her. This revulsion for heterosexual contact parallels the homosexual panic he suffered with Giovanni.

Frightened and perplexed by the changes in David, Hella begs him to
confide in her, to tell her the truth. But, characteristically, he is unable
either to give of himself or to be honest. Once again, he flees—this time to
Nice, where, "blind with alcohol and grim with lust," he spends a lost
weekend with a sailor and where Hella finally discovers him in a gay bar.
With some justice, John Shawcross complains that the focal detail of Hella's appearance in the gay bar is not well prepared for and, therefore, seems
unexplainable—at least how she would be able to discover the particular
bar to which David had fled.[22] But there could not have been a large number of gay bars in Nice in the 1950s, and Hella certainly has reason to be
suspicious of David's sexual orientation by this point in their relationship.

When they confront each other in the bar, David tells Hella, "now you
know," and she replies, "I think I've known it for a long time." Later, she
elaborates: "I *knew* . . . I knew. This is what makes me so ashamed. I
knew it every time you looked at me. I knew it every time we went to
bed." With understandable bitterness, she attacks David for his dishonesty
and failure of responsibility. "If only you had told me the truth *then*. Don't
you see how unjust it was to wait for *me* to find it out? To put all the
burden on *me*." David's selfishness and evasions in his relationship with
Hella are predictable from his past relationships with Joey, Sue, and, especially, Giovanni. Declaring that "Americans should never come to Eu-

rope," Hella departs for the safety of America. "I wish I'd never left it," she says, and adds: "If I stay here much longer, I'll forget what it's like to be a woman." Disillusioned and defeated, Hella retreats to the comfort of American conformity.

Giovanni's Room ends, however, not on a note of defeat but of hope. David's apparent defeat is translated into a subjective victory. Alone in the great house that he has cleaned, abandoned by his mistress and devastated by the imminent death of his former lover, David finally looks at the naked sun. By accepting his loss of innocence and embracing the world of experience, he learns the means to his salvation. From the contemplation of the suffering of Giovanni and the dishonesty of his own life, he experiences a revelation that promises a rebirth, a kind of paradise within. He goes into the bedroom, undresses, and stares into the mirror. What he sees, swinging before him "like an unexpected lantern on a dark, dark night," is Giovanni's face, as he prepares to exit "this dirty world, this dirty body." At this moment of revelation—this epiphany to which the whole book has been leading—David identifies with the anguish and terror of Giovanni in agony. In return, the death of Giovanni, the man of sorrows, expiates David's guilt.

In his epiphany, David achieves a new maturity. He remembers the biblical verse "*When I was a child, I spake as a child, I understood as a child, I thought as a child: but when I became a man, I put away childish things.*" His longing to make this prophecy come true indicates his hope to abandon the romantic nostalgia for innocence that has paralyzed his interchanges with others. Confronting directly the terror within, he contemplates his body, "the incarnation of a mystery." He examines his penis, "his troubled sex," in the mirror and wonders "how it can be redeemed." Realizing that "the key to my salvation . . . is hidden in my flesh," he accepts his nakedness, "which I must hold sacred, though it be never so vile." By implication, this acceptance includes both the fact of his homosexuality and the unavoidable "stink of love" attendant on all human intimacy. It is an acceptance of the world of experience, including his own troubled past. By both remembering and forgetting the Garden of Eden, David becomes a hero and says Yes to life.

The tone of the closing paragraph, with its mingling of sadness and hope, is reminiscent of the ending of *Paradise Lost,* in which Adam and Eve are escorted from Eden: "The World was all before them, where to choose/Thir place of rest, and Providence thir guide:/They hand in hand with wandring steps and slow,/Through Eden took thir solitarie way."[23] Just as they are guided by Providence, so David is sustained by a belief in the "heavy grace of God, which has brought me to this place." And just as the original couple leave Eden remembering the past but looking forward to the future, so David leaves the great house for the world, which lies all before him. The morning weighing on his shoulders "with the dreadful weight of hope," he tears up the blue envelope announcing the date of Giovanni's execution and makes his way toward the world of his new beginning. That the wind blows some of the torn pieces of the envelope back into his face indicates that he can never be entirely free of his past, that it will necessarily impact on all the days and nights that stretch before him. But by the end of the novel David has acknowledged his sins against love, accepted his homosexuality, and achieved a kind of heroism. The painful self-inquisition that is his meditation on the failures and evasions of his past has yielded a hopeful future. By looking into the naked sun, David has discovered a world of possibility.

That *Giovanni's Room* ends with the promise of David's salvation is altogether appropriate, for throughout the novel religious language and symbols abound. The presence of crucifixes and images of suffering, the echoes of biblical language, and the frequent references to religious concepts such as guilt and innocence, anguish and shame, damnation and salvation all suggest the possibility of a religious dimension to the novel. Moreover, the names of the central characters are meaningful. As noted previously, the name David means "loving" and the name Giovanni means "God has given." In addition, the names evoke the biblical David and Jonathan, whose love is described as "passing the love of women" (2 Sam. 1:26). And when David enters Guillaume's bar on the evening that he meets Giovanni, he feels that the patrons "were the elders of some strange and austere holy order and were watching me in order to discover, by means of signs I made but which only they could read, whether or not I had a true vocation." Baldwin, thus, dramatizes the issue of David's homosexuality as a question of religious vocation. The religious allusions and ideas that permeate the novel make possible an interpretation of the work as an allegory of betrayal and redemption in which homosexuality is salvific. The book may be seen as a dramatization of the *felix culpa*, or fortunate fall, in which good is created from evil.

The novel focuses on the issue of David's "vocation," but, as Robert A. Bone points out, "It is Giovanni . . . who is the true priest. For a priest is nothing but a journeyman in suffering."[24] Anticipating his later role as martyred saint, Giovanni, whose eyes are "like morning stars," is described as wearing a halo when David recalls his appearance the night they met: "so vivid, so winning, all of the light of that gloomy tunnel trapped around his head." In Baldwin's allegory, David rejects the burden of Giovanni's salvation and becomes a Judas-figure ("Judas and the Savior had met in me," he admits) only, ironically, to be saved by the very martyr he betrays. Refusing the priestly office of scapegoat, David is ultimately redeemed by Giovanni's assumption of that role. More precisely, by identifying with the suffering of Giovanni, by belatedly making his lover's pain his own, David works his own salvation.

Establishing a recurrent pattern in which the homosexual plays the role of redemptive figure, *Giovanni's Room* occupies a key position in Baldwin's canon, anticipating the later novels in which the suffering of the black and the gay are significantly linked. But the novel is not merely a trial run of *Another Country* or important only for its anticipation of Baldwin's more fully developed philosophy of the paradoxical nature of suffering.[25] It is an impressive achievement in its own right. A brooding and painful anatomy of the destructiveness of external and internal homophobia, the novel bespeaks the need for self-knowledge and self-acceptance. As an original contribution to the Jamesian formula of Americans in Europe, the work offers an insightful critique of American evasion and exposes the fear and doubt concealed beneath the veneer of American self-confidence and certainty. Although set in Paris and barren of explicit political content, it is nevertheless a devastating yet clear-sighted analysis of the American malaise of the 1950s, diagnosing the pressure for conformity as a fear of the terror within and a symptom of a widespread hostility to love.

Marred by its flirtation with melodrama and by the inadequate development of Giovanni, who remains more of a symbol than a believable character, the work is nevertheless extraordinarily accomplished. Carefully crafted and meaningfully structured, the novel masterfully controls the first-person narration and maintains sympathy for a protagonist who is often not very likeable, transforming an anti-hero guilty of repeated betrayals into a hero who dares finally to look at the naked sun. The epiphany on which the book ends is at once surprising and satisfyingly credible. Shaped in the crucible of his own suffering, David's ultimate identification with Giovanni's pain is the redemptive reversal of a long history of self-deception and self-torment. Written in prose of unusual beauty and power, *Giovanni's Room* is a compassionate but unsentimental exploration of the terror within. Although it is often dismissed as narrow and theatrical, it is a significant achievement.

As a gay fiction, *Giovanni's Room* is especially important for its insistence, in the midst of the homophobic 1950s, that homosexual love need not be sordid. Even as the novel sketches the gay underworld of its day as a decadent hell, it depicts *le milieu* as a product of a widespread hostility to love, the result not of any moral flaw inherent in homosexuality but of repression and fear. Better than any other work of its time, it conveys the psychological pain of internalized homophobia and the destructiveness of self-denial. Played out against a social background of rigid categories and sex-role expectations, the novel depicts the overwhelming pressures for conformity and movingly dramatizes their destructive effects on a sensitive young man.

But for all the intensity of its concentration on the internal life of its protagonist and his failures, *Giovanni's Room* is not merely a psychological study. It anatomizes homophobia as a manifestation of fear and exposes the romanticization of innocence as a form of evasion. More broadly, it offers an alternative to corruption and self-contempt and discovers in love the power to transform the "five dirty minutes in the dark" into an act of lasting value. Most boldly of all, it illustrates the possibility of self-affirmation through confrontation of the terror within and discovers in homosexuality a salvific potential, casting the homosexual as a redemptive figure. By forcing his reader's vicarious identification with the suffering of David and Giovanni, Baldwin evokes a compassionate response to the plight of homosexuals in an anti-gay society. A gay fiction that documents the devastating social and personal effects of homophobia, *Giovanni's Room* also envisions a positive solution. It creatively translates pain into compassion and suffering into redemption.

A central text in the American literature of homosexuality, *Giovanni's Room* is a greater artistic achievement than either *The City and the Pillar* or *The Charioteer.* Like them it is a coming-out narrative that both confirms and challenges stereotypical ideas about the gay experience, and it too could be described as a "homosexual problem novel." But in its confrontation with the homophobia of its time it is at once bolder and more sophisticated than Renault's earnestly accommodationist approach and less cool and detached than Vidal's ironic and unapologetic challenge to hypocritical attitudes. By telling the story from the perspective of his troubled protagonist, Baldwin vividly captures the painful reality of internalized homophobia and subtly translates apparent defeat into subjective victory. But despite the fact that Vidal's novel ends melodramatically and Baldwin's hopefully, *The City and the Pillar* is actually far more optimistic about social progress than is *Giovanni's Room.* This may reflect both the higher level of homophobia in the mid-1950s than in the late 1940s and Baldwin's more realistic perspective as an Afro-American, who entertained fewer illusions about the pace of social change in the United States. Baldwin's optimism is, finally, individual rather than social. In the face of widespread hostility to love, the paradise must necessarily be within. A dark and brooding novel, *Giovanni's Room* nevertheless attests to a world of possibility attained by looking at the naked sun and saying Yes to life.

9

"The Waters of the Pool": Christopher Isherwood's *A Single Man*

More forthrightly than any other major writer of his generation, Christopher Isherwood embraced the contemporary gay liberation movement. By the time of his death on January 4, 1986, he had become, as a result of his outspoken advocacy of equal rights and his solidarity with other members of his "tribe," a kind of gay icon and courage teacher. Although he did not come out openly in print until 1971—in *Kathleen and Frank*, ostensibly a biography of his parents, but "chiefly about Christopher"[1]—his homosexuality was never a secret. Indeed, it is a crucial element of his work, which cumulatively constitutes what Angus Wilson described as "one of the important Anglo-Saxon literary legends of our time."[2] Even when it is suppressed or disguised for legal or artistic reasons, homosexuality makes its presence felt in the novels and memoirs, for it is an indispensable aspect of the personal and literary myth of the outsider that Isherwood cultivated so assiduously. But Isherwood's importance as a gay writer finally lies not merely in his portrait of the homosexual as alienated outsider. More significantly, it resides in his insistence that homosexuality is also a faithful mirror of the human condition. His work anticipates the gay-liberation perspective that would flower in the aftermath of Stonewall.

In his 1976 reassessment of his life and work in the 1930s, *Christopher and His Kind,* Isherwood makes clear his acute awareness of the homophobia of Western society and how this homophobia necessarily invested his sexuality with political significance. "Girls are what the state and the church and the law and the press and the medical profession endorse, and command me to desire," he writes.

> My mother endorses them, too. She is silently brutishly willing me to get married and breed grandchildren for her. Her will is the will of Nearly Every-

195

*body, and in their will is my death. My will is to live according to my nature,
and to find a place where I can be what I am.*[3]

For Isherwood, homosexuality is not only part of the essential core of personality, his nature, but also his way of protesting the heterosexual dictatorship that falsely assumes a sameness to human nature and insists on conformity. "If boys didn't exist," he admits, "I should have to invent them." Yet if homosexuality is a means of defining himself against the Others and rebelling against their will—a means, that is, of asserting individuality and uniqueness—it also, paradoxically, functions as a way to broaden the concept of human nature itself. Throughout his work, the presence of homosexuals witnesses to the variousness of human possibilities, and in his most sustained exploration of homosexuality, *A Single Man* (1964), he accomplishes the considerable task of forcing his readers' identification with his gay hero even as he documents the homosexual's alienation and bitterness.

Homosexuality features in the early novels in many guises, ranging from the self-conscious innuendos of *All the Conspirators* (1928) to the fuller depictions of homosexual characters and situations in *The Memorial* (1932); from the coyly comic portrait of Baron Kuno von Pregnitz, whose secret fantasies revolve around English-schoolboy adventure stories in *The Last of Mr. Norris* (1935), to the spoiled homosexual idyll of Peter Wilkinson and Otto Nowak in *Goodbye to Berlin* (1939). In the early works, homosexuality is presented unapologetically and without the *Sturm und Drang* that marks contemporaneous treatments of the issue. In these novels, Isherwood refrains from sensationalizing the gay subculture; he deftly defuses and domesticates aspects of gay life that lesser writers might have rendered as decadence or depravity; and he reveals considerable insight into the dynamics of gay relationships. At the same time, however, he depicts his gay characters as infected (along with many others) with the soul sickness that denies life and distorts reality. They manifest symptoms of the obscure dread that pervades post–World War I England and pre-Hitler Germany, respectively. Homosexuals in the early fiction are an important constituency of "The Lost," a group that he describes in the preface to *The Berlin Stories* as including "those individuals respectable society shuns in horror."[4] But even in the early works the gay characters are juxtaposed with the heterosexual characters to reveal beneath their apparent polarities a shared reality of the deadened spirit. As one character in *Goodbye to Berlin* remarks, "Eventually we're all queer."[5]

In the later novels, beginning with *The World in the Evening* (1954), Isherwood probes more deeply and focuses more intently on the plight of the homosexual in a homophobic society. In these works, gay characters are both more numerous and their homosexuality defined more sharply in terms of their social roles and the obstacles they face. As the bisexual protagonist of *The World in the Evening* concludes, it is difficult to be a homosexual: "[I]t takes so much character—more than I've got—to be a good one."[6] The dilemma faced by the gay characters of the later novels is epitomized by their apparently incompatible needs to assert their individuality and to feel a sense of community, a conundrum that is at the heart of the recurrent debates about the social role of homosexuals in gay fiction from Wilde's *De Profundis* and Cather's "Paul's Case" onward.

This dilemma is clear in the character of Bob Wood, the Quaker artist of *The World in the Evening,* one of the earliest sympathetic portraits of a gay militant in Anglo-American literature. Although he is a minor character who functions primarily to help guide the novel's protagonist, Stephen Monk, on his spiritual journey from egoist to committed participant in life, Wood articulates the frustration and anger of gay men in the homophobic 1950s. His understanding of the political dimension of being homosexual in a world that systematically falsifies the gay experience differentiates him from the apologetic attitude of most gay characters of the period, such as Laurie Odell of Renault's *The Charioteer* or David of Baldwin's *Giovanni's Room.* The angriest of Isherwood's gay characters, Bob quickly reveals his homosexuality to Stephen, describing himself as "a professional criminal." When Stephen mouths a liberally tolerant caution—suggesting that the young man should not be "so aggressive. That's what puts people against you"—Bob bitterly attacks the heterosexual majority for its failure to accept the gay minority:

"Maybe we ought to put people against us. Maybe we're just too damned tactful. People just ignore us, most of the time, and we let them. We encourage them to. So the whole business never gets discussed, and the laws never get changed."

This passionate outburst reveals the extent of Bob's alienation. He has rejected his Quaker heritage because the Friends refuse to confront the issue of gay oppression, and he has been criminalized by the larger society. Estranged from a meaningful sense of community, his chief characteristic is a "quality of loneliness."

Significantly, Bob's response to the stigma he feels as a homosexual is the desire to take political action. Sick of the futile discussions of the etiology of homosexuality, he would like to "march down the street with a banner saying, 'We're queer because we're queer because we're queer' "; but even this protest, wildly unlikely in the early 1940s, when the action of the novel takes place, is impossible: his lover, Charles, Stephen's physician, a Jew who has changed his name, "is sick of belonging to these whining militant minorities." Charles's prescription for Bob's dilemma is the improbable creation of "Quaker Camp," but, tellingly, the solution Bob finds for himself is political at base. At the end of the novel, he joins the Navy, declining noncombatant status as a conscientious objector because "if they declared war on the queers—I'd fight." His motives are not conventionally patriotic: "Compared with this business of being queer, and the laws against us, and the way we're pushed around even in peacetime—this war hardly seems to concern me at all." But he refuses to accept exemption from military service on the basis of his homosexuality, "because what they're claiming is that us queers are unfit for their beautiful pure Army and Navy—when they ought to be glad to have us." The solidarity that Bob feels with his fellow homosexuals is a refreshingly new stance in the gay fictions of the period. Isherwood's conception of homosexuals as a legitimate minority with real grievances anticipates the emerging gay liberation movement of the late 1960s and his own fuller treatment of the issue in *A Single Man*.

In the "Ambrose" section of *Down There on a Visit* (1962), Isherwood creates a haunting portrait of the homosexual as persecuted victim, and depicts a response to the social dilemma of homosexuals that is nearer to Wilde's rejection of society than to Cather's accommodationism. The title character is an expatriate Englishman who has created a self-sufficient anarchic community on the Greek island of St. Gregory. Described in terms suggesting saintliness and otherworldly absorption, Ambrose retreats to his island, where he reigns over his disorderly menagerie like "one of Shakespeare's exiled kings."[7] Like Prospero's in *The Tempest*, his retreat is not voluntary. Permanently scarred by the trashing of his rooms at Cambridge by a group of undergraduate hearties, he has been frequently harassed and evicted from a series of lodgings. "I never want to move," he explains.

> "But they won't let me stay—*anywhere*. . . . That's what makes most places utterly impossible—the people. They're so completely hateful. They want everybody to conform to their beastly narrow little way of looking at things. And if one happens not to, one's treated as something unspeakable."

On St. Gregory, Ambrose attempts to create a brave new world of his own imagining. His fantasy of a self-created homosexual kingdom is revealing as a parody of the unjust reality that provokes his alienation:

> "Of course, when we do get into power, we shall have to begin by reassuring everybody. We must make it clear that there'll be absolutely no reprisals. Actually, they'll be amazed to find how tolerant we are. . . . I'm afraid we shan't be able to make heterosexuality actually legal, at first—there'd be too much of an outcry. . . . But meanwhile it'll be winked at, of course, as long as it's practiced in decent privacy. I think we shall even allow a few bars to be opened for people with those unfortunate tendencies, in certain quarters of the larger cities."

This comic fantasy cannot be taken wholly seriously, yet it is of great importance, embodying as it does the homosexual's bitterness at being excluded from the larger society. Moreover, the vengeful fantasy also betrays Ambrose's hidden desire for involvement in the world, albeit at a level beyond the reality that he finds unacceptable. Indeed, it is Ambrose's awareness of the injustice and cruelty of the majority culture that both fuels his parody and accounts for his attempt to create an alternate world.

At the end of the section, when the island community has been mostly abandoned, Ambrose is asked, "Don't you mind being alone here—with nobody but the boys?" His revealing reply, "But one's always alone, ducky. Surely you know that," indicates his existential isolation. It indicts the dominant culture for its failure to extend a sense of community beyond its "beastly narrow little way of looking at things" and perhaps even questions the possibility of community. Like Wilde in *De Profundis*, Ambrose—branded and cast out by society for his homosexuality—has developed insight into the way society attempts to impose arbitrary forms. He has reached an awareness of the need to translate his exclusion into anarchic self-sufficiency. His rejection of the world is similar to that in Wilde's work and, similarly, results in a perverse saintliness. And like Wilde's in *De Profundis*, Ambrose's critical intelligence, his existential insight, is also a measure of the failure of community and its pressing need. His rejection of society is, thus, simultaneously a cry for help. Ambrose, no less than Bob Wood, suffers from the absence of community—an absence that will eventually be addressed by the gay liberation movement.

If Isherwood explores various solutions to the homosexual's problematic relationship to society in the complementary dilemmas of Bob Wood in *The World in the Evening* and of Ambrose in *Down There on a Visit*, his most profound treatment of the question is *A Single Man*. In this "masterpiece of a comic novel,"[8] he humorously and movingly captures the essence of homosexual resentment against a society that routinely denies the validity of gay love. The protagonist of *A Single Man* is the most fully human of all Isherwood's gay characters. He shares the alienation and anger of figures like Bob Wood and Ambrose, but he is a more central and more rounded character than they. In addition, *A Single Man* more fully develops the context of gay oppression than do the earlier novels, and places it within a still larger context of spiritual transcendence. Dealing with universal themes of commitment and grief, alienation and isolation, the book concretely explores the minority sensibility and masterfully balances worldly and religious points of view. A classic of gay literature, *A Single Man* is also a profound meditation on death and decay and on the disparity between the body and the spirit. It regards the assertions of individual uniqueness and of minority consciousness as indispensable worldly and political goals, but it finally subsumes them in the Vedantic idea of the oneness of life.[9]

Set in Los Angeles in early December, 1962—soon after the Cuban missile crisis, in the midst of the Cold War and the craze for fallout shelters—*A Single Man* portrays the tensions of American life at a particular time with remarkable specificity and evocativeness. The virulent homophobia of the McCarthy years has lessened somewhat, but fear of homosexuality stalks the land. Limited as it is to one day in the life of a single character in a single city, the book is the most concentrated and narrowly circumscribed of Isherwood's novels. The day begins with the protagonist's awakening in his bed and it ends with his falling asleep in the same bed. Although the outward events that the novel records are unremarkable, the day turns out to be significant indeed. And in tracing this one day in the life of an unlikely but endearing hero, Isherwood, with characteristically deceptive ease, casually exposes the entire fabric of a single man's existence and the full texture of life in twentieth-century America. His portrait of Los Angeles in the early 1960s is comparable in irony and insight to his portraits of Berlin in the early 1930s.

The novel follows a day in the life of George, a late-middle-aged and lonely expatriate Briton who teaches English at San Tomas State College in a suburb of Los Angeles. He is a homosexual who lives alone following the recent death in an automobile accident of Jim, his lover of many years, whose painful absence constitutes a palpable presence in the novel. Wracked by grief and tormented by the children of his neighbors, George is bitter and isolated, and near the end of his endurance. In the course of the book, his daily routine is assiduously catalogued, from his first moments of awakening through the various personae he assumes and the many roles he plays to his last conscious thoughts.

After waking and dressing and partaking of a lonely breakfast, George distractedly drives via freeway to the burgeoning college, where he meets students, teaches a class, eats lunch, and converses with colleagues. When he leaves the campus, he stops at a hospital to visit Doris, a friend who several years previously had seduced Jim and who is now dying of cancer. Depressed by the visit, he makes an unscheduled detour to a gymnasium, where he works out more vigorously than usual. Leaving the gym, he impulsively drives through the hills overlooking the city. He stops the car "and looks out over Los Angeles like a sad Jewish prophet of doom, as he takes a leak."[10] He drives on to a supermarket, where he is overcome with despair and suddenly decides to accept an invitation extended earlier by Charlotte, who is "like him . . . a survivor."

After a sentimental and alcoholic evening with Charlotte, whom he calls Charley, George decides to walk down to the Starboard Side, a bar where he and Jim met in 1946. At the bar, he is surprised to find Kenny, a flirtatious student who had earlier bought him a pencil sharpener. When, as an obscure test of his own, Kenny dares him to a swim in the ocean, George immediately complies, proving that he is as silly as he claimed to be. During the "baptism of the surf," he feels himself purified by the water. Cold and wet, George and Kenny walk to the professor's home, where, after much conversation, George eventually passes out from an excess of alcohol. Kenny puts him to bed and then leaves. George awakens, masturbates, decides to fly to Mexico for Christmas, and then drifts off into a sleep that might also be his death.

The key to the book's extraordinary power resides in Isherwood's masterful control of narrative technique. Narrated dispassionately in the omniscient third person, in a voice that is both commanding and comforting, the novel is written in a style that alternates between poetic intensity and gentle irony. The narrator at first presents George with what appears to be clinical detachment: as a kind of biological exhibit to be contemplated by narrator and reader alike. As the book proceeds, George develops from a depersonalized object—"Obediently, it washes, shaves, brushes its hair"—into a "three-quarters-human thing," and finally into full humanity. George is first referred to as an "it" devoid of individual personality, then acknowledged as a partially conscious automaton, and finally recognized as a "he," whose personality is more fluid than it appears to casual observers as he goes through the day performing a variety of roles, sometimes on automatic pilot. Concurrently, the narrator becomes increasingly less clinical and detached, and the distance between him and the narrator gradually narrows, until the reversion to medical terminology in the final scene.

The narrative technique functions complexly to accomplish a number of effects. First of all, the distance between narrator and protagonist helps establish the book's double vision,[11] its simultaneous concern with the mundane and the transcendent, with the worldly questions of individual identity and the religious perspective into which such questions are finally absorbed. Examining George as a biological specimen, the narrator seems to speak with more than human authority. By observing George *sub specie aeternitatis*, he unobtrusively underlines the crucial body–soul dichotomy and prepares for the philosophical distinction between the *Maya*, or mundane reality, and the *Brahman*, or higher reality, that informs the novel. Moreover, because the narrator frequently addresses the reader directly, the book becomes "a symbolic dialogue between the author as guru and the reader as a disciple meditating on the ephemera of George's day."[12] In this dialogue, George is regarded with wry gravity as a beleaguered, occasionally ludicrous specimen of humanity, who arouses (sometimes simultaneously) pathos, humor, concern, admiration, dismay, and affection.

Significantly, the dispassionate narration actually fosters the reader's identification with the alienated, homosexual hero. The narrator's persistent and flagrant violations of George's privacy—even following him into the bathroom and frequently reporting on his bodily functions—create an enforced intimacy between reader and protagonist. However different the circumstances of George and any particular reader, the reader is still, like George, a mortal animal, whose spirit is housed in a body that is destined eventually to become "cousin to the garbage in the container on the back porch. Both will have to be carted away and disposed of, before too long." This recognition of a common mortality helps bridge all the barriers that separate the reader and the minority-conscious hero. As Jonathan Raban asks, "Dare we judge that decaying biological thing when it is we ourselves who may be George?"[13] The narrative technique contributes to the book's success in depicting George, despite all his crotchets and idiosyncrasies, including his sexuality, as an Everyman figure.

The title of the novel not only justifies its relentless focus on one character, but also identifies its dual concern with George as an idiosyncratic individual and as a representative figure. He is single in many senses of the term (though ironically the entity known as George is hardly a single phenomenon but consists—like all of us—of multiple selves). His singleness reflects the essential loneliness of the human condition—the apartness from one another on which individual identity is based—as well as his particular sense of alienation as a gay man in a society that devalues homosexuals.

More specifically, however, George is single as the result of the loss of his lover. Early in the novel, the narrator records the pain of grief with poignant intensity:

> And it is here, nearly every morning, that George, having reached the bottom of the stairs, has this sensation of suddenly finding himself on an abrupt, brutally broken off, jagged edge—as though the track had disappeared down a landslide. It is here that he stops short and knows, with a sick newness almost as though it were for the first time: Jim is dead. Is dead.

One of the great distinctions of the novel is the moving and economical way in which it captures both the texture of the gay couple's life together and the depth of George's grief. The relationship of George and Jim gradually emerges to become the most deeply felt love story in all of Isherwood's fiction.

The obsession with and constant rediscovery of his loss throughout the day cripple George. At the beginning of the novel, he is "a live dying creature" who "will struggle on and on until it drops. Not because it is heroic. It can imagine no alternative." He is a "prisoner for life." He recognizes his reflection in the mirror as not "so much a face as the expression of a predicament. Here's what it has done to itself, here's the mess it has somehow managed to get itself into during its fifty-eight years." George's continuing love for Jim invests the novel with great tenderness, as when he imagines his dead lover "lying opposite him at the other end of the couch, also reading; the two of them absorbed in their books yet so completely aware of each other's presence.'' These memories of a shared life starkly emphasize the reality of George's loss, his singleness. But his grief serves to enforce his isolation, to chain him in memories, to imprison him in the past. Although after his visit to Doris, George momentarily exults in the life energy he feels, for most of the day he is less a fully committed member of "that marvelous minority, The Living" than merely a stubborn survivor. By the end of the book, however, he accepts the fact that "Jim is in the past, now" and concludes: "It is Now that he must find another Jim. Now that he must love. Now that he must live."

Unlike most gay fictions of its day, *A Single Man* is not a *Bildungsroman* focused on the protagonist's acceptance of his sexuality. George's homosexuality is a simple given in the novel, not the source of agonizing self-examination, as it is in *Maurice, The City and the Pillar, The Charioteer,* or *Giovanni's Room.* Isherwood frustrates attempts to discover the roots of George's homosexuality by revealing almost nothing of his early childhood or family relationships, and George mocks the popular psychological explanations of his neighbor Mrs. Strunk. Well adjusted and comfortable with his sexuality, he is neither guilt-ridden nor indecisive about his sexual orientation. Homosexuality is depicted as part of the wholeness of George's personality, an integral part of his identity, neither open to question nor a subject of contention. But George's homosexuality is not on that account merely an incidental aspect of his personality, as it might be in a novel less aware of the homophobia that afflicts American society. Though George is by no means defined solely by his homosexuality, it is, in fact, the characteristic that most pervasively defines his life. Constantly aware of being gay in a straight world, he reveals his minority consciousness throughout the day.

The conception of homosexuality as a legitimate minority among the diverse minorities that constitute the fabric of American society is essential to the novel and to its treatment of homosexuality. Minorities of all kind abound in the book, from senior citizens ('' 'old,' in our country of the bland, has become nearly as dirty a word as 'kike' or 'nigger' '') to expatriates like George, Charley, and Mr. Stoessel. The student population of San Tomas State College is made up of minorities: "Negroes, Mexicans, Jews, Japanese, Chinese, Latins, Slavs, Nordics, the dark heads far predominating over the blond." The student body itself is described as a "tribe," though only the minority of eager beavers actually identify themselves as such; the rest are only "willing to pretend that they do on special occasions." The minorities included in the novel range from an albino (Buddy Sorenson) to a Negro (Estelle Oxford), from a nun (Sister Maria) to a Jew (Myron Hirsch), from a Nisei whose family was interned during

World War II (Lois Yamaguchi) to a Hispanic divorcée (Mrs. Netta Torres). The homosexual minority is represented among the student body by Wally Bryant, George's "little minority-sister," whom he hopes to inspire to "throw away his nail file and face the truth of his life."

One purpose of the presence of so many minority members in the novel is simply to make the point that, in some sense, almost everyone is a member of a minority group. This recognition helps ease reader identification with the minority-conscious George—who as a foreigner, an intellectual, a teacher, and an old man, as well as a homosexual, is actually a member of several minorities—and makes possible the important balance the novel strikes between assertions of individual and tribal identity, on the one hand, and, on the other, a wider view in which such differences are merely circumstantial and ultimately insignificant. As Brian Finney observes, "What gives everyone a sense of identity is membership of a minority. It segregates the living from the dead. It also isolates individual consciousness from universal consciousness."[14] Moreover, a crucial reason for Isherwood's high valuation of diversity is his belief that only through respect for differences can individuals and groups learn from one another. As Kenny tells George in the Starboard Side, "What's so phony nowadays is all this familiarity. Pretending there isn't any difference between people. . . . If you and I are no different, what do we have to give each other? How can we ever be friends?"

Another reason for Isherwood's minority consciousness, however, is clearly political. To portray homosexuals as simply another tribe in a nation composed of many different tribes is both to soften the stigma linked to homosexuality and to encourage solidarity among gay people. And by associating the mistreatment of homosexuals with the discrimination suffered by other minorities in America, such as the blacks, the Jews, and the Japanese, Isherwood legitimizes the grievances of gay people. He also implies the possibility of a political redress to injustice by forming alliances of minorities. As George exits the freeway on the way to the college, he passes through a colorful neighborhood populated by blacks and Mexicans. "George would not care to live here," the narrator remarks, "because they all blast all day long with their radios and television sets. But he would never find himself yelling at their children, because these people are not The Enemy." He adds: "If they would ever accept George, they might even be allies." Anticipating the gay liberation movement's conception of homosexuals as an oppressed minority, A Single Man—despite the apparently detached understatement of its narration—is politically engaged.

George's minority consciousness is defined most explicitly when he focuses on the issue of persecution in a classroom discussion of Aldous Huxley's After Many a Summer. "A minority," George says, "is only thought of as a minority when it constitutes some kind of threat to the majority, real or imaginary. And no threat is ever quite imaginary." He insists on the concept of difference in defining minorities, rejecting the bland liberalism that would deny diversity by pretending to believe that there is no difference between, say, a Negro and a Swede. He points out that living under the threat of persecution hardly improves one's character. In defense, a minority "has its own kind of aggression. It absolutely dares the majority to attack it. It hates the majority—not without a cause, I grant you." Indeed, the inevitable result of persecution is hatred. "Do you think it makes people nasty to be loved?" George asks the class. "You know it doesn't! Then why should it make them nice to be loathed? While you're being persecuted, you hate what's happening to you, you hate the people who are making it happen, you're in a world of hate."

These characteristics of persecution are mirrored in George's own experience, as they were in the lives of Bob Wood and Ambrose. As a homosexual, George threatens the majority's sense of psychological security. In the increasingly conformist society depicted in the novel, where individualists and bohemians of all stripes have been banned from the "new and better breeding grounds in the sunny Southland," the homosexual implicitly rebukes the heterosexual majority's desperate need to believe that heterosexuality is the best of all possible choices in the best of all possible worlds. George attributes his neighbors' unease in the "kingdom of the good life upon earth" (as he refers to the middle-class utopia that is Southern California) to the fear of nonconformity. As a homosexual who refuses to fit the preordained pattern of respectable life in the American utopia, George represents a challenge to his neighbors' own choices. "Oh yes indeed, Mr. Strunk and Mr. Garfein are proud of their kingdom," George muses.

> But why, then, are their voices like the voices of boys calling to each other as they explore a dark unknown cave, growing ever louder and louder, bolder and bolder? . . . They are afraid of what they know is somewhere in the darkness around them, of what may at any moment emerge into the undeniable light of their flashlamps, nevermore to be ignored, explained away. The fiend that won't fit into their statistics. . . . Among many other kinds of monster, George says, they are afraid of little me.

Beneath the confident materialism of early-1960s America lurks barely concealed doubt that is expressed, among other ways, in a homophobic demand for sameness. Like Baldwin, Isherwood diagnoses the fear and hatred of homosexuality as a national neurosis.

Like Ambrose, George expresses his hatred in comic fantasies of vengeance. As he drives along the freeway, he plans to form "Uncle George's" terrorist organization to kidnap the newspaper editor who has launched a vicious campaign against sex deviates ("by which he means people like George"), his staff writers, the police chief, the head of the vice squad, and the ministers who encourage the campaign. Wouldn't it be amusing, he thinks, to

> take them all to a secret underground movie studio where, after a little persuasion—no doubt just showing them the red-hot pokers and pincers would be quite sufficient—they would perform every possible sexual act, in pairs and in groups, with a display of the utmost enjoyment. The film would then be developed and prints of it would be rushed to all the movie theaters. George's assistants would chloroform the ushers so the lights couldn't be turned up, lock the exits, overpower the projectionists, and proceed to run the film under the heading of Coming Attractions.

This relatively benign fantasy is replaced with altogether more bloody ones, requiring "at least five hundred highly skilled killers and torturers," when George realizes that "These people are not amusing. They should never be dealt with amusingly. They understand only one language: brute force."

George works himself up into a frenzy of hatred for three-quarters of the population of America, whom he defines as "The Enemy." He blames them collectively for the loss of Jim. "All are, in the last analysis, responsible for Jim's death," he decides, "their words, their thoughts, their whole way of life willed it, even though they never knew he existed." But however revealing of his alienation and bitterness, George's hatred is not simply an expense of spirit. It is also a stimulant that allows him to face life without Jim, and it exemplifies George's dogged commitment to life even in the depths of his grief and despair, the fact that *"he hasn't given up."* "Rage, resentment, spleen," the narrator observes, "of such is the vitality of middle-age." Moreover, George's response to the homophobia that he feels around him is more various than simply blind hatred. It is also expressed in his "acute criminal complex," which makes him "hyperconscious of all bylaws, city ordinances, rules and petty regulations," and in the flipness and gentle parody of gay humor, as when he complains, "Why can't these modern writers stick to the old simple themes—such as, for example, boys."

Rather than being subject to overt persecution, George most commonly experiences attitudes of condescending tolerance or studied indifference to his sexuality. He decides that his students probably guess that he is homosexual, but that the fact does not interest them. "They don't want to know about my feelings or my glands or anything below my neck," he thinks. "I could just as well be a severed head carried into the classroom to lecture to them from a dish." This striking image of the divided self crystallizes the difficulty homosexuals face in forming a sense of wholeness in a homophobic society. George contrasts the attitude of his neighbor, Mr. Strunk—who would, he thinks, "nail him down with a word. *Queer,* he doubtless growls"—with that of Mrs. Strunk, who is trained in the new tolerance, the technique of annihilation by blandness. Out comes her psychology book—bell and candle are no longer necessary. Reading from it in sweet singsong she proceeds to exorcise the unspeakable out of George. No reason for disgust, she intones, no cause for condemnation. Nothing here that is willfully vicious. All is due to heredity, early environment (Shame on those possessive mothers, those sex-segregated British schools!), arrested development at puberty, and/or glands. Here we have a misfit, debarred forever from the best things of life, to be pitied not blamed.

Mrs. Strunk's position illustrates well Dennis Altman's observation that "the difference between tolerance and acceptance is very considerable, for tolerance is a gift extended by the superior to the inferior."[15] George's reply to her in his imaginary dialogue firmly rejects both her condescension and her psychology: "But your book is wrong . . . when it tells you that Jim is the substitute I found for a real son, a real kid brother, a real husband, a real wife. Jim wasn't a substitute for anything. And there is no substitute for Jim, if you'll forgive my saying so, anywhere."

Living alone in the secluded, island-like little house he and Jim chose "because you could only get to it by the bridge across the creek," George is isolated and embattled. His isolation is emphasized by his decision not to share the news of Jim's death. He first learns of the accident from Jim's uncle, who even admitted "George's right to a small honorary share in the sacred family grief." But George refuses to betray any emotion and declines an invitation to the funeral. Although Mrs. Strunk "would enjoy being sad about Jim" (in her liberal tolerance, she believes that a homosexual relationship "can sometimes be almost beautiful—particularly if one of the parties is already dead, or better yet, both"), George tells her merely that Jim will be remaining in the East indefinitely. Only with Charley does he share his grief. But after sobbing in her arms and accepting her comfort, George has second thoughts. He fears that he has made Jim "into a sob story for a skirt." Only when he realizes that "you can't betray . . . a Jim, or a life with a Jim, even if you try to" does he allow Charley to participate fully in the ritual of grief.

George's singleness is particularly underscored by his lack of a homosexual community. For all his tribal consciousness, George has very little connection with a gay community beyond the bars he contemplates visiting and the young hustlers he notices and rejects. The absence of a viable homosexual community in the days before the Stonewall riots and the gay activist movements, when the homosexual minority is "one that isn't organized and doesn't have any committees to defend it," underlines the poignancy of George's need for community and facilitates Isherwood's use of homosexuality as a metaphor for the alienation endemic to the human condition. At any rate, in *A Single Man* George encounters no fellow homosexuals with whom he might share a common identity or from whom he might receive support and understanding in his rituals of grief. Only in his visits to two women who know of his relationship with Jim is George free to be open about his sexual orientation. But these visits, each in a different way, serve to shrink rather than to expand his sense of community.

George's first visit is to Doris, who had once attempted to lure Jim from him. She is now dying in a hospital bed, a "yellow shriveled mannequin with its sticks of arms and legs, withered flesh and hollow belly, making angular outlines under the sheet." He contrasts her present decay with her former state, particularly "that body which sprawled naked, gaping wide in shameless demand, underneath Jim's naked body." For George, Doris is "Bitch-Mother Nature," the female prerogative for which the Church, the Law, and the State exist and before which he is expected to bow and hide "his unnatural head in shame." She is "Woman the Enemy," who arrogantly asserted her fully sanctioned right to Jim. George shrewdly defeated her by yielding, by allowing Jim "to satisfy all his curiosity and flattered vanity and lust (vanity mostly) on the gamble that he would return (as he did) saying, *She's disgusting,* saying, *Never again.*" But despite his triumph, George has nurtured his hatred for Doris, believing that as long as "one tiny precious drop of hate" remained, he could still find some residue of Jim in her. Now, however, he discovers that he can no longer hate Doris. For all their polarities, they are both nearing the end of the road. "*I shall follow you soon,*" George thinks as he holds her hand. He leaves her deathbed diminished. One more bit of Jim is lost.

Having come face-to-face with mortality in his visit to Doris, George momentarily exults in being numbered among the ranks of "that marvelous minority, The Living." Rejoicing in "the tough triumphant old body of a survivor," he enjoys the "easygoing physical democracy" of the gym. But afterward, as he drives up into the hills overlooking the city, he becomes painfully aware of the transience of all things, including the ravenous city. As he looks out at the city spread below him, while urinating, he remembers the biblical description, "*Babylon is fallen, is fallen, that great city,*" and thinks, "But this city is not great, was never great, and has nearly no distance to fall." Thoroughly depressed, he ventures into a supermarket, whose bright lights promise sanctuary from loneliness and the dark. But "ambushed among its bottles and cartons and cans, are shockingly vivid memories of meals shopped for, cooked, eaten with Jim." Overwhelmed with loneliness, he calls Charley and belatedly accepts her invitation to dinner. They suddenly "are linked, are yet another of this evening's lucky pairs, amidst all of its lonely wanderers."

The relationship of George and Charley illustrates the rapport that gay men and heterosexual women often enjoy, despite George's conception of women as "The Enemy." Their friendship is based on their common English background and on their having shared each other's troubles. Both dogged survivors who have not quite given up on life, each is dependent on the other for support and comfort and the "magic" that allows them to pursue quite separate dreams while pretending that they are identical. Charley, for all her problems with a failed marriage and a rebellious son and despite her penchant for self-pity, is nevertheless capable of creating

> this utterly mysterious, unsensational thing—not bliss, not ecstasy, not joy—just plain happiness. *Das Glueck, le bonheur, la felicidad*—they have given it all three genders, but one has to admit, however grudgingly, that the Spanish are right; it is usually feminine, that's to say, woman-created.

With Charley, George reminisces about the trip to England he and Jim had taken and the crazy plans they had made, and he allows her to indulge in fantasies of her own. They are both imprisoned in the past, George in his memories of Jim, Charley in her romanticization of England. Significantly, however, while indulging Charley's nostalgia for the past, George realizes that "The past is just something that's over." This is an important lesson that he will finally apply to his own life.

Paradoxically, the extended encounter with Charley, which brings George *la felicidad*, also increases his awareness of isolation. She is not content with being one of the links to George's past with Jim. Just as Cora in Williams's "Two on a Party" is in love with Billy, so Charley would like George to need her in a more personal, even sexual way, as she makes abundantly clear in a number of broad hints. As he leaves her house, tellingly located on Soledad Way, "she kisses him full on the mouth. And suddenly sticks her tongue right in. . . . It's one of those drunken long shots which just might, at least theoretically, once in ten thousand tries, throw a relationship right out of its orbit and send it whizzing off on another." For all her sympathy and genuine love, Charley fails to accept a crucial dimension of the wholeness of George's personality. Charley's hope to replace Jim in George's affection is a measure both of her famous failure of perception and of her emotional neediness, but insofar as George fails to evince a sexual interest in her, it is also an indication of his continuing isolation, a reminder of his loss.

George's singleness even when with a friend like Charley is emphasized by the memory he has, soon after leaving her house, of the beach months of 1946:

> The magic squalor of those hot nights, when the whole shore was alive with tongues of flame, the watchfires of a vast naked barbarian tribe—each group or pair to itself and bothering no one, yet all a part of the life of the tribal

encampment—swimming in the darkness, cooking fish, dancing to the radio, coupling without shame on the sand. George and Jim (who had just met) were out there among them evening after evening, yet not often enough to satisfy the sad fierce appetite of memory, as it looks back hungrily on that glorious Indian summer of lust.

But this memory of a tribal past is more than a nostalgic reminiscence of youthful lust. It is a vision of community that is in pointed contrast to George's current singleness. Embedded in it is an allusion to the "cloven tongues like as of fire" through which the Holy Spirit appeared at Pentecost, symbolizing the unity within diversity of mankind and the universality of God's offer of grace (Acts 2:1–21). As a vision of community that reconciles the conflicting needs of tribal acceptance and individual assertion, this memory plays a vital role in George's decision to embrace life and to seek identity with others, while at the same time preserving the integrity of his individuality.

George's actual decision to embrace life results from the evening encounter with Kenny, whom he had earlier told, "there are some things you don't even *know* you know, until you're asked." A tall, skinny young man, Kenny is one of George's most enigmatic students. Sometimes George suspects him of "understanding the innermost meaning of life—of being, in fact, some kind of genius," and at other times thinks that he may simply be "misleadingly charming and silly." As he walks across campus after his class, George notices Kenny and his girlfriend, Lois Yamaguchi, sitting on the lawn. The professor and his students wave at each other—"The old steamship and the young castaways have exchanged signals," George thinks—and then Kenny catches up with the older man and begins questioning him about whether he had ever taken mind-altering drugs. Accusing George of a kind of caginess, of never revealing all that he knows, Kenny leads him to a bookstore, where he buys him a pencil sharpener. Their conversation on campus establishes a kind of impersonal intimacy between them, "a readiness to remain at cross-purposes," that makes possible the symbolic dialogue in which they engage later, at the Starboard Side. In this dialogue, Kenny represents youth and the future, George age and experience.

Kenny's motivations for seeking out George are not entirely clear, perhaps not even to himself. It may be, as Stephen Adams suggests, that Kenny deliberately sets himself up for a seduction.[16] Certainly he is flirtatious, even provocative, and there clearly is a sexual tension in the encounter between pupil and teacher that results. But whatever the conscious or unconscious motivations that bring Kenny to the bar, he responds to George's assumption of the role of father-figure. He tells George, "I *like* calling you sir." Looking to George as a surrogate father, what Kenny really wants to know is the use of experience. George tells him that "I, personally, have gotten steadily sillier and sillier" and that experience can't be *used,* only accepted. Prodded by Kenny's questions, George begins to realize the value of the present as the sum of the past.

Kenny challenges George to a midnight swim as a test of his silliness, and George accepts with alacrity. In the "stunning baptism of the surf," he escapes "across the border into the water-world," symbolic of the oceanic consciousness that is the novel's higher reality. Intent upon his "rites of purification," George gives himself wholly to the water: "he washes away thought, speech, mood, desire, whole selves, entire lifetimes; again and again he returns, becoming always cleaner, freer, less." He is suddenly swallowed by "a great, an apocalyptically great wave." He stands naked and tiny and unafraid in the mystery of the ocean's vastness, accepting the revelation of the wave's apocalypse. Although George is unable to articulate the significance of this spiritual experience—which lifts the burden of the past from his shoulders—he reveals its impact in his new courage and confidence.

Rejuvenated by the "baptism in the surf," George is transformed. He becomes "An oracular George, who may shortly begin to speak with tongues." He comes to reject "dreary categories" that separate human beings. "I mean," he asks Kenny, "what is this life supposed to be *for?* Are we to spend it identifying each other with catalogues, like tourists in an art gallery? Or are we to try to exchange *some* kind of a signal, however garbled, before it's too late?" These questions are at the heart of the novel's perspective on the value of minority consciousness and its corollary dangers. Diversity is important, for only if we value difference can we learn from others, and only if we respect our own experience can we convey its significance to others. But if we are only the sum of our labels, then we have no signals to communicate; and if we mistakenly confuse labels with the complexity of experience, then we remain superficial tourists, unable to penetrate beyond our stereotypical expectations of others. Unfortunately, Kenny, for all his flirtatiousness, is shocked when George suggests a solution to the youth's problem of trying to find a place to sleep with his girlfriend, and he silently labels George a "dirty old man."

George desperately longs to explain the value of experience in order to make Kenny understand its importance and its limitations. He knows that Kenny wants him "to tell you *what I know,*" but he also realizes that he cannot do that: "Because, don't you see, *what I know is what I am.* And I can't tell you that. You have to find it out for yourself. I'm like a book you have to read. A book can't read itself to you. It doesn't even know what it's about. I don't know what I'm about." He chides Kenny for being too passive to take the effort to read him, to find out what he's about. He accuses Kenny of committing

> "the inexcusable triviality of saying 'He's a dirty old man,' and turning this evening, which might be the most unforgettable of your young life, into a *flirtation.* . . . It's the enormous tragedy of everything nowadays: flirtation.

Flirtation instead of fucking, if you'll pardon my coarseness. All any of you ever do is flirt, and wear your blankets off one shoulder, and complain about motels. And miss the one thing that might really . . . *transform your entire life.*"

But if Kenny's life is not transformed by the evening, George's is. He accepts himself here as the total of his experiences.

This acceptance causes George to value not only the past, but also the present. He decides to fly to Mexico for Christmas, to find love, to move beyond the exile of his solitariness, to seize the present. Even the comic masturbation scene, so often in literature an emblem of loneliness and isolation, here symbolizes George's transformation from passive observer to active participant. He begins by imagining others in sexual play. After rejecting Kenny, who refuses "to take his lust seriously," George focuses on the two tennis players whose beauty had brightened his day on campus. Then he freely substitutes himself for them: he "hovers above them, watching; then he begins passing in and out of their writhing, panting bodies. He is either. He is both at once." After the orgasm, George falls asleep with a smile on his face, and in the "partial surfacings" of sleep, he decides that "Jim is in the past now. . . . Jim is death." He cedes the past to Charley and the future to Kenny, but clings to Now: "It is Now that he must find another Jim. Now that he must love. Now that he must live. . . ."

Paradoxically, at least to Western minds, George's decision to embrace life in the present, to seek community with others, prepares him for death. Death, only suppositional in the novel, involves becoming part of a community larger than the gay minority or the heterosexual majority or even the marvelous minority of the living. All individuals are single in their separateness one from another, yet they are finally united in an oceanic consciousness. In death, George's spirit will merge with the universal consciousness, "that consciousness which is no one in particular, but which contains everyone and everything, past, present, and future, and extends unbroken beyond the uttermost stars." The Vedantic idea of the oneness of life is the higher reality in which the *Maya* of mundane life is finally subsumed. Thus, even as the novel charts George's growth from isolation toward worldly commitment, it also traces his emergence from the narrow confines of individual identity into an otherworldly union with the universal consciousness.

The novel's religious vision is stated most explicitly in an extended passage that uses rock pools and ocean as analogues for individual identity and impersonal universality:

Up the coast a few miles north, in a lava reef under the cliffs, there are a lot of rock pools. . . . Each pool is separate and different, and you can, if you are fanciful, give them names. . . . The rocks of the pool hold their world together. And throughout the day of the ebb tide, they know no other.

But that long day ends at last; yields to the nighttime of the flood. And, just as the waters of the ocean come flooding, darkening over the pools, so over George and the others in sleep come the waters of that other ocean. . . . We may surely suppose that, in the darkness of the full flood, some of these creatures are lifted from their pools to drift far out over the deep waters. But do they ever bring back, when the daytime of the ebb returns, any kind of catch with them? Can they tell us, in any manner, about their journey? Is there, indeed, anything for them to tell—except that the waters of the ocean are not really other than the waters of the pool?

In this passage, Isherwood distinguishes between the rock pools—the *Maya*, or mundane reality in which George exists as an individual person— and the ocean—the *Brahman*, or higher reality in which George is part of the universal consciousness. But the *Maya* is illusory and impermanent, and the differences isolating the individual rock pools are also illusory when measured in terms of the higher reality: "the waters of the ocean are not really other than the waters of the pool." Thus, for all George's fierce insistence on his individuality, the *Maya* of personal identity finally yields to the *Brahman* of impersonal universality, just as the waters of the rock pool are eventually merged with the waters of the ocean. In the suppositional death that ends the novel, George is no longer a single man, in any of that term's many senses. His spirit escapes the confines of the rocks; it joins the "deep waters," unable any longer to associate with "what lies here, unsnoring on the bed . . . cousin to the garbage in the container on the back porch." In the nighttime of the flood, the waters of the pool merge with the waters of the ocean.

Concerned as it is with decay and death and the disparity between the body and the spirit, *A Single Man* has been described accurately as a *memento mori* sermon.[17] But it is more: the awareness of death heightens the need to live fully and to love. *A Single Man* is surely as much about living as about dying. It confronts the most vital issues of contemporary fiction and of modern life and offers in resolution to the problems of alienation and isolation a vision of community, of self-transcendence through universal consciousness and through involvement in the lives of others. In making concrete this resolution, Isherwood's great gay fiction presents a sustained and moving portrait of male homosexual love—perhaps the most honest of such portraits in contemporary literature—and plumbs insightfully and revealingly the homosexual plight. Deftly combining a deeply felt minority consciousness and a transcendent religious vision, the novel brilliantly portrays its idiosyncratic, antiheroic hero as a type of Everyman with whom all readers can identify. In understated prose, tinged with humor, irony, and compassion, Isherwood not only captures the fullness of an individual life in a particular place at a specific time but also translates it into an emblem of the human condition in any place at any time.

As a gay fiction, *A Single Man* is especially important for its presentation of homosexuality as simply a human variation that should be accorded value and respect, and for its recognition of homosexuals as a legitimate minority with grievances that should be redressed politically. From a teleological point of view, the differences that separate individuals and groups may be insignificant, but from a worldly vantage point they are crucial, for they make possible the exchange of signals that may be the purpose of life itself. Isherwood's dual insistence on the common humanity of gay people and on the need for a tribal identity among homosexuals are vital contributions to gay fiction before Stonewall. Presaging the contemporary gay liberation movement, Isherwood recognizes the need for gay community even as he articulates a transcendent vision in which a universal consciousness subsumes individuality itself.

Isherwood's recognition of the need for community and his incisive analysis of the context of oppression in which gay people lived in 1962 are particular distinctions of *A Single Man* as a gay fiction. Even as the novel posits the similarity of homosexuals to other minorities it is also painfully aware of the fact that in the early 1960s gay people were not regarded as a legitimate minority. Whereas the feelings of inferiority and oppression felt by other minorities could be at least partially assuaged by the acceptance and support of their respective communities, the homosexual's outcast state before the gay liberation movement is underscored by the absence of such support. Moreover, unlike other minorities, who may be defined as outsiders but who were nevertheless assigned symbolic qualities of status and worth that connected them to the majority experience, homosexuals were given no such qualities: in the popular mind there were no terms in which homosexuals were represented as valuable members of the human community. Isherwood's penetrating awareness of these realities renders his novel an important social document.

But *A Single Man* has far more than sociological or historical interest. A tour de force in which every nuance is deftly controlled, it is both Isherwood's finest novel and a masterpiece of gay fiction. It movingly conveys the resentment of homosexuals at their mistreatment by the larger community, yet its anger is leavened by humor and its minority consciousness is qualified by its transcendent vision. Forcing its readers to identify with its alienated hero, it presents George not simply as a homosexual Everyman but as Everyman himself.

Afterword

Edmund White's 1988 novel *The Beautiful Room Is Empty* traces its protagonist's emergence from the painful obscurities of his youth to the self-doubt and oppression of his early manhood in the 1960s. The novel concludes with the hero's somewhat bewildered participation in the Stonewall Inn riots of 1969. The morning after the uprising, when the protagonist and his friend rush out to buy newspapers to see how the event—"our Bastille day"—had been described, they discover that it had in fact been ignored. "We couldn't find a single mention in the press of the turning point of our lives," the narrator reports.[1] In this simple sentence, on which the novel ends, White captures well both the pivotal importance of the gay liberation movement to the self-esteem of homosexuals and its marginalization by the larger society. A similar observation is made by Armistead Maupin in *Sure of You*, the 1989 conclusion to his popular *Tales of the City* series, in an exchange between a heterosexual journalist and a gay activist. The journalist compares the level of social consciousness in the 1960s and the 1970s, summarizing the latter decade as "a great big blank." This assessment is challenged by the gay activist, who points out that the most significant social movement of the 1970s was gay liberation, by which he means more than discos and bathhouses. A "whole new culture" emerged, he argues, and adds: "You guys [in the press] didn't cover it, but that doesn't mean it didn't happen."[2] The frustration expressed by Maupin's character at the reluctance of the mainstream news media to take gay liberation seriously is justifiably shared by many homosexuals. In October 1987, when hundreds of thousands of people marched on Washington in support of gay rights and the fight against AIDS, neither *Newsweek* nor *Time* covered the largest civil rights demonstration in American history.

Precisely because of the repeated (and continuing) attempts to relegate gay men and lesbians to the margins of society and the persistent refusals to recognize the legitimacy of their experience, the gay fictions explored in this book acquire an importance far beyond the narrowly literary. Affirming homosexual identity at times when such affirmations were perilous, these texts bespeak both the tenacious persistence of the homosexual impulse and

215

its heroic resistance to the larger cultural fictions that brand homosexuality as something unspeakable. Taken together, the gay fictions in the period from Wilde to Stonewall chart the development of homosexual consciousness from the individualistic to the collective. Without ever abandoning the emphasis on self-knowledge as the crucial issue on which both personal and social identity hinges, the texts examined herein move from the view of erotic response as an element of self-realization to a view of sexuality as a distinguishing social characteristic. They help document the gradual shift from conceiving homosexuality exclusively as a personal problem to understanding it in terms of social justice. However limited by virtue of their almost exclusive focus on white, middle-class males, these gay fictions nevertheless constitute an imaginative (though by no means comprehensive) history of gay people in the period between Wilde and Stonewall, and help explain how the contemporary gay liberation movement was made possible and why it was inevitable.

Although the texts examined in this book, some well known, others not, are especially important as social documents in which the various representations of gay men attest to the different experiences of being homosexual at particular times and places, these gay fictions have more than merely social or historical significance. In their explorations of the experience of *otherness*, they probe with unusual depth and insight the pain of exclusion, finding in the tribulations and joys of homosexual men faithful reflections of the human condition. By depicting gay people as complete human beings and taking seriously the homosexual's problematic relationship to society, these texts resist their consignment to any category of special pleading or parochial interest.

The same can be said of gay fiction generally, of which the works examined in this book are only broadly representative. Although gay literature has not been sufficiently appreciated, it is remarkably rich and various, especially considering the obstacles with which its authors had to contend in writing honestly about a controversial subject. A more comprehensive account of serious twentieth-century British and American fiction dealing with male homosexuality would, for example, include texts by such diverse authors as Sherwood Anderson, D. H. Lawrence, Evelyn Waugh, Djuna Barnes, Denton Welch, John Horne Burns, J. R. Ackerley, Paul Goodman, Michael Campbell, Paul Bowles, Sanford Friedman, William Burroughs, Francis King, Angus Wilson, Robin Maugham, John Rechy, James Purdy, and Iris Murdoch, as well as such post-Stonewall writers as Edmund White, Andrew Holleran, Armistead Maupin, David Plante, and David Leavitt, among many others. That the several homosexual literary traditions have frequently been dismissed as lacking universality is more revealing of the narrowness of the dismissers' notion of what is universal than an accurate reflection of the limits of gay literature.

The gay fictions with which this book has been concerned vary as to their literary accomplishment, but each is a significant attempt to illuminate the human experience in all its complexity and richness, and they deserve critical study and appreciation as works of art. By focusing on such perennial questions as the value of self-knowledge, the individual's relationship to his or her society, the conflicting appeals of innocence and experience, the need to escape the stifling pressures of conformity, and the yearning for wholeness and for connectedness, the novels and stories explored in this book transcend both their alleged smallness of appeal and their particular historical moments. Although they focus on issues of specific and immediate relevance to homosexuals, these works should be of interest to all people concerned with the importance of self-realization, with issues of justice and diversity, and with the sometimes difficult pursuit of human happiness. For the depth of their analyses, the breadth of their visions, and the integrity of their art, these gay fictions merit an honored place not only in the history of representations of homosexuality, but also in the broad range of the Anglo-American literary tradition.

Notes

Chapter 1: Introduction: From Wilde to Stonewall

1. This study is confined to the representation of homosexual men. The representation of lesbians in literature is equally interesting and important, but beyond the scope of this book. In order to understand my own contribution to the study of the representation of gay men in Anglo-American literature, it may be helpful to review briefly the five book-length studies of the subject that have appeared over the past decade or so. In *Playing the Game: The Homosexual Novel in America* (Indianapolis: Bobbs-Merrill, 1977), Roger Austen provides a pioneering guide to American gay fictions and exposes the mischief and harm that homophobia has wrought over the past century. As criticism, Austen's book is limited by its scope. The attempt to survey over two-hundred novels necessarily leads to superficiality in the discussion of important works. James Levin's *The Gay Novel: The Male Homosexual Image in America* (New York: Irvington, 1983) builds on Austen's work, but is not nearly as successful, lacking Austen's wit, liveliness, and literary sensitivity, while suffering even more from superficiality. Georges-Michel Sarotte's *Like a Brother, Like a Lover: Male Homosexuality in the American Novel and Theatre from Herman Melville to James Baldwin* (New York: Doubleday/Anchor, 1978) is also as much a work of social history as of literary criticism, and it is also superficial in its discussion of particular works of literature. Sarotte is mainly interested in exploring the American psyche, and considers homosexuality a kind of failed masculinity.

My own work is most similar to two books that are self-consciously critical explorations of serious literature: Jeffrey Meyers's *Homosexuality and Literature 1890–1930* (London: Athlone Press, 1977) and Stephen Adams's *The Homosexual as Hero in Contemporary Fiction* (New York: Barnes & Noble, 1980). Meyers's book deserves some credit as a pioneering study, but it is vitiated by homophobia. Adams's study is altogether superior: it is a thoughtful and sympathetic analysis of the homosexual theme in literature from Vidal to Angus Wilson. For a more detailed critique of these previous contributions to the study of gay male literature, see my review essay, "*GSN* Omnibus Review: Studies of Gay Fiction," *Gay Studies Newsletter* 12, No. 2 (July 1985):15–18.

2. Louie Crew and Rictor Norton, "The Homophobic Imagination: An Editorial," *College English* 36 (1974):272.

3. The development of homosexual identity has been studied by psychologists and sociologists. See, e.g., Richard R. Troiden, "The Formation of Homosexual

Identities," *Journal of Homosexuality* 17, Nos. 1/2 (1989):43–73, which includes an extensive bibliography.

4. John D'Emilio, *Sexual Politics, Sexual Communities: The Making of a Homosexual Minority in the United States, 1940–1970* (Chicago: University of Chicago Press, 1983), p. 239. See also Barry D. Adam, *The Rise of a Gay and Lesbian Movement* (Boston: Twayne, 1987), which provides a transnational perspective.

5. Jeffrey Weeks, *Coming Out: Homosexual Politics in Britain, from the Nineteenth Century to the Present* (London: Quartet Books, 1977), p. 3.

6. Michel Foucault, *The History of Sexuality, Volume 1: An Introduction*, trans. Robert Hurley (New York: Vintage, 1980), p. 43. See also Weeks, *Coming Out*, pp. 25–32; and Jonathan Ned Katz, *Gay/Lesbian Almanac: A New Documentary* (New York: Harper & Row, 1983), pp. 147–74.

7. For discussions of the social constructionist/essentialist debate, see John Boswell, "Revolutions, Universals, Categories," *Salmagundi* 58–59 (1982–83):89–113; David F. Greenberg, *The Construction of Homosexuality* (Chicago: University of Chicago Press, 1988), pp. 484–93; and Will Roscoe, "Making History: The Challenge of Gay and Lesbian Studies," *Journal of Homosexuality* 15, Nos. 3–4 (1988):1–40.

8. Although the 1885 Criminal Law Amendment Act was enacted during a period of increasing hostility toward homosexuality, it is not clear that the members of Parliament who voted for it fully understood its provisions. See Greenberg, *The Construction of Homosexuality*, p. 400. On the context and consequences of the Act, see Weeks, *Coming Out*, pp. 14–22.

9. Havelock Ellis, *Studies in the Psychology of Sex, Volume 2: Sexual Inversion* (Philadelphia: F. A. Davis, 1920), p. 352.

10. On the literary manifestations of the Uranian movement, see Brian Reade, ed., *Sexual Heretics: Male Homosexuality in English Literature from 1850 to 1900* (London: Routledge & Kegan Paul, 1970) and Timothy D'Arch Smith, *Love in Earnest: Some Notes on the Lives and Writings of English 'Uranian' Poets from 1889 to 1930* (London: Routledge & Kegan Paul, 1970). Previous to the Uranian movement, the most trenchant analysis of homosexuality in English is that undertaken by Jeremy Bentham, who in a series of (unpublished) essays and notes written between 1774 and 1824 acutely anatomized the evils of antihomosexual hysteria and anticipated a gay-liberationist perspective. For a summary and expert analysis, see Louis Crompton, *Byron and Greek Love: Homophobia in 19th-Century England* (Berkeley: University of California Press, 1985).

11. On Whitman's homosexuality, see, e.g., Joseph Cady, " 'Not Happy in the Capitol': Homosexuality and the Calamus Poems," *American Studies* 19 (Fall 1978):5–22; Robert K. Martin, *The Homosexual Tradition in American Poetry* (Austin: University of Texas Press, 1979); and Michael Lynch, " 'Here is Adhesiveness': From Friendship to Homosexuality," *Victorian Studies* 29 (1985):67–96.

12. D'Emilio, *Sexual Politics, Sexual Communities*, p. 24.

13. Alfred C. Kinsey, Wardell B. Pomeroy, and Clyde E. Martin, *Sexual Behavior in the Human Male* (Philadelphia: W. B. Saunders, 1948), p. 627.

14. Donald Webster Cory [pseudonym of Edward Sagarin], *The Homosexual in America* (New York: Greenberg, 1951), pp. 13–14.

15. On the oppression of homosexuals in England and America during the 1950s,

see Weeks, *Coming Out,* pp. 151–82, and D'Emilio, *Sexual Politics, Sexual Communities,* pp. 40–53.

16. For an account of the struggle within the homophile organizations during the early 1960s between the moderate leaders and the more militant ones, see D'Emilio, *Sexual Politics, Sexual Communities,* pp. 149–75. For sketches of some of these militant leaders, see Kay Tobin and Randy Wicker, *The Gay Crusaders* (New York: Paperback Library, 1972).

Chapter 2: "In Such Surrender There May Be Gain": Oscar Wilde and the Beginnings of Gay Fiction

1. Richard Le Gallienne, Introduction, *The Works of Oscar Wilde* (New York: Lamb, 1909), p. 1.

2. See André Gide, "In Memoriam," in *Oscar Wilde: A Collection of Critical Essays,* ed. Richard Ellmann (Englewood Cliffs, NJ: Prentice-Hall, 1969), p. 34.

3. Quoted in H. Montgomery Hyde, *Oscar Wilde: A Biography* (London: Eyre Methuen, 1976), p. 38. Unless otherwise noted, throughout this chapter I rely on Hyde's biography and on Richard Ellmann, *Oscar Wilde* (New York: Viking, 1987), for information about Wilde's life.

4. Wilde, *The Soul of Man Under Socialism,* in *Complete Works of Oscar Wilde,* intro. by Vyvyan Holland (London: Collins, 1948), p. 1101.

5. James Joyce, "Oscar Wilde: The Poet of *Salome,*" in *Oscar Wilde: A Collection of Critical Essays,* ed. Ellmann, pp. 59–60.

6. Quoted in Hyde, *Oscar Wilde: A Biography,* pp. 257–58.

7. George Woodcock, *The Paradox of Oscar Wilde* (New York: Macmillan, 1950), p. 169.

8. Quoted in Hyde, *Oscar Wilde: A Biography,* p. 293. Tellingly, Sir John Bridges, the magistrate before whom Wilde and Alfred Taylor were arraigned, made a similar comment as he denied bail: "With regard to the gravity of the case, I think there is no worse crime than that with which the prisoners are charged" (quoted in Hyde, p. 228).

9. On the Victorian legal sanctions against sodomy and "gross indecency," see H. Montgomery Hyde, *The Other Love: An Historical and Contemporary Survey of Homosexuality in Britain* (London: Heinemann, 1970), pp. 90–93, 134–37. For an excellent survey of British homophobia earlier in the century, see Crompton, *Byron and Greek Love,* pp. 12–62.

10. Hyde, *Oscar Wilde: A Biography,* p. 294.

11. Wilde, *Complete Shorter Fiction,* ed. Isobel Murray (New York: Oxford University Press, 1979), p. 12. All quotations from "The Portrait of Mr. W. H." in this essay are from *Complete Works,* pp. 1150–1201. The earlier version of the story was first published in the July 1889 issue of *Blackwood's Magazine.* Near the end of 1893, Wilde's publisher Mathews & Lane announced the imminent publication of the revised version, but when the Mathews-Lane partnership was dissolved in 1894, Mathews declined to publish it. Although Lane agreed to "accept all responsibility assumed by the firm," the story never appeared. See Wilde's letters to Mathews and Lane in *Selected Letters of Oscar Wilde,* ed. Rupert Hart-Davis (Oxford: Oxford University Press, 1979), pp. 122–24.

12. The best discussion of the differences between the two versions is in Rodney Shewan, *Oscar Wilde: Art and Egotism* (London: Macmillan, 1977), pp. 83–85.

13. *The Letters of Oscar Wilde*, ed. Rupert Hart-Davis (New York: Harcourt, Brace and World, 1962), p. 247. Ellmann suggests that the story is, at least in part, inspired by Wilde's relationship with Ross: "He imagined Shakespeare, a married man with two children like himself, captivated by a boy as he had been captivated by Ross" (*Oscar Wilde*, pp. 297–98).

14. Lewis J. Poteet, "Romantic Aesthetics in Oscar Wilde's 'Mr. W. H.,' " *Studies in Short Fiction* 7 (1970):458.

15. Wilde, "The Decay of Lying," in *Complete Works*, p. 992.

16. Linda Dowling, "Imposture and Absence in Wilde's 'Portrait of Mr. W. H.,' " *Victorian Newsletter* 58 (1980):458. An essay that came to my attention too late to influence my own discussion makes a similar point about Wilde's novella illustrating the inextricability of literature from interpretation: William A. Cohen, "Willie and Wilde: Reading *The Portrait of Mr. W. H.*," *South Atlantic Quarterly* 88 (1989):219–45.

17. Wilde, "The Rise of Historical Criticism," in *Complete Works*, p. 1105.

18. Poteet, "Romantic Aesthetics," p. 460.

19. Wilde, "The Critic as Artist," in *Complete Works*, p. 1027.

20. Matthew Arnold, "The Buried Life," *The Poems of Matthew Arnold*, ed. Miriam Allott (London: Longman, 1979), p. 291.

21. Chatterton was an important figure for Wilde, and the subject of an unpublished, fragmentary essay. For a discussion of Wilde's fascination with Chatterton, see Shewan, *Oscar Wilde: Art and Egotism*, pp. 70–78.

22. Wilde, *Complete Shorter Fiction*, ed. Murray, p. 12.

23. On the ambiguity of the deaths of Cyril and Erskine, see Herbert Sussman, "Criticism as Art: Form in Oscar Wilde's Critical Writings," *Studies in Philology* 70 (1973):118.

24. On the chronology of composition and on the similarities between the two works, see Donald L. Lawler and Charles E. Knott, "The Context of Invention: Suggested Origins of *Dorian Gray*," *Modern Philology* 73 (1976):389–98. For additional parallels between the two works, see Shewan, *Oscar Wilde: Art and Egotism*, pp. 114–15, 126–27.

25. The cited reviews are reproduced in *Oscar Wilde: The Critical Heritage*, ed. Karl Beckson (London: Routledge & Kegan Paul, 1970), pp. 76, 68, and 75. On the Cleveland Street scandal, see Colin Simpson, Lewis Chester, and David Leitch, *The Cleveland Street Affair* (Boston: Little, Brown, 1976). For an excellent analysis of the controversy surrounding the publication of *The Picture of Dorian Gray*, see Regenia Gagnier, *Idylls of the Marketplace: Oscar Wilde and the Victorian Public* (Stanford: Stanford University Press, 1986), pp. 51–65.

26. Reprinted in *Oscar Wilde: The Critical Heritage*, ed. Beckson, p. 78.

27. Throughout, I quote the novel from *The Picture of Dorian Gray*, ed. Isobel Murray (London: Oxford University Press, 1974).

28. *The Letters of Oscar Wilde*, ed. Hart-Davis, p. 259.

29. Philip K. Cohen, *The Moral Vision of Oscar Wilde* (Rutherford, NJ: Fairleigh Dickinson University Press, 1978), p. 118. Although I disagree with many of Cohen's interpretations and conclusions, I am indebted to his documentation of many instances of moral ambivalence in the novel.

30. Jeffrey Meyers, *Homosexuality and Literature 1890–1930* (London: Athlone Press, 1977), p. 20. For a stimulating account of how "Wilde's 'obviously' homoerotic text signifies its 'deviant' concerns while never explicitly violating the dominant norms for heterosexuality," see Ed Cohen, "Writing Gone Wilde: Homoerotic Desire in the Closet of Representation," *PMLA* 102 (1987):801–13. In *A Problem in Modern Ethics* (privately printed, 1891), John Addington Symonds refers to the homosexuality of "the early Dorians, those martial founders of the institution of Greek Love," adding that "it is notorious to students of Greek civilization that the lofty sentiments of their chivalry was intertwined with singular anomalies in its historical development." Wilde probably chose the name "Gray" in homage to John Gray, a young poet with whom he was in love during the composition of the book. See Ellmann, *Oscar Wilde*, pp. 307–8.

31. *The Letters of Oscar Wilde*, ed. Hart-Davis, p. 266.

32. For a stimulating discussion of Basil's role as initiator of the tragedy and of the novel as a meditation on the moral role of the artist, see Joyce Carol Oates, "*The Picture of Dorian Gray:* Wilde's Parable of the Fall," *Critical Inquiry* 7 (1980):419–28.

33. For a reading of the novel as "chiefly a study of various Victorian art movements corresponding to different stages in the development of Victorian human nature," see Christopher S. Nassaar, *Into the Demon Universe: A Literary Exploration of Oscar Wilde* (New Haven: Yale University Press, 1974), pp. 37–72. Nassaar's argument is not convincing as an account of the novel as a whole, but its emphasis on Pater's problematic influence is well taken. On the novel as simultaneously a tribute to and parody of Pater, see Robert K. Martin, "Parody and Homage: The Presence of Pater in *Dorian Gray*," *Victorian Newsletter* 63 (Spring 1983):15–18.

34. *Selected Letters of Oscar Wilde*, ed. Hart-Davis, p. 240. *De Profundis* was not mailed from prison; Wilde presented it to Ross on the day after he was released. Ross had copies of the document made and claimed to have sent one of the copies to Douglas, who claimed not to have received it. In 1905, Ross published an expurgated version of the letter and a somewhat fuller version appeared in 1908. In 1949, Vyvyan Holland, Wilde's son, published what was described as the "first complete and accurate version" of the work, but a truly complete and accurate text did not appear until 1962, in the Hart-Davis edition of Wilde's letters. All quotations from *De Profundis* in this chapter follow the text established by Hart-Davis.

35. *Selected Letters of Oscar Wilde*, ed. Hart-Davis, p. 152, n. 1. It may also be relevant that the first poem sent to Wilde by Douglas was entitled "De Profundis." See Ellmann, *Oscar Wilde*, pp. 385–86.

36. Regenia Gagnier, "*De Profundis* as *Epistola: in Carcere et Vinculis:* A Materialist Reading of Oscar Wilde's Autobiography," *Criticism* 26 (1984):335. See also the slightly fuller version of this article in Gagnier, *Idylls of the Marketplace*, pp. 179–95.

37. On Wilde's structuring *De Profundis* around Satanic and Christic figures, see Nassaar, *Into the Demon Universe*, pp. 147–63, and Cohen, *The Moral Vision of Oscar Wilde*, pp. 235–64.

38. Joseph Cady, "Oscar Wilde and the Homosexual Potential for 'Imagination,' " unpublished paper presented at the 1974 Gay Academic Union Conference, New York City.

39. For parallels between Christ and Wilde as depicted in *De Profundis*, see

Meredith Cary, "*De Profundis:* Wilde's Letter to the World," *Tennessee Studies in Literature* 16 (1971):94–95, and Cohen, *The Moral Vision of Oscar Wilde,* pp. 243–44. The study that takes Wilde's Christology most seriously is G. Wilson Knight, *The Christian Renaissance* (1933; rpt. London: Methuen, 1962).

40. Although discredited today, Lomboroso's theories helped turn the discourse about homosexuality from moral to psychological and congenital issues. They may have contributed to Italy's decriminalization of consensual homosexual activity in 1889 and they deeply influenced Havelock Ellis. See Jeffrey Weeks, *Coming Out,* pp. 27, 58–59. On the degeneracy theory, see David Greenberg, *The Construction of Homosexuality,* pp. 411–15.

41. On Wilde's use of the dual image of Christ and the clown, see Joseph Butwin, "The Martyr Clown: Oscar Wilde in *De Profundis,*" *Victorian Newsletter* 42 (Fall 1972):1–6.

42. Quoted from a letter to Ross in *Oscar Wilde: The Critical Heritage,* ed. Beckson, p. 244.

43. Wilde canonized himself not long before his death, when he referred to himself as "the infamous St. Oscar of Oxford, Poet and Martyr" (*The Letters of Oscar Wilde,* ed. Hart-Davis, p. 720). The term *homintern* was apparently coined—in analogy with the Comintern, or Third International, the organization established in 1919 to foster international Marxism—by Harold Norse and appropriated by W. H. Auden, who uses it in an essay on Shakespeare's *Sonnets,* where he writes of gay readers being determined "to secure our Top-Bard as a patron saint of the Homintern." (See Auden, "Shakespeare's Sonnets," in *Forewords and Afterwords,* selected by Edward Mendelson [New York: Random House, 1973], p. 99.) I employ the term with an awareness of Auden's irony, even as I find it suggestive in ways that Auden may have intended only mockingly, but which the more politically militant Norse probably meant seriously. Interestingly, Auden's comment disparaging attempts by gay readers to enlist Shakespeare in the homintern probably reflects temporizing on his part, for he remarked at an evening spent at the Stravinskys' on January 31, 1964, that "it won't do just yet to admit that the top Bard was in the homintern" (Robert Craft, *Stravinsky: Chronicle of a Friendship, 1948–1971* [New York: Knopf, 1972], p. 257).

44. W. H. Auden, "An Improbable Life," in *Forewords and Afterwords,* p. 323.

45. John Cowper Powys, "Wilde as a Symbolic Figure," in *Oscar Wilde: The Critical Heritage,* ed. Beckson, p. 357.

46. *Selected Letters of Oscar Wilde,* ed. Hart-Davis, p. 327. It is interesting to note that several members of the Wilde circle, including Alfred Douglas and More Adey, believed Wilde's prosecution and conviction to be politically motivated. See Appendix B, "Alfred Douglas's Political Interpretation of Wilde's Conviction," in Gagnier, *Idylls of the Marketplace,* pp. 205–7.

Chapter 3: "A Losing Game in the End": Willa Cather's "Paul's Case"

1. Sharon O'Brien, *Willa Cather: The Emerging Voice* (New York: Oxford University Press, 1987), p. 215. For other discussions of Cather as a lesbian, see Jane Rule, *Lesbian Images,* pp. 74–87, and Deborah Lambert, "The Defeat of a Hero:

Autonomy and Sexuality in *My Antonía*," *American Literature* 53, No. 4 (January 1982):676–90. In *Willa: The Life of Willa Cather* (New York: Doubleday, 1983), Phyllis Robinson discusses Cather's romantic attachments with women, but does not use the term "lesbian."

2. Roger Austen, *Playing the Game*, pp. 31–33.

3. Larry Rubin, "The Homosexual Motif in Willa Cather's 'Paul's Case,' " *Studies in Short Fiction* 12 (1975):131.

4. All quotations of Cather's journalistic writings are taken from *The Kingdom of Art: Willa Cather's First Principles and Critical Statements 1893–1896*, ed. Bernice Slote (Lincoln: University of Nebraska Press, 1966).

5. On the connection between "the Love that dare not speak its name" and "the thing not named," and on Cather's difficulty in naming Wilde, see O'Brien, *Willa Cather*, pp. 126–27 and 142n.

6. On the models for her portrait of Paul, see Kathleen D. Byrne and Richard C. Snyder, *Chrysalis: Willa Cather in Pittsburgh* (Pittsburgh: Historical Society of Western Pennsylvania, 1980), pp 64–66; James Woodress, "Introduction," *The Troll Garden*, ed. James Woodress (Lincoln: University of Nebraska Press, 1983), p. xx; and Marilyn Arnold, *Willa Cather's Short Fiction* (Athens: Ohio University Press, 1984), p. 67n. Woodress suggests that Cather may have been influenced by an incident reported in the Pittsburgh newspapers involving the theft of an employer's money by two boys who ran off to Chicago.

7. The story was first published in Cather's collection of stories, *The Troll Garden*, and then in *McClure's Magazine* in May 1905. *The Troll Garden* appeared in April or May 1905; it is not known exactly when Cather composed "Paul's Case," but it is generally dated near the end of 1904. Wilde's *De Profundis* appeared in February 1905, so it may be unlikely that Cather read *De Profundis* before writing "Paul's Case," and my argument suggesting a similarity between the two works does not depend on the one influencing the other. Nevertheless, involved as she was in literary journalism, Cather would certainly have been aware of so important a literary event as the publication of Wilde's vindication, and this awareness alone may have stimulated her thinking about issues posed by his imprisonment and disgrace; and it is, of course, possible that she may have had access to a prepublication review copy of *De Profundis*.

8. All quotations from "Paul's Case" are from *Willa Cather's Collected Short Fiction 1892–1912*, ed. Virginia Faulkner, rev. ed. (Lincoln: University of Nebraska Press, 1970), pp. 243–61.

9. Another of the stories in *The Troll Garden*, "The Sculptor's Funeral," also has a homosexual theme. Indeed, "The Sculptor's Funeral" and "Paul's Case" may be viewed as companion pieces. As Alice Hall Petry observes, "The Sculptor's Funeral" is "a remarkably astute study of a family, a town, a society failing to come to terms, not with a young man's artistic inclinations, but rather with his homosexuality" ("Harvey's Case: Notes on Cather's 'The Sculptor's Funeral,' " *South Dakota Review* 11 [1986]:108–9). In contrast, the emphasis in "Paul's Case" is equally on a homosexual's failure to come to terms with his society.

10. Cather, "The Novel Démeublé," *Not Under Forty* (New York: Knopf, 1936), p. 50. Cather's remark in a 1918 interview is also pertinent: "It is always hard to write about the things that are near your heart. From a kind of instinct of self-

protection you distort and disguise them" (Grant Overton, *The Women Who Make Our Novels* [New York: Moffat, Yard, 1918], p. 259).

11. O'Brien, *Willa Cather*, p. 127.

12. Rubin, "The Homosexual Motif," pp. 127–31.

13. On Cather's use of these terms, see O'Brien, pp. 225–26.

14. Rubin conjectures that the frostiness of the parting may have been the result of a sexual overture on Paul's part that the Yale freshman rejects. "Given the lack of any further elucidation of the situation, on Cather's part," Rubin writes, "the reader is left with an unshakable sense of innuendo" (p. 130).

15. It should be stressed that Cather invented the name Cordelia Street: the actual street in Pittsburgh that probably inspired Cather's setting is Aurelia Street. See Byrne and Snyder, *Chrysalis*, pp. 83–84.

Chapter 4: "The Flesh Educating the Spirit": E. M. Forster's Gay Fictions

1. Forster, "The Challenge of Our Time," in *Two Cheers for Democracy* (London: Edward Arnold, 1951), p. 56. Unless otherwise cited, all biographical information on Forster is taken from P. N. Furbank, *E. M. Forster: A Life*, 2 vols. (London: Secker and Warburg, 1977–78; rpt., 2 vols. in 1, New York: Harcourt Brace Jovanovich, 1978).

2. Edward Carpenter, *The Intermediate Sex* (London: Allen & Unwin, 1908), p. 114. In 1893, John Addington Symonds wrote to Carpenter that "The blending of Social Strata in masculine love seems to me one of its most pronounced, and socially hopeful features. Where it appears, it abolishes class distinctions, and opens by a single operation the cataract-blinded life to their futilities" (quoted in Weeks, *Coming Out*, p. 41).

3. Quoted in "Editor's Introduction," Forster, *Arctic Summer and Other Fiction*, ed. Elizabeth Heine (New York: Holmes & Meier, 1981), p. xxx.

4. Furbank, *E. M. Forster*, II, 155.

5. Forster, *Pharos and Pharillon* (London: Hogarth Press, 1923; New York, Knopf, 1962), p. 92.

6. Cynthia Ozick, "Forster as Homosexual," *Commentary* 52 (December 1971):85. As Judith Scherer Herz comments, following Furbank's biography, "No mention could be made in essay or book review of Burgess or Blunt, for example, no discussion of MI5 could be conducted, without the writer trotting out the (in)famous line, 'if I had to choose between betraying my country and betraying my friend I hope I should have the guts to betray my country,' as if Forster were somehow the progenitor of a generation of vipers." In addition to a host of homophobic attacks, Forster was also assailed by some gay activists, who argued that his reticence in publishing his gay fictions undermined his authority. For a spirited attempt to "restore to Forster some of the importance, both literary and ethical, that has been gradually leached away in the succession of belittling essays and reviews that have appeared since his death," see Herz, *The Short Narratives of E. M. Forster* (London: Macmillan, 1988). The quotations are from pp. 120 and 4–5, respectively.

7. June Perry Levine, "The Tame in Pursuit of the Savage: The Posthumous Fiction of E. M. Forster," *PMLA* 99 (1984):72.

8. Quoted in Furbank, *E. M. Forster*, I, 48.

9. Ibid., I, 259.

10. For a responsible statement of this view, see Judith Scherer Herz, "The Double Nature of Forster's Fiction: *A Room with a View* and *The Longest Journey,*" *English Literature in Transition* 21 (1978):254–65; for a homophobic formulation, see Meyers, *Homosexuality and Literature,* p. 106.

11. Christopher Isherwood, *Christopher and His Kind* (New York: Farrar, Straus and Giroux, 1976), p. 126.

12. Forster, "The Curate's Friend," in *Collected Short Stories* (London: Sidgwick & Jackson, 1947; Harmondsworth, Middlesex: Penguin, 1954, p. 86). All quotations from "The Curate's Friend" follow this edition. For the first suggestion of a homosexual dimension to "The Curate's Friend," credit goes to Alan Wilde, *Art and Order: A Study of E. M. Forster* (New York: New York University Press, 1964), pp. 74–76.

13. Oscar Wilde, *The Importance of Being Earnest,* in *The Portable Oscar Wilde,* ed. Richard Aldington (New York: Viking, 1946), p. 481.

14. For a discussion of the priapic ethos of Forster's gay fictions, see Alan Wilde, *Horizons of Assent: Modernism, Postmodernism, and the Ironic Imagination* (Baltimore: Johns Hopkins University Press, 1981), pp. 50–89.

15. Forster, *Maurice* (London: Edward Arnold, 1971), p. 249. All quotations from *Maurice* follow this edition. For an excellent account of the novel's evolution and complex manuscript history, see Philip Gardner, "The Evolution of E. M. Forster's *Maurice,*" in *E. M. Forster: Centenary Revaluations,* ed. Judith Scherer Herz and Robert K. Martin (Toronto: University of Toronto Press, 1982), pp. 204–23.

16. See Dixie King, "The Influence of Forster's *Maurice* on *Lady Chatterley's Lover,*" *Contemporary Literature* 23 (1982):65–82.

17. See Alan P. Bell, Martin S. Weinberg, and Sue Kiefer Hammersmith, *Sexual Preference: Its Development in Men and Women* (Bloomington: Indiana University Press, 1981). On the homosexual milieu of Edwardian England, see Ira Bruce Nadel, "Moments in the Greenwood: *Maurice* in Context," in *E. M. Forster: Centenary Revaluations,* ed. Herz and Martin, pp. 177–90.

18. Symonds actually wrote two different kinds of apologia for homosexuality, directed toward two distinct audiences. In his commercial publications, such as *Studies of the Greek Poets* (1873, augmented 1876) and *Renaissance in Italy* (1877–1886), his collection of poetry, *Many Moods* (1888), and his translation of the *Sonnets of Michaelangelo* (1878), he is circumspect and evasive, frequently treating homosexual subjects but nearly always platonizing the homoerotic or otherwise concealing physical passion. In his privately printed publications—sometimes issued anonymously and in very small editions—Symonds is more explicit. These privately printed works include two important prose treatises, *A Problem in Greek Ethics* (1883) and *A Problem in Modern Ethics* (1891); a collection of essays, *In the Key of Blue* (1893); his collaboration with Havelock Ellis, *Sexual Inversion* (issued anonymously in 1897); and numerous volumes of poetry, including the long poem in honor of Whitman, "The Song of Love and Death" (written 1871, printed 1875?), that served as an important source for the homoerotic ideology of *A Room with a View.* Carpenter's works include a long Whitmanesque poem, *Towards Democracy* (1883, augmented 1885, 1892, 1895), and such books as *Homogenic Love* (1894), *Iolaus: An Anthology of Friendship* (1902), and *The Intermediate Sex* (1908). The difference between Carpenter and Symonds is actually more a matter of style than

substance; written under the direct influence of Carpenter, *Maurice* reflects Carpenter's view that Symonds was excessively cautious and timid in his public comments on homosexuality.

19. Robert K. Martin, "Edward Carpenter and the Double Structure of *Maurice*," *Journal of Homosexuality* 8 (Spring/Summer 1983):35–46. On Carpenter's influence on the novel, see also Roger Ebbatson, *The Evolutionary Self: Hardy, Forster, Lawrence* (Brighton, Sussex: Harvester, 1982), pp. 57–75, and Levine, "The Tame in Pursuit of the Savage."

20. My subsequent quotations from *De Profundis* are from the text that Forster would have known, the abridged version published by Methuen in 1905. Wilde and *De Profundis* were much in the news in 1913, the year that Forster began work on *Maurice*. In 1912, Arthur Ransome published *Oscar Wilde: A Critical Study*, in which he alleged that Wilde blamed Alfred Douglas for his ruin. Douglas promptly sued Ransome for libel; the case was heard in April 1913. As justification for his allegations, Ransome produced the unpublished full version of *De Profundis*, portions of which were read aloud in court. The jury found in Ransome's favor. Widely reported, the trial served to rehash the Wilde scandal of 1895 and to focus attention on *De Profundis*. For an account of the Ransome libel action, see H. Montgomery Hyde, *Cases That Changed the Law* (London: Heinemann, 1951), pp. 164–76.

21. Thomas Carlyle, *Sartor Resartus*, ed. Charles Frederick Harrold (New York: Odyssey), pp. 53–54.

22. See "Alexis" in "A Pronouncing Vocabulary of Common English Given Names," in *Webster's New Collegiate Dictionary* (Springfield, Mass.: Merriam, 1959), p. 1131.

23. Martin, "Edward Carpenter and the Double Structure of *Maurice*," p. 40. See also Kathleen Grant, "*Maurice* as Fantasy," in *E. M. Forster: Centenary Revaluations*, ed. Herz and Martin, p. 200.

24. The color blue was frequently evoked by Uranians, and Forster's use of the Blue Room as the scene of Maurice's exchange with Clive fittingly links their relationship with the apologia of Symonds, whose collection of essays is entitled *In the Key of Blue*. Certainly Forster intends a contrast between the spiritual communion in the Blue Room and the later physical communion in the Russet Room. As Bonnie Blumenthal Finkelstein writes, "Maurice's cool, platonic affair . . . in the Blue Room . . . is finally superseded by a more complete, hot, passionate, and physical love in the Red" (*Forster's Women: Eternal Differences* [New York: Columbia University Press, 1975], p. 172).

25. On this point, see Martin, "Edward Carpenter and the Double Structure of *Maurice*," p. 41.

26. James S. Malek, "Tackling Tribal Prejudices: Norms in Forster's Homosexual Fiction," unpublished essay, p. 38. On this passage, see also Ebbatson, *The Evolutionary Self*, pp. 63–64.

27. This incident may have been inspired by an 1838 letter from Thomas Carlyle to his mother in which he recounts having seen Queen Victoria driving through a park. (*New Letters of Thomas Carlyle*, ed. Alexander Carlyle [London: John Lane, 1904], I, 119). Ebbatson, *The Evolutionary Self*, pp. 68–69, traces the phrase "inside a ring fence" to Carpenter's *Love's Coming of Age*.

28. In the late nineteenth and early twentieth centuries, the word "comrade"

itself possessed strong homoerotic connotations. Edward Carpenter begins *Homogenic Love* (1894; rpt. in *Sexual Heretics,* ed. Reade) by declaring that "Of all the many forms that Love delights to take, perhaps none is more interesting . . . than that special attachment which is sometimes denoted by the word Comradeship." Throughout he uses "comrade-love" as a synonym for homosexuality.

29. Malek, "Tackling Tribal Prejudices," p. 38. On the flawed ending of *Maurice,* see also Stephen Adams, *The Homosexual as Hero,* pp. 116–19. For an account of the importance of the greenwood in Forster's fiction, see Elizabeth Wood Ellem, "E. M. Forster's Greenwood," *Journal of Modern Literature* 5 (1976):89–98. In an interesting but perverse and inattentive reading that refuses to accept the novel's political and psychological realities, Wilfred Stone denies that the ending is really happy at all, finding it not sentimental but fantastic (" 'Overleaping Class': Forster's Problem in Connection," *Modern Language Quarterly* 39 [1978]:386–404). Crucial to Stone's strained argument are his unsubstantiated assumptions that Forster was guilt-ridden about his homosexuality and that he really loathed the lower classes. Both the novel and the evidence of Forster's life suggest precisely the opposite.

30. Glen Cavaliero, *A Reading of E. M. Forster* (London: Macmillan, 1979), p. 137.

31. Meyers, *Homosexuality and Literature,* p. 102. Meyers's discussion of *Maurice* is particularly offensive, containing not only an abysmally insensitive reading of the novel but also an ill-informed and contemptuous account of Forster's personal life. For a rebuttal to Meyers's objections to *Maurice,* see Adams, *The Homosexual as Hero,* pp. 118–19.

32. Martin, "Edward Carpenter and the Double Structure of *Maurice,"* p. 43. Forster clearly repudiates the elitism of Clive's claim of special insight by virtue of his homosexuality, but he recognizes that gay people, particularly if they become aware of their mark of difference in adolescence, are frequently unusually introspective. This thoughtfulness is, again, not the result of any particular quality of homosexuality but of the homosexual's peculiar relationship to society. Clive's claim of aesthetic superiority is at one with his elitism, and to that extent is not taken seriously by the novel. But Forster does accept the proposition that sexual orientation affects aesthetic response, though exactly how remains elusive.

33. For instance, Donald Salter, in an otherwise sympathetic survey, regards several of the gay fictions as pornographic; see " 'That is My Ticket': The Homosexual Writings of E. M. Forster," *London Magazine* 14 (1975):16–22. But Salter bases this judgment on a misunderstanding of the "facetious tales" and on a too literal interpretation of Forster's remark in a diary entry about some stories that he destroyed in 1922: "They were written not to express myself but to excite myself." It is questionable whether a story written to "excite" the author is necessarily pornographic, but in any case Forster's remark does not refer to the stories in *The Life to Come.* Furbank reports that Forster was excited while writing "The Story of a Panic" and the scene in *Where Angels Fear to Tread* in which Gino twists Philip's broken arm (*E. M. Forster,* I, 114); these scenes reverberate with violence and sexuality, but they certainly are not pornographic. Neither are the posthumously published tales.

34. Stone, " 'Overleaping Class,' " p. 404. Equally inaccurate is Barbara Rose-

crance's smug assertion: "The homosexual stories concern themselves not with the meaning of life but with a byway of experience, the thrills and punishments of homosexual passion. . . . Their orgies of rape, mutilation, and death project anguish, but also a questionable pleasure in violence, self-punishment, and destruction" (*Forster's Narrative Vision* [Ithaca, N.Y.: Cornell University Press, 1982], pp. 182–83). Such assertions reflect remarkable innocence of complex psychological issues and apparently willful misreadings of the fiction. Because they reduce the important social and political and sexual issues at the heart of Forster's gay fictions to symptoms of neurosis and to "a byway of experience" irrelevant to "the meaning of life," such assertions are also fundamentally homophobic.

35. Forster, "The Life to Come" in *The Life to Come and Other Stories*, ed. Oliver Stallybrass (London: Edward Arnold, 1972), p. 69. All quotations from the stories in this book follow this edition.

36. In the nineteenth century, Jeremy Bentham diagnosed ascetic morality as the force that most supported homophobia, and he located its root in Pauline Christianity. See Crompton, *Byron and Greek Love*, pp. 268–83.

37. Judith Scherer Herz, "From Myth to Scripture: An Approach to Forster's Later Short Fiction," *English Literature in Transition* 24 (1981):210; the subsequent quotation is from p. 209.

38. J. I. M. Stewart, "Old and Gay," *Spectator*, October 21, 1972, p. 629; Stone, " 'Overleaping Class,' " p. 397. For a refutation of Stone's position, see Levine, "The Tame in Pursuit of the Savage," pp. 79–80.

39. Forster, *A Passage to India* (London: Edward Arnold, 1924; New York: Harcourt, Brace, Jovanovich, n.d.), p. 103.

40. James S. Malek, "Forster's 'Arthur Snatchfold': Respectability vs. Apollo," *Notes on Contemporary Literature* 10 (September 1980):9.

41. James S. Malek, "Persona, Shadow, and Society: A Reading of Forster's 'The Other Boat,' " *Studies in Short Fiction* 14 (1977):21–27.

42. See Stone, " 'Overleaping Class,' " and Rosecrance, *Forster's Narrative Vision*, pp. 182–83. For a refutation of these views, see Levine, "The Tame in Pursuit of the Savage," especially pp. 79–87. There is something naive and parochial about the charges of Stone and Rosecrance, since however violent Forster's gay fictions are, they are actually far less violent than the work of most of his major contemporaries.

Chapter 5: "The Cabin and the River": Gore Vidal's *The City and the Pillar*

1. The period 1945–55 is labeled the "crucial decade" by Eric C. Goldman in *The Crucial Decade: America 1945–1955* (New York: Knopf, 1956). For a brief but suggestive study of homosexuality in the work of Norman Mailer, Gordon Merrick, and Gore Vidal in this period, see S. James Elliott, "Homosexuality in the Crucial Decade: Three Novelists' Views," in *The Gay Academic*, ed. Louie Crew (Palm Springs: ETC, 1978), pp. 164–77. On the postwar burst of American novels with gay themes, see also Roger Austen, *Playing the Game*, pp. 93–94.

2. Vidal, *The City and the Pillar Revised* (New York: Dutton, 1965), p. 155. All subsequent quotations from the Afterword and from the revised version of the novel are from this edition.

3. Vidal, *The City and the Pillar* (New York: Dutton, 1948), p. 246. All subsequent quotations from the original version of the novel are from ths edition. Vidal's 1965 revision substantially improves the novel's style and conclusion, but because my interests are historical as well as aesthetic, I refer throughout to the original version except where clearly indicated.

4. The arrest of Tilden, perhaps the greatest tennis player of all time, for homosexual offenses involving minors sent shock waves through the sports world and challenged the widely held assumption that athletes could not be homosexual. In January 1947, Tilden was sentenced to nine months in jail for contributing to the delinquency of a minor. In 1949, he was sentenced to one year in jail for a similar offense.

5. *The Diary of Anaïs Nin, Volume IV, 1944–1947*, ed. Gunther Stuhlmann (New York: Harcourt Brace Jovanovich, 1971), p. 175.

6. The term is that of Bernard F. Dick in *The Apostate Angel: A Critical Study of Gore Vidal* (New York: Random House, 1974), p. 38. But because Dick does not recognize the homosexual myths that Vidal uses in the novel, he seriously misleads by creating a false antinomy when he remarks that Vidal's book is "important as a mythic novel, not a homosexual one." He is challenged on this count by Austen, *Playing the Game*, pp. 123–24, and by Adams, *The Homosexual as Hero*, p. 18.

7. Modern scholarship has questioned the traditional interpretation of the Sodom story as a condemnation of homosexuality, seeing it instead as a condemnation of inhospitality or rape. See, e.g., Derrick S. Bailey, *Homosexuality and the Western Christian Tradition* (London: Longman, Green, 1955); John McNeill, *The Church and the Homosexual* (Kansas City: Sheed, Andrews & McMeel, 1976); and John Boswell, *Christianity, Social Tolerance, and Homosexuality* (Chicago: University of Chicago Press, 1980).

8. Dick, *The Apostate Angel*, p. 39. The previous quotation is from page 31. For a challenge to Dick's thesis, see Adams, *The Homosexual as Hero*, p. 18. In *Gore Vidal* (New York: Ungar, 1982), Robert F. Kiernan links Jim Willard with George Willard of Sherwood Anderson's *Winesburg, Ohio* and other "boy-men" of American literature (pp. 39–40).

9. Walt Whitman, "Song of Myself," 1. 200, in *Walt Whitman: The Complete Poems*, ed. Francis Murphy (Harmondsworth, Middlesex, Eng.: Penguin, 1975), p. 3. Among the late-nineteenth-century homoerotic paintings of bathing scenes are *The Swimming Hole* by Thomas Eakins and *August Blue* by H. S. Tuke. Austen explains the prevalence of bathing scenes in gay American literature in practical terms: "Since the one sensuous nude/near nude experience American society permits young males to have with each other is related to some variation of 'the old swimming hole,' it is not surprising that many of the more autobiographical novels contain swimming scenes. The traumatic shock of recognition that one is 'different' often goes back to some early and indelible fascination with the naked body of a slightly older male . . . and furthermore it is not uncommon for the physical characteristics of this person to serve as the ideal against which all later love objects are measured. . . . Sharing some golden moments with an adored near-naked buddy is the closest many gay males come to perfection during their peculiarly troubled adolescence, and thus it seems that the appearance of these poignant pool scenes can

also be understood in terms of the novelist recapturing the golden moments of his youth" (*Playing the Game*, p. 141, n. 40).

10. Austen, *Playing the Game*, p. 124; Adams, *The Homosexual as Hero*, p. 18. The Hylas ritual is outlined and explained by Rictor Norton, *The Homosexual Literary Tradition: An Interpretation* (New York: Revisionist Press, 1974), pp. 1–27. See also his discussion of "The Love-Battle," pp. 56–74. It is unlikely that Vidal consciously intended to evoke the Hercules–Hylas myth, but he was certainly aware that wrestling is frequently a metaphor for homoeroticism.

11. See *The Symposium*, tr. W. H. D. Rouse, in *Great Dialogues of Plato*, ed. Eric H. Warmington and Philip G. Rouse (New York: New American Library, 1956), pp. 85–89.

12. Kiernan, *Gore Vidal*, pp. 42–43.

13. Kiernan, *Gore Vidal*, pp. 41–42.

14. It should be pointed out that the epithet "queer" is much more wounding in American than in British English. In British usage, the term lacks some of the contempt that it has in American slang, probably because it is a word that is used more commonly and benignly in England than in America. The characters in Renault's *The Charioteer*, for example, refer to themselves as "queers," and while this usage does reflect their internalized homophobia, it does not have the same force as it would were the characters American.

Chapter 6: "The Charm of the Defeated": The Early Fiction of Truman Capote and Tennessee Williams

1. Truman Capote, *Other Voices, Other Rooms* (New York: Random House, 1948; New York: Signet, 1960), p. 82. All subsequent quotations from *Other Voices, Other Rooms* are also from the 1960 paperback edition.

2. Carson McCullers, *The Ballad of the Sad Cafe* (1943; Boston: Houghton, Mifflin, 1951), p. 24.

3. Adams, *The Homosexual as Hero*, p. 59.

4. Both *One Arm* and *Hard Candy* were published in limited editions of fifteen hundred copies each. It is doubtful that widely distributed editions would have been permitted at the time; at the very least, they would have encountered censorship difficulties. The books were not issued in trade editions until the late 1960s. In his *Memoirs*, Williams recounts his being shocked by Paul Bowles's short story "The Delicate Prey" when he read it in manuscript in 1948: "This seems odd, I know. And I think it was quite incomprehensible to Paul that I, who had published such stories as 'Desire and the Black Masseur' should be shocked by 'The Delicate Prey.' I recognized it as a beautiful piece of prose but I advised him against publication in the States. You see, my shocking stories had been published in expensive private editions by New Directions and never exhibited on a bookstore counter" (*Memoirs* [Garden City, N.Y.: Doubleday, 1975], p. 159). In an interesting essay, John M. Clum speculates that Williams made a distinction between private art—poetry and fiction—and the public art of theater; hence, he felt freer to treat homosexuality in his nondramatic writings, though even there he employed a homophobic discourse. See " 'Something Cloudy, Something Clear': Homophobic Discourse in Tennessee Williams," *South Atlantic Quarterly* 88 (1989):161–79.

5. William H. Peden, "Mad Pilgrimage: The Short Stories of Tennessee Williams," *Studies in Short Fiction* 1 (1964):243.

6. See, for example, Tom S. Reck, "The Short Stories of Tennessee Williams: Nucleus for His Drama," *Tennessee Studies in Literature* 16 (1971):141–54. Other discussions of Williams's short fiction include: Benjamin Nelson, *Tennessee Williams: The Man and His Work* (New York: Obolensky, 1961), pp. 185–97; Signi Falk, *Tennessee Williams* (New York: Twayne, 1961), pp. 38–41; Luke M. Grande, "Metaphysics as Alienation in Tennessee Williams' Short Stories," *Drama Critique* 4 (1961):118–22; Peden, "Mad Pilgrimage," pp. 243–50; Ren Draya, "The Fiction of Tennessee Williams," in *Tennessee Williams: A Tribute*, ed. Jac Tharpe (Jackson: University Press of Mississippi, 1977), pp. 647–62; Thomas J. Richardson, "The City of Day and the City of Night: New Orleans and the Exotic Unreality of Tennessee Williams," in *Tennessee Williams: A Tribute*, pp. 631–46; and Edward A. Sklepowich, "In Pursuit of the Lyric Quarry: The Image of the Homosexual in Tennessee Williams' Prose Fiction," in *Tennessee Williams: A Tribute*, pp. 525–44. Of these, by far the best discussion is that of Sklepowich.

The fullest consideration of Williams as a writer of short stories appeared only after this chapter was completed: Dennis Vannatta, *Tennessee Williams: A Study of the Short Fiction* (Boston: Twayne, 1988). Vannatta's book is a general introduction to the short stories, but his discussions of individual stories are very brief, sometimes perfunctory. Vannatta rejects labeling Williams as a homosexual writer on the revealingly homophobic grounds that "surely this label is absurdly narrow for a writer of Williams's expansive and profound sympathies" (p. 78). Throughout, he sentimentalizes Williams as a failed artist. For example, he remarks that in the last two decades of Williams's life, everything deserted him "but the desire to write. When at last that left him, he died" (p. 37). What this romantic scenario overlooks is the fact that despite the sadness of his final years, Williams did not pine away or commit suicide; in a freak accident he choked to death on a bottle cap.

7. All quotations from "One Arm" are from *One Arm and Other Stories* (New York: New Directions, 1948), pp. 7–29.

8. All quotations from "Desire and the Black Masseur" are from *One Arm and Other Stories*, pp. 83–94.

9. See, for example, Edmund Fuller, *Man in Modern Fiction* (New York: 1958), pp. 70–72. For an early defense of the story, see Paul J. Hurley, "Williams' 'Desire and the Black Masseur': An Analysis," *Studies in Short Fiction* 2 (1964):51–55.

10. William Butler Yeats, "The Second Coming." The story is also vaguely reminiscent of Eliot's *The Wasteland*.

11. Nelson, *Tennessee Williams*, p. 191.

12. Williams, "Introduction to Carson McCullers's *Reflections in a Golden Eye*," in *Where I Live: Selected Essays*, ed. Christine R. Day and Bob Woods (New York: New Directions, 1978), p. 46.

13. All quotations from "The Angel in the Alcove" are from *One Arm and Other Stories*, pp. 137–49.

14. All quotations from "The Night of the Iguana" are from *One Arm and Other Stories*, pp. 169–96.

15. Sklepowich, "In Pursuit of the Lyric Quarry," p. 531.

16. All quotations from "The Mysteries of the Joy Rio" are from *Hard Candy:*

A Book of Stories (New York: New Directions, 1954), pp. 203–20. In subsequent editions, the title was changed to *Hard Candy and Other Stories*.

17. According to the notes in *Tennessee Williams: Collected Stories* (New York: Ballantine, 1986), "The Mysteries of the Joy Rio" was written in 1941, while "Hard Candy" was begun in 1949 and completed in 1953.

18. All quotations from "Hard Candy" are from *Hard Candy: A Book of Stories*, pp. 103–21. For a stimulating but somewhat unbalanced discussion of "Hard Candy," see Clum, " 'Something Cloudy, Something Clear,' " pp. 165–68.

19. All quotations from "Two on a Party" are from *Hard Candy: A Book of Stories*, pp. 47–78.

20. For some reason, in nearly all discussions of the story, Cora is described as a prostitute (see, e.g., Nelson, p. 194; Peden, p. 247; and Sklepowich, p. 534); but she emphatically is not. While it may be true that Cora's characterization may owe something to the literary tradition of "the proverbial whore with the heart of gold," as Sklepowich suggests (p. 535), she is not a prostitute. She is dependent on a trust fund controlled by her brother; hence, her concern when the hotel clerk threatens to write her family about her life in New York. The dynamics of the story, and of her relationship with Billy, would be considerably different were she engaged in selling sex rather than in attempting to give it away.

21. As Sklepowich points out, "Several of Williams' comments in the *Memoirs* on his own life of cruising are especially pertinent to an understanding of the bond between Billy and Cora" (p. 535). At one point in the *Memoirs*, Williams reflects, "I wonder, sometimes, how much of the cruising was for the pleasure of my cruising partner's companionship and for the sport of the pursuit and how much was actually for the pretty repetitive and superficial satisfactions of the act itself" (p. 53). Later, he describes his "sublimated love" for a 1939 cruising buddy, whom he calls "Dreamy Eyes." Their cruising activity in Times Square ended abruptly after they were beaten up following sex with two sailors.

Chapter 7: "The Plain of Truth": Mary Renault's *The Charioteer*

1. See Bernard F. Dick, *The Hellenism of Mary Renault* (Carbondale: Southern Illinois University Press, 1972), p. 30, and Peter Wolfe, *Mary Renault* (New York: Twayne, 1969), p. 121.

2. As Gore Vidal noted, "in a dozen popular books Mary Renault has made the classical era alive, forcing even the dullest of bookchat writers to recognize that bisexuality was once our culture's norm and that Christianity's perversion of this human fact is the aberration and not the other way around" ("The Ashes of Hollywood II: The Top 6 of the Top 10," *New York Review of Books*, May 31, 1973, p. 15).

3. For information about the status of homosexuals and homosexuality in the 1950s, see Weeks, *Coming Out*, pp. 151–82, and D'Emilio, *Sexual Politics, Sexual Communities*, pp. 40–125.

4. Weeks, *Coming Out*, pp. 158–62. On the sensational Montagu–Wildeblood trials of 1953 and 1954, see Peter Wildeblood, *Against the Law* (Harmondsworth, Eng.: Penguin, 1957). Andrew Hodges's biography of the mathematician and phys-

icist Alan Turing, *Alan Turing: The Enigma* (New York: Simon and Schuster, 1983), gives an excellent account of homophobic hysteria in England in the 1950s as well as of Turing's own prosecution and conviction in 1954. Turing's sentence—he avoided prison, but only by accepting court-ordered hormone injections that caused him to grow breasts—neatly illustrates the convergence of legal and medical approaches to homosexuality in the decade.

5. D'Emilio, *Sexual Politics, Sexual Communities*, p. 57.

6. Kenneth Fink, "The Psychodynamics of the Homosexual," *Mattachine Review*, July 1960, p. 11.

7. Wolfe, *Mary Renault*, p. 114. W. C. McWilliams, in an untitled article in *Commonweal*, December 7, 1973, extravangantly praises *The Charioteer* as "the most sensitive and accurate treatment of homosexuality that I know of" (p. 271).

8. Renault's account of Ralph's expulsion from prep school is similar in some respects to Vidal's 1950 short story "The Zenner Trophy."

9. Plato, *Phaedrus*, tr. Benjamin Jowett, in *The Works of Plato*, ed. Irwin Edman (New York: Modern Library, 1930), p. 296.

10. Renault, *The Charioteer* (New York: Pantheon, 1959), p. 32. All quotations are from this, the first American edition. *The Charioteer* was originally published in England in 1953, but was rejected by Renault's American publisher, William Morrow and Co.—a rejection that she ascribed to the rise of McCarthyism in the United States.

11. This explanation of the origins of homosexuality was codified in Irving Bieber's *Homosexuality: A Psychoanalytic Study of Male Homosexuals* (New York: Vintage, 1962). The medical model of the 1950s and 1960s has been discredited by a host of studies that have shown repeatedly that there are no discernible differences in psychological adjustments between homosexuals and heterosexuals in nonclinical populations. These studies, pioneered by Evelyn Hooker, finally led to the American Psychiatric Association's 1973 decision to declassify homosexuality as a mental illness. For an excellent historical overview of homosexuality and psychoanalysis, see Kenneth Lewes, *The Psychoanalytic Theory of Male Homosexuality* (New York: Simon and Schuster, 1988).

12. D'Emilio, *Sexual Politics, Sexual Communities*, p. 242.

13. Wolfe, *Mary Renault*, p. 118. In *The Hellenism of Mary Renault*, Dick also finds the conclusion pessimistic, claiming that the novel "ends on a twin note of inevitability and resignation" (p. 36).

14. Plato, *Phaedrus*, in *The Works of Plato*, p. 289.

Chapter 8: "Looking at the Naked Sun": James Baldwin's *Giovanni's Room*

1. James Baldwin and Nikki Giovanni, *A Dialogue* (Philadelphia: Lippincott, 1973), pp. 88–89.

2. James Baldwin and Richard Avedon, *Nothing Personal* (New York: Athenaeum, 1964), n.p.

3. Dorothy H. Lee, "The Bridge of Suffering," *Callaloo* 6 (Spring/Summer 1983):92–99. Lee's brief article concentrates on *Just Above My Head* (1979), but it is wonderfully suggestive for a reading of all Baldwin's novels. For an overwrought

analysis of homosexuality in Baldwin's work, see John S. Lash, "Baldwin Beside Himself: A Study in Modern Phallicism," in *James Baldwin: A Critical Evaluation*, ed. Therman B. O'Daniel (Washington, D.C.: Howard University Press, 1977), pp. 47–55. An altogether more insightful discussion than Lash's is that by Stephen Adams, *The Homosexual as Hero*, pp. 35–55.

4. As suggested, for example, by John T. Shawcross, "Joy and Sadness: James Baldwin, Novelist," *Callaloo* 6 (Spring/Summer 1983):102.

5. Eldridge Cleaver, "Notes on a Native Son," *Soul on Ice* (New York: McGraw-Hill, 1968), p. 110.

6. Austen, *Playing the Game*, pp. 48 and 150, respectively.

7. Donald B. Gibson, "James Baldwin: The Political Anatomy of Space," in *James Baldwin: A Critical Evaluation*, ed. O'Daniel, p. 10.

8. Baldwin, *Giovanni's Room* (New York: Dial Press, 1956; rpt. New York: Dell, 1985), p. 1. All quotations from the novel are from the 1985 reprint.

9. Robert F. Sayre, "James Baldwin's Other Country," in *Contemporary American Novelists*, ed. Harry T. Moore (Carbondale: Southern Illinois University Press, 1964), p. 163.

10. Shawcross, "Joy and Sadness," pp. 106–7.

11. Baldwin, "The Male Prison," in *The Price of the Ticket: Collected Nonfiction, 1948–1985* (New York: St. Martin's, 1985), p. 104. "The Male Prison" was originally published in 1954 as "Gide as Husband and Homosexual."

12. George E. Kent, "Baldwin and the Problem of Being," in *James Baldwin: A Collection of Critical Essays*, ed. Keneth Kinnamon (Englewood Cliffs, N.J.: Prentice-Hall, 1974), p. 24.

13. Baldwin, "A Question of Identity," in *The Price of the Ticket*, p. 93.

14. Colin MacInnes, "The Dark Angel: The Writings of James Baldwin," *Encounter* 21 (August 1963):27; Adams, *The Homosexual as Hero*, p. 42.

15. Adams, *The Homosexual as Hero*, p. 42.

16. Baldwin, "Disturber of the Peace: James Baldwin," an interview with Eve Auchincloss and Nancy Lynch, *Mademoiselle*, May 1963; rpt. *The Black American Writer*, ed. C. W. E. Bigsby (Baltimore: Penguin, 1971) 1:213–14. In an important interview with Jere Real in the American gay newsmagazine *The Advocate*, Baldwin remarked that "I think Americans are more uptight about homosexuality than about any other subject," and he located the source of this uptightness in an inability to love: "I think . . . that the inability to love *is* the central problem, because that inability masks a certain terror, and that terror is the terror of being touched. And if you can't be touched, you can't be changed. And if you can't be changed, you can't be alive. I don't mean to imply that Europeans are more loving and less afraid than Americans, but there's something about the structure of this country and something in the nostalgia that's at the basis of the American personality, it seems to me, that prohibits a certain kind of maturity and entraps the person, or the people, in a kind of dream love that can never stand the weight of reality." These comments, made almost thirty years after the publication of *Giovanni's Room*, are a remarkably apt gloss on the novel. See Jere Real, "James Baldwin: A Rare Interview with a Legendary Writer," *The Advocate*, May 27, 1986, pp. 42–46.

17. Baldwin, "The Black Boy Looks at the White Boy," in *The Price of the Ticket*, p. 290.

18. Baldwin, "A Question of Identity," in *The Price of the Ticket*, p. 95.

19. Kent, "Baldwin and the Problem of Being," p. 23.

20. Baldwin, "Disturber of the Peace," p. 214.

21. For a discussion of David's rejection of the "stink of love," see Charlotte Alexander, "The 'Stink' of Reality: Mothers and Whores in James Baldwin's Fiction," in *James Baldwin: A Collection of Critical Essays*, ed. Kinnamon, pp. 77–95. See also Louis H. Pratt, *James Baldwin* (Boston: Twayne, 1978), pp. 62–63.

22. Shawcross, "Joy and Sadness," p. 102.

23. Quoted from *The Complete English Poetry of John Milton*, ed. John T. Shawcross (Garden City, N.Y.: Doubleday/Anchor, 1963), p. 489.

24. Robert A. Bone, "James Baldwin," in *James Baldwin: A Collection of Critical Essays*, ed. Kinnamon, p. 39. Bone points to a crucial distinction throughout Baldwin's work: "there are the relatively innocent [in the sense of being naive]—the *laity* who are mere apprentices in human suffering—and the fully initiated, the *clergy* who are intimate with pain. Among the laity may be numbered Americans, white folks, heterosexuals, and squares; among the clergy, Europeans, Negroes, homosexuals, hipsters, and jazzmen" (p. 40). On religion in *Giovanni's Room*, see also the skeptical remarks of Edward Margolies, "The Negro Church: James Baldwin and the Christian Vision," in *James Baldwin: Modern Critical Views*, ed. Harold Bloom (New York: Chelsea House, 1986), pp. 67–70. On suffering in Baldwin's work, see also Lee, "The Bridge of Suffering."

25. As alleged by, for example, Bone, "James Baldwin," p. 38, and implied by Sayre, "James Baldwin's Other Country," p. 165.

Chapter 9: "The Waters of the Pool": Christopher Isherwood's *A Single Man*

1. Isherwood, *Kathleen and Frank: The Autobiography of a Family* (New York: Simon & Schuster, 1971), p. 510.

2. Angus Wilson, "Insights into Isherwood," *London Observer*, March 20, 1966, p. 26.

3. Isherwood, *Christopher and His Kind, 1929–1939* (New York: Farrar, Straus and Giroux, 1976), p. 12.

4. Isherwood, *The Berlin Stories [The Last of Mr. Norris* and *Goodbye to Berlin]* (New York: New Directions, 1954), p. v. Isherwood's preface first appeared in this edition.

5. Isherwood, *Goodbye to Berlin*, in *The Berlin Stories*, p. 193.

6. Isherwood, *The World in the Evening* (New York: Simon & Schuster, 1954), p. 187. All quotations from the novel are from this edition.

7. Isherwood, *Down There on a Visit* (New York: Simon & Schuster, 1962), p. 100. All quotations from the novel are from this edition.

8. Carolyn G. Heilbrun, *Christopher Isherwood*, Columbia Essays on Modern Writers 53 (New York: Columbia University Press, 1970), p. 42.

9. Isherwood converted to Vedantism in 1939; this philosophy influences all of Isherwood's later novels, which frequently feature a struggle between the ego of individual identity and the *Atman* of universal consciousness, the impersonal God within each individual. On Vedantism in Isherwood's work, see Alan Wilde, *Chris-*

topher Isherwood (New York: Twayne, 1971), pp. 99–101. See also S. Nagarajan, "Christopher Isherwood and the Vedantic Novel: A Study of *A Single Man*," *Ariel: A Review of International English Literature* 3 (1972):63–72.

10. Isherwood, *A Single Man* (New York: Simon and Schuster, 1964; New York: Avon, 1978), p. 92. All quotations are from the paperback edition.

11. On Isherwood's double vision, see Wilde, *Christopher Isherwood*, pp. 127–38.

12. Paul Piazza, *Christopher Isherwood: Myth and Anti-Myth* (New York: Columbia University Press, 1978), p. 150.

13. Jonathan Raban, *The Technique of Modern Fiction* (London: Edward Arnold, 1968), p. 32.

14. Brian Finney, *Christopher Isherwood: A Critical Biography* (New York: Oxford University Press, 1979), p. 254.

15. Dennis Altman, *Homosexual Oppression and Liberation* (New York: Avon, 1973), pp. 50–51.

16. Adams, *The Homosexual as Hero*, pp. 152–53.

17. Wilde, *Christopher Isherwood*, pp. 128–29.

Afterword

1. Edmund White, *The Beautiful Room Is Empty* (New York: Knopf, 1988; New York: Ballantine, 1989), p. 199.

2. Armistead Maupin, *Sure of You* (New York: Harper & Row, 1989), p. 91.

Index